W9-BKO-210

The Library of
Southern
Civilization

LEWIS P. SIMPSON

EDITOR

*Southerners
and
Europeans*

Southerners and Europeans

ESSAYS IN A TIME OF DISORDER

Andrew Lytle

FOREWORD BY LEWIS P. SIMPSON

Louisiana State University Press

BATON ROUGE AND LONDON

Designer: Diane B. Didier
Typeface: Goudy Old Style
Typesetter: Composing Room of Michigan
Printer: Thomson-Shore, Inc.
Binder: John H. Dekker & Sons

10 9 8 7 6 5 4 3 2 1

Library of Congress Cataloging-in-Publication Data

Lytle, Andrew Nelson, 1902–
    Southerners and Europeans: essays in a time of disorder / Andrew
Lytle; foreword by Lewis P. Simpson.
        p.   cm. — (The Library of Southern civilization)
    ISBN 0-8071-1420-0
    I. Title. II. Series.
PS3523.Y88S6 1988
814'.52—dc19

To Deaderick C. Montague | FIDEI DEFENSOR

Contents

Acknowledgments

"THE HERO WITH THE PRIVATE Parts" originally appeared in *Daedalus*, 92 (Spring, 1963), 281–96. "The Subject of Southern Fiction" originally appeared as the Foreword to Andrew Lytle, *A Novel, a Novella, and Four Stories* (New York: McDowell, Obolensky, 1957). "The Working Novelist and the Mythmaking Process" originally appeared in *Daedalus*, 88 (Spring, 1959), 326–38. "Caroline Gordon and the Historical Image" was originally published in the *Sewanee Review*, LVII (Autumn, 1949). Copyright 1949, 1977, by the University of the South. "The Displaced Family" was originally published in the *Sewanee Review*, LXI (Winter, 1958). Copyright 1958, 1986, by the University of the South. "Helen's Last Stand: Faulkner's *The Town*" was originally published in the *Sewanee Review*, LXV (Summer, 1957). Copyright 1957, 1985, by the University of the South. "The Son of Man—He Will Prevail: Faulkner's *A Fable*" was originally published in the *Sewanee Review*, LXIII (Winter, 1955). Copyright 1955, 1983, by the University of the South. "Regeneration for the Man: Faulkner's *Intruder in the Dust*" was originally published in the *Sewanee Review*, LVII (Winter, 1949). Copyright 1949, 1977, by the University of the South. "John Crowe Ransom" was originally published in the *Sewanee Review*, LVI (Summer, 1948). Copyright 1948, 1976, by the University of the South. "Allen Tate" was originally published in the *Sewanee Review*, LX (Autumn, 1959). Copyright 1959, 1987, by the University of the South. "History and Vision in Tolstoy's *War and Peace*" was originally published in the *Sewanee Review*, LXI (Summer, 1953). Copyright 1953, 1981, by the University of the South. "In Defense of a Passionate and Incorruptible Heart: Flaubert's *Madame Bovary*" was originally published in the *Sewanee Review*, LXXIII (Autumn, 1965). Copyright 1965 by the University of the South. Reprinted by permission of the editor. All of the above essays plus "Fiction and the Essence of Things: Stephen Crane's 'The Open Boat'" also appeared in *The Hero with the Private Parts: Essays by Andrew Lytle* (Louisiana State University Press, 1966).

"The State of Letters in a Time of Disorder" was originally published in the *Sewanee Review*, LXXIX (Autumn, 1971). Copyright 1971 by the University of the South. "Caroline Gordon's *The Forest of the South*" originally appeared in *Critique*, I (Winter, 1956), 3–9. "Concupiscence and Power: Warren's *All the King's Men*" originally appeared as the introduction to the Southern Classic Library edition of Robert Penn Warren, *All the King's Men* (Birmingham, Ala: Southern Living Gallery, 1984). "Caroline Gordon" is reprinted from *Dictionary of Literary Biography Yearbook 1981*, edited by Karen Rood and others (Copyright © 1982 by Gale Research Company; reprinted by permission of the publisher), Gale Research, 1982, p. 80. "Flannery O'Connor" originally appeared in *Esprit*, undergraduate literary magazine of the University of Scranton, Pennsylvania, vol. VIII (Winter, 1964), 33–34. "Three Ways of Making a Saint: Flaubert's *Three Tales*" originally appeared in the *Southern Review*, n.s., XX (Summer, 1984), 495–527. "The Divinity of Love: Joyce's 'The Dead'" was originally published in the *Sewanee Review*, LXXVII (Spring, 1969). Copyright 1969 by the University of the South. "The Hero as an Old Furniture Dealer: Ford Madox Ford's *Parade's End*" originally appeared in Sondra J. Stang (ed.), *The Presence of Ford Madox Ford*. University of Pennsylvania Press, 1981.

Foreword

WE HAVE TENDED, SO TO speak, to write off the man of letters in the twentieth century. (I use the term *man*, I should hasten to explain, not in the sexist but in the generic sense.) But while he has been a declining presence, the man of letters has nonetheless manifested his presence strongly in this century, nowhere more so than in the South of the brilliant group of writers who formed the core of the Agrarian movement: John Crowe Ransom, Donald Davidson, Allen Tate, Robert Penn Warren, and Andrew Lytle. Putting on various literary hats—those of historian, memoirist, novelist, literary critic, editor, and teacher, not to mention that of actor on the legitimate stage—Lytle has faithfully continued what I take to have been a basic work of the Agrarians: namely, the representation of the man of letters and the preservation of that entity of Western civilization, both mystical and real, in which he essentially holds his citizenship—the cosmopolitan community of letters. No doubt the most significant work Lytle has done toward preserving the integrity, authority, and fraternity of the literary order has been as a novelist, the capacity in which we know him best. Yet, though the practice of criticism has at no stage of his career been Lytle's major preoccupation, and the total body of his criticism is comparatively small, he has expressed through it a knowledge of the literary art, and an intensity of commitment to this art, that gives him a distinct place among American critics.

I am not sure that Lytle himself has ever quite recognized this fact. Several years ago when Louis D. Rubin, Jr., solicited a collection of his essays for the Southern Literary Studies Series of the Louisiana State University Press, Lytle seemed surprised that his essays might be considered to have a permanent value. In his preface to the book that resulted from Rubin's suggestion, *The Hero with the Private Parts* (1966), Lytle observed that "it is dangerous" for a novelist "to do much writing about others who write." It is, he said, "so much easier to try to interpret something finished and done than it is to do it yourself," adding, "The discipline of a craft is always imperilled when it is being practiced by a lesser use of the mind." There is only one justification for the novelist to engage in critical interpretation. This lies in its being a necessary part of his discipline, for the novelist must "read well" if he would write well, and he can read fully and effectively only when he "writes down" what he reads. Doing this—explicating and commenting as a critic—the novelist may "explore and develop" in the work of another (or in his own work) "the first glimmer of meaning which by refraction flashes out of the abyss, that matrix of all knowledge." Acting as the critic, the novelist approaches what can never be plumbed to its depths, never truly explained, the mystery of the imagination and the creating word.

The tension between the discipline, or the craft, of art and the mystery of its inspiriting motive is in Lytle's sensibility integrally related to a complex, germinal tension in his thought and emotion between Europe and America or, more particularly, between the American South and Europe. A controlling concept underlying this tension is cogently embodied in an old marshal of Madrid who appears in the first chapter of *At the Moon's End.* Condemning the corrupting influence of the lust for gold that is obviously the dominant motive of the expedition about to embark from Spain for the New World under the leadership of De Soto, the marshal says Columbus has made "a hole in Christendom" that "can never be plugged." Suggesting as it does that the quest to conquer the New World has resulted in the depletion of the spiritual dominion that had unified Western civilization for eight hundred years—that the experience of a New World by the Old World had not proved to be redemptive but to be at best of mixed benefit and at worst a damnation—the old marshal's metaphor is central to Lytle's novelistic imagination. As Lytle declares in his foreword to *A Novel, a Novella, and Four Stories*, "The westward movement of Europeans, beginning with Columbus, not only shattered the narrow physical boundaries of Christendom but, like all extension, weakened it by reducing a union composite of spiritual and temporal parts to the predominance of material ends."

Interpreting the exploration, settlement, and development of America as integral to the historical decline of Christendom, Lytle has treated the Edenic version of America with an irony that varies in tone from the condemnatory to the nostalgic. Vividly present in his celebration of the small farmers of the South in "The Hind Tit," Lytle's lively contribution to the Agrarian symposium *I'll Take My Stand* (1930), the nostalgic note is struck most explicitly in *A Wake for the Living* (1975), his affectionate memoir of his native community, that of the plain folk of Middle Tennessee during the early part of the twentieth century. But as M. E. Bradford has observed, Lytle can salute the "Tennessee of his father" with "elegiac affirmation chiefly because it never seriously imagined itself to be an Eden." Understanding that it "could be no more than an extension and perhaps a very modest improvement of and upon an older England, not the Zion of the 'new' Jerusalem of the eschatologists," the world in which Lytle was reared was a stable "civil polity."

Even though Lytle has continued to revere the long-vanished provincial community of Middle Tennessee—remote from Europe and comparatively distant from the factories and cities of the northern and eastern United States—as no other place on earth, he has never amended his overall vision of southern history to include the image of the South or any part of it as an Edenic reversal of Europe. That he has been tempted to do so may be indicated by what he refers to as his "theological musings" about the archetypal Myth of the Garden, in which he seems to be not so much concerned about the nature of primal guilt as about the quality of primal innocence, and its persistence as the condition of love.

But America has no premium on innocence in Lytle's moral vision, which has always embraced European and American writers as necessarily constituting one community. This vision is reflected in the organization of the present collection of his literary essays for the Library of Southern Civilization series of the LSU Press. Beginning with several essays of general thematic character and moving to a number that focus primarily on individual writers, the volume concludes with a final group of essays on European writers who have been important influences on the way Lytle sees literature and history: Tolstoy, Flaubert, Joyce, and Ford Madox Ford. Two of the essays in the last group of five, it will be noted, are devoted to Flaubert—in one instance to *Madame Bovary* and in the other to the trilogy of short fictions Flaubert brought together in one volume under the simple title *Trois Contes*. Possibly the most profoundly evocative of his literary essays, these searching meditations—"A Passionate and Incorruptible Heart" and "Three Ways of Making a Saint"—deal with Flaubert's comprehension of the relationship between the literary artist and the drama of the last days of Christendom.

In the first—a compelling explication of Flaubert's drama of the destruction of a fundamentally innocent heart by society—Lytle, who has great affection for Emma Bovary, discovers nothing wrong with her "demand for affection." She was, Lytle contends, undone by the "corrupt means" the "sensibility" of her world drives her to employ in her search for love. This sensibility—and the whole complex of ideology and emotion associated with what it represents: a modern, fully developed bourgeois social order—Lytle interprets as Flaubert's vision of the "second fall of man, the fall into history." The second fall occurred, according to Lytle, when in the sixteenth century the "entire order of Christendom" was upset by the alteration of the "relationship between the lords temporal and the lords spiritual." The crucial signs of this change, he points out, are the appearance of Machiavelli's *The Prince* and the execution of Sir Thomas More. *The Prince* was a supreme rationalization of secular power; More's death was the end of the insistence on the duality of the spiritual and temporal orders. After More, instead of

> a theology for the whole, history—man judging man's acts, and explaining them too—became the reward of behavior. Gradually the world came to be looked upon not as the grounds for the drama of the soul but as the end in itself. The Christian vision dimmed. Estates became classes; that is, man was

defined by his economic status, the heresy being that the economic man assumed the posture of the whole man, the Christian. The state is still Christian. It has entered its Satanic phase of false illusions. A part is taken for the whole. This is the oldest lie of all, appearance not representing reality. Man is made in God's image. To say that man is only matter, only a sensibility, is the subtlest lie of all.

Insisting, in opposition to Allen Tate's opinion that she is a "silly, sad, and hysterical little woman," Lytle conceives that Flaubert invests Emma with the dignity of a "nature incorruptible and inviolate." Although in defending the character of Emma, Lytle does not see in Flaubert's story any implication of an attempt to save her soul, it is plain, I believe, that Lytle reads Flaubert, without qualification or reservation, as a writer who is profoundly imbued with the Christian tradition as this had been understood before the fall into history.

In his later years Andrew Lytle has found in the stories comprising Flaubert's *Three Tales*—"Herodias," "St. Julian the Hospitator," and "A Simple Heart"—what, without acknowledging it, Flaubert himself must have divined while writing them: a Christian resolution of the crisis of culture in the modern Western world. As viewed by Lytle in his reading of *Madame Bovary*, this crisis would appear to be doomed to end eventually in the annihilating fall of the creative imagination into the abyss of the modern sensibility. In his interpretation of the symbolic meaning of the last scene in Emma's story, Lytle emphasizes Flaubert's implication that its context is the transformation of Christendom into a spiritual wasteland: "The priest and the atheist sit up with the dead body. . . . The priest sprinkles holy water; the druggist, chlorine solution. The priest says we will end by understanding each other. They already understand. Bread and wine is spread for their repast. Not the blood and body of our Lord ends the action, but the worldly bread and wine to appease their carnal appetites as it diverts them from the smell of decay, which, being exuded by the dead flesh, becomes the final symbol of death in life, the description of the society that has undone Emma."

Yet, Lytle has consistently held that as artist the novelist no less than the poet has the capacity to see what others do not see—to see, like Yeats, that the linear pattern of history is enveloped in a transcendent pattern of cultural cycles. The modern materialistic age seems permanent, but it will yield to another cycle and an age of faith will return. Adapting the argument in his explication of *The Velvet Horn*, "The Working Novelist and the Mythmaking Process," to his reading of Flaubert, we are justified in saying that Lytle envisions Flaubert, a generation before Yeats, as a beholder of the "trembling of the veil" and a major prophet of the recovery of faith. Indeed Lytle reads the *Three Tales* as the embodiment of a vision of such a recovery through the rediscovery—never to be accomplished by doctrinaire theology—of the *feeling* for the Christian drama of the Trinity. Each of the tales

> ends in death, and the meaning of each renders the original properties of the Trinity. Although the enveloping action for all is the same, the form for each differs. "Herodias," with its dance of death, Salome's dance, is informed by the First Person of the Trinity, God the Father; "St. Julian the Hospitator," Christ the Son; and "A Simple Heart," the Holy Ghost. The three in one, as they differ in their actions, reveal the distinction of each member of the Trinity not as an abstract definition but as it affects the body of the world; that is, technically not by summary alone but through scenes and all the discrete uses of fiction.

Inextricably linked in their metaphorical embodiment of the Trinity, each of Flaubert's stories, Lytle says, "gives differing conditions for the making of a saint." In "Herodias" the conditions are historical; in "The Legend of St. Julian," mythic; in "A Simple Heart," the lives of the ordinary people of the bourgeois society of Flaubert's—and Emma Bovary's—time. In offering the crudely stuffed, grotesque semblance of her parrot, Loulou, which she has come to associate with the Holy Ghost, on the Corpus Christi altar, Félicité fulfills, Lytle says, the "story of the Trinity, of God, the Father loving the child, and the Holy Ghost the love that played between them." In the very world of Emma Bovary's frustrated quest for love, Felicity becomes the exemplification of divine love and attains sainthood. Through the power of the artist's imagination—in Flaubert's case this includes the power to transcend his former powerful countervision of modern man and society—man's fall into history has been redeemed.

In allowing for the capacity of the artistic imagination, I should add, Lytle is by no means unaware that the modern artist is heir to the Puritan heresy that the individual man may have direct communion with God and thus may succumb, and at times has succumbed, to the delusion that he is the special object of God's grace. But even as he implicitly acknowledges this peril, Lytle assumes—perhaps feels he must assume—that the mind of the literary artist may be almost the last mind articulately open to history as a mystery that unfolds out of God. In no sense the confidant of God, the artist—if I correctly read this son of Middle Tennessee reading Flaubert— may be the last credible witness to his grace visible in the deep twilight of Christendom.

LEWIS P. SIMPSON

Part I

The State of Letters
in a Time
of Disorder

FOR THOSE WHO LOVE LITER-
ature—a big word, I grant you—
and especially the making of it,
there is cause to worry these days.
There has never been so much published and so little worth reading.
One might think that computers
are doing the writing. So much is
allotted to these machines that we
may look forward to the next stage,
when they will also do the reading
for us. That will do away with any
worry about letters—or anything
else.

A poet of great reputation asked
me not long ago if I didn't think
literary quarterlies were out of fashion. I was taken aback, naturally. I
told him I didn't think so, that neither a monthly nor a weekly served
the same purpose. That purpose, I
went on to say (and while I was talking, I thought I was stating the obvious), allowed for several uses: one,
the most obvious, that it gave the
needed time for reflection in the
writing of reviews, so that a book
could receive a sane and balanced
estimate, free of the temporary pressures that follow it into the market;
and second, the important consideration that the editor must
distinguish between manuscripts

which are first-rate and those which only seem so. A hurried reading is no help in this. So it is that editors sometimes judge by formulae or editorial boards. It is worse when the formulae pass disguised as principles. Finally, someone has to say yes or no.

There is another service the quarterlies perform. They can help young writers find a publisher. Madison Avenue is beset by agents and writers offering their wares; but the senior editors do not always, and indeed cannot, see what is offered, especially manuscripts which, as they say, come over the transom. But many of these senior editors do read the good quarterlies. A week after distribution oftentimes a letter will pass through the office to some writer an editor wants to pursue. The *Sewanee Review* makes it a policy to keep space for young people of talent and skill. But talent is just the beginning. Without luck and the slow, hard learning of a craft, talent is wasted. Without talent, of course, no amount of work will do any good. A magazine also has its physical limits. At the *Review* some five or six thousand manuscripts pass over the editors' desks each year. Only eighty are printed. Obviously, good things must be rejected. Nevertheless, the quarterlies are needed today more than ever. Their care for language and style and the protection of what is eternal in letters makes them a kind of supreme court of literary judgment.

This brings us back to the distinguished poet. His attitude merely impinges upon the situation. A graver plight in letters is found at the very source: the creative act itself. I don't like the phrase. The Middle Ages would not have understood it. Creation cannot properly belong to man; it belongs to God. Hence its reflection is too pervasive to be usurped by man. It cannot be restricted to the arts, since it is the true source of all things. It was the Creative Word whispered into the ear of Her Ladyship the Virgin (I use this description deliberately, because Heaven is no democracy) which united matter with the divine and so made God incarnate. This is the rock beneath the ground of the Christian community. This reminds us that the soul is the form of the body. Since this is so, form of necessity inheres in the imagination, where the soul becomes concrete. Else the mysterious Word could never become flesh, made manifest through the sensibility; nor would the artist be able to imitate. He would find himself baffled by abstractions which come close to theological heresy and literary absurdity. Hence the fiction writer, for example, only seems to be inspired by the objective world.

It is the mind which selects what it wants from the discrete phenomena the eye takes in. Not the other way around.

From the beginning the soul and the more material partner are inseparable. This is the mystery which the artist must confront, whether he knows it or not. The imagination contains every aspect of form, and all subjects lie therein. It is the act of the artist seeking his subject which leads him to the unique form which encloses the subject. Often a related theme misleads him, but just as mysteriously this may bring him into the center of his material. A transverse entry sadly may mislead him forever if he grows deaf to the admonishing poetic voice. Fiction, unlike verse, is discursive and perhaps makes the risk more extravagant. Once the subject is found and under way, the craft may be consciously used, so long as he remembers it is only a tool.

One of the risks is using the symbol as an end in itself, which means, in fiction at least, the substitution of the symbol for the act. An entire action is symbolical of something. The symbol, always concrete, crowns and gives definition to the action. Its misplaced function makes for confusion. By itself it remains idea, and ideas cannot act, although they are the cause for action. The use of a wrong symbol also makes for confusion: a king holding a bishop's crozier rather than a sword or scepter. This is the confusion of office. On the other hand, a sword may as symbol have a double meaning: the promise of life by the sacrifice of life, the crusader's weapon and the symbol of the cross for which it kills.

But the symbol, being a technical matter, is not our true concern. What should grieve us all is the increasing emphasis on sensation as the only subject for the arts. This is most brutally seen in the films from the underground. Behind the lenses of the camera stands Peeping Tom. Not only in the underground has he gained respectability. Aboveground he is not only tolerated; at times he is embraced as the true meaning of behavior. All of us, being human, have curiosity about Tom's interests, but we should not forget that he makes what is private public and in so doing destroys the distinctions between these two parts of being and behavior. My complaint is not so much the obscenities; it is the conscious effort, on the part of producers, writers, and actors, to eliminate categories and bring forth a succession of unrelated images, distorted or salacious, as meaning. This is formlessness for its own sake. It resembles art for art's sake, for both practices make the work of art personal to the artist and his cult of sympathizers, not public to society as a whole. This is literary narcissism. But there is a difference between this formlessness for formlessness's sake and art for art's sake. Art for art's sake did not dispense with form. Lacking form, the subject is dissolved into sensation or monotony. Finally only monotony, because the bestial, the infantile, the erotic, removed from all other events or knowledge, turn the means into the end. The tool, whether a hammer or a mind, cannot be the thing it makes or transmits, with all due respect to Mr. McLuhan. Binet's lathe in *Madame Bovary* turns out napkin rings. Even though these rings are without utility (for he neither sells, uses, nor gives them away), nevertheless the ring is an object apart from the machine and the man turning.

This monotony is the death of an art. Among books the pornography which passes for fiction enhances the monotony. Sentences lack the concentration of the picture made instantly visible. But words are dangerous, because they mean what they say. There will always be an appeal in honest pornography; but it must be received for what it is and not, under the confusion of forms, as serious writing. In fiction, by serious writing I suppose we mean a total action whose form makes perfect the essence of experience, or tries to. The artifact then will be round and smooth and whole. Pornography only pretends to be round and smooth and whole. It pretends that copulation and its variants are the entire preoccupation of people. An early creative myth has the world parents in an embrace which lasts three hundred years. Nobody I know is so mythological. If by some miracle such could be the case, it would be wicked to interrupt or intervene. But for most of us, with the usual imperfections and frailer appetites, the question must arise: What can we do in the meanwhile? What we do is find shelter and food, make a living, worship God, keep the state in order or disorder, make war and peace, performing all those operations which bind man to his community. As a matter of fact the myth does not stop with the three-hundred-year-old embrace. One of the children gets between the parents and pushes the father upwards and the mother down. Thus we have heaven and earth. This separation became the first sin, because it interrupted a paradisal state whose loss all cultures regret. The loss of innocence is our secret grief, and some earthly paradise our deepest longing. But I think the time has come to remind ourselves that there are two sexes, male and female, and that the erotic act is no true synecdoche for mankind.

This breakdown of forms is a breakdown in meaning. It is a desperate effort at survival within the secular state. It is the profane driven back upon the nervous system, abusing the sensibility and mistaking the nervous system for life. And what makes life bearable is love. Love manifests itself not as the sensibility but through it. The sensibility is only an agency, for *caritas* suffuses being, both animal and human, and perhaps even vegetable life. Of this last we cannot be sure, as few of us speak any vegetarian language. But there is somebody—I wish I could call his name—who has heard a beet scream when its top was cut off. I do know that a young cousin of mine who milked the family cow induced in her the warmest affection for him. When he went away to college, she would kick anybody who tried to milk her. Indeed he did very poorly in college and ended up in the Marine Corps, trying to find in the names of all his class the lost intimacy he had known at home. Those of you who read Faulkner find in *The Hamlet* the most lyrical love affair between the idiot Snopes boy and her who wore the bright horns of morning. This is not only saying that an idiot is reduced to his animal nature and so is upon the same level as a cow. It is saying as an emphasis upon the action, insofar as the Snopes family is concerned, that the idiot Snopes, though mindless and reduced in nature, is superior to his kin, especially Flem, who show some human qualities but no humanity. Only money do they have in mind, whereas the idiot boy commits himself to something outside himself. It can be called neither lust nor love, but a feeling or instinct out of which lust or love can grow to be.

Money is either a medium of exchange or, taken as an end in itself, power. Pure power is always sterile, since it depends upon the shrinkage of those qualities which describe humanity. A human being committed to one idea or pursuit or feeling at the expense of the rest of his nature becomes monstrous. A miser is monstrous in a passive way. Money never used accumulates as a growing self-worship, and this denies a full life, a full life implying communion with others. The active use of money as power against an individual or the state is always satanic. It usurps through the private will God's order, in the state of man and in the state of the realm. Usury was forbidden in the Middle Ages because it violated the nature of man by allowing him to get something for nothing. But radically it deprived a man of his part in the Christian economy; *i.e.*, he had no craft. It usurped also the proper use of authority. Louis XIV understood this when he came to the

throne and found his kingdom in pawn to moneylenders. In advice to his
heir he says: "From three quarters I reduced to a half all the new mortgages
which were charged upon my revenue, which had been effected at a very
extortionate rate during the War and which were eating up the best of my
resources. . . . This action of mine was perfectly just, for a half constituted
a substantial premium. . . . It was just that public utility should take the
place of all other considerations and reduce everything to its legitimate and
natural order."

There was no such authority to temper Flem Snopes's greed for power in
Faulkner's *The Town*. Since Christian order had been distorted by secular
rule, Flem as banker was the authority, because money unrestrained is never
going to restrain money. But at what a cost! Flem made himself impotent in
his pursuit of this kind of power: that is, he made himself monstrous. With a
wife in name only, a child not his, the reward is an empty convention. The
irony lies just here: in his quest for money Flem becomes a kind of inverted
hero. The citizens of the town regard money as does Flem, since the town
has lost its religious sense, listening only to those who make a travesty of it.
But the citizens could never make the heroic sacrifice that Flem does, the
sacrifice of his humanity, to obtain it. They still keep their humanity,
degraded as it is, with love reduced to sentimentality. Flem is a fool as the
Old Testament understands the word: he is impious. He is a fool in the
ordinary sense, too. He takes the symbol for the action; so everything he is
and does substitutes appearance for reality.

You remember how Caroline Gordon notices, in "Spotted Horses," the
space around Flem when he is standing near the barn-lot fence. There is
never any immediate contact between the devil and his victims. The space
here is to indicate this fact, for the devil releases in their hearts folly and
madness. (He tempts through the Texan, indirectly.) But all about us the
arts and pseudoarts are seriously accepting folly as meaning. Surely to
reduce life to sensation is consummate folly. Allen Tate calls "that human
imagination angelic which tries to achieve direct knowledge of essences
without going through the senses." I would add that the mind which tries to
reach knowledge only through the sensibility is satanic. To take the part for
the whole, or to use it as an end in itself, creates a false illusion about nature
and human nature. One of the devil's titles is the Great Liar. A lie is
nothing, no thing, and cannot exist until somebody accepts it as the truth.

This is the opposite of the divinity fusing with the body of the world. A lie can only seize the mind of that man who has forgotten the Incarnation. This presumes the neglect of his own soul, and we know the soul loves tempta- tion because of the frequency of its fall from grace. To be explicit, we still live within the confines of Christendom. Only now we are in its satanic phase. This reminds us that we have been promised only one thing: that the gates of hell will not finally prevail.

Not hate but power is the opposite of love. Lust, for example, is an instance of this. It uses for its temporary ends the chosen object and after- wards discards it, giving nothing of itself. If lust is mutual, then each discards each and both discover the apathy of emptiness. In every sense unrestrained power inflates the ego in all the ways that this kind of power operates. You may say that power is common to experience, which is true. But the question which follows is, How are we to avoid its maleficent properties? In the Christian economy it is very clear how this is done. Power cannot only be restrained but can be properly used by confining it to its office. No office, even the highest political office, should use more than the power needed to execute it. To do so is to long for absolute power, which Lord Acton complained was corrupting. Lord Acton's axiom is a half-truth. Power corrupts absolutely only when it goes beyond formal usage. It also corrupts when the officer uses the office for his personal ends. These are old truths, but we have neglected them. By neglecting them, we have also confused two other categories directly connected with sensation. We dis- tinguish less and less between what is public and what is private. The stability of civic order, personal being, the possibility of communion be- tween neighbors, is directly dependent upon keeping what is public public and what is private private. Unless the distinction is kept clear, the arts will languish and be lost in the formlessness we have been discussing. Indeed, without knowledge of this distinction we would be deprived of much great drama, such as *King Lear* and *Oedipus Rex*. Look what happened to Lear when, as private subject, he still tried to exercise the office he had given away. The exposure of the domestic life of Oedipus at a time of public crisis brought the play to its climax and Oedipus to his sightless dependent wandering.

There is one very cogent exemplum of the confusion between the limits of offices and the use of a public office for private ends which should stand as the parable for all such violations. When Henry II appointed Becket, his playboy and intimate, to the archbishopric of Canterbury, the priests reproved Becket for what they thought would be a profane violation and impious use of that high office. He showed in return great humility, admitting his unworthiness but saying, "I hope by external discipline to mould my reluctant heart." Henry said, "Now that you are playing at being my lord Archbishop . . ." He replied, "Sire, I am the Lord Archbishop." These words reproved the king's usurpation of spiritual power, and they also brought Becket to his death; yet the bloody outrage at the foot of the altar only stressed again the sanctity of the office and the necessary distinction between crozier and scepter. Henry's going through England in sackcloth and ashes, whether he repented or not, made vivid his impiety, his wrongful tampering with God's institutions for private and selfish reasons.

Most great literature has crime for its subject. I am not referring to the crime of man against man or man against things. It represents the loss in the heart and mind of any belief, even in the self. The criminal takes what he wants or thinks he needs, and enjoys the risk, because he belongs nowhere and to nobody. He drifts in the vacuum of sensation, among a kind of hierarchy of losers. But the crimes which great literature exhibits are acts against the divine order of the universe. These crimes have to do with the disobedience by man of God's will, or the substitution of his own will for the divine will. The protagonist in this last instance is most often the Puritan. To praise the self, to serve the self instead of God, evokes a divine vengeance. Job comes to mind, but nothing can equal the full-turned drama of Saul and David and Jonathan, unless you feel that this is the beginning of an action which David's life and rule can only complete. But the sin of self is universal, not just limited to our mythology. It lies behind Theseus' journey to Crete with the condemned maids and youths. You remember how it was with Minos, king of Crete. He took the white bull which the god had given him, and instead of sacrificing the animal to Poseidon (or Zeus), he kept it to improve his herd. As a punishment his queen, Pasiphaë, was made to lust after the bull's strength and beauty. But there was a practical difficulty. How could she, frail human nature, receive the full weight of nature's bestial power? Daedalus the artist was called in and made a cowlike frame covered with cowhide and no doubt exuding the aroma of the lush meadow and that scent which makes any bull slobber. Within this the queen cowered as she was bred. The birth was as monstrous, the Minotaur, as the act was perverse, and the cause impious. And notice that, unlike the Centaur, that symbol for man's dual nature, the animal body with the human head, the Minotaur is just the reverse: sensation doubled in strength, reason absent, manhood at the mercy of instinct brought to its highest and most willful power, the bull's head upon the man's body. This makes for the perfect symbol for impotence: the human form unequal to the requirements of brute strength and the nostrils of the bull wasted upon the savorless and odorless instinctual needs of the human appetite. Minos ordered the artist to make the labyrinth to hide the disgrace, putting both the queen and her misbegot offspring inside it. Minos, like any ruler who has lost his faith in the divine, never learned. To use a more obvious method of instruction, the god turned the white bull loose on Crete, and it ravaged the entire island in its gallop.

You might ask: What part does the artist play here? How far was he responsible for the catastrophe? The clue is the discreet modesty he showed by withdrawing and not bearing witness to the mésalliance. He might have remained to test his craftsmanship—that is, to see if the framework would hold. But of course he knew that it would hold. To watch for any other reason would have confused the connection he had with the queen. Since their contract was impersonal, he would have invaded her privacy; so he quietly withdrew from the scene. In other words, he acted like the traditional craftsman: he accepted the commission of his patron and delivered the artifact. This ended what they had in common. He had not intruded and so could not be morally involved. It was the king, irresponsibly using his office for private gain, who was morally guilty. He later showed again the stupidity of one who uses power without restraint: to punish Daedalus, he confined the artist within the labyrinth, the thing he had made; in other words, he confined him within his proper knowledge, of which Daedalus promptly made use to escape with Icarus his son, but not before he had given into Ariadne's hand the key to the maze, the magical ball of twine which would unroll to the heart of the matter.

This fable presents as sensational a crime as any the underground or the top-of-the-ground pornography offers us. But it does not make its appeal to our sensation. It is presented through traditional means, those conventional distinctions of the office, the public and private divisions, and the traditional meeting between artist and patron. Nowhere here is the personal and unique appetite treated as if it alone mattered. The action comes out of a metaphysical origin. The sin is against the divine order, the reckless self-indulgence in man's will, that blind reliance upon and use of mortal power, which defies the divine. We have an antagonist and a protagonist. That formless obscenity restricting itself to sensation has only an antagonist. There can be no action in the proper sense of drama with just an antagonist. There is action of a sort, and this sort exhibits the appeal of that which takes the place of the protagonist. And that is the secret and guilty corruption of the psyche of the spectator. Because of this the spectator can never become a part of an audience or feel the catharsis of seeing and being moved in common with others by a dramatic performance. Such a communal response binds together and never separates the observers by turning each into a solitary.

Let us call these reveries of the solitary the secret reveries of the latter-day Puritan. Now this latter-day Puritan has lost the satanic theology of his ancestors; but he still puts evil in the object, in a bottle of whiskey, "a fix," a deck of cards, a woman's hair, or the suggestive curves of the body. He puts evil there but no good. The good is all taken up by his own nature. And since he has all the good, he can do no wrong. And since he can do no wrong, he must have all knowledge and a perfect will. Of necessity he must judge all others, since by their very natures, *i.e.*, not his nature, they are all bad and so all wrong. He sees no obscenity in the obliteration of the public-private distinction. Since he is engaged with himself and is all actor—all spectator, he has no public or private life. His life is the life of the good and therefore without restriction, for who can say that the good is bad? But the good must have substance; so we have the sensibility as the end in itself, communication as its own meaning, the object as the subject. At last witchcraft has achieved its apotheosis: the most extravagant use of power, no longer suppressed but visibly witnessed.

With such a rule sensation increasingly becomes all that the secular state can offer. This state operates from moment to moment, without principles or cohesion among its parts, disjunctive because it has lost its vision of the divine, exchanging the belief in the God-man for the little man who plays god and aspires to conquer Heaven and earth. It is no wonder that serious young men and women devote themselves to the underground in the arts. The underground is imitating in the largest sense the general condition of Western society, and particularly our branch of it, for our branch has re-

versed the process and returns to Europe what Europe once gave us, materialism as the end in itself, but in what a perverse and magnified way. There
are the French existentialists, the nihilists, shall we say, who have made
themselves the philosophers of the carnal world. The French are a very
remarkable people. They have the gift of making their defects virtues in the
eyes of others. If I mistake it not, this mere existence as the end in itself
comes out of their great defeat and humiliation which has Vichy for its
symbol. As an army and a nation they lost honor, freedom, pride, were put
to a servile existence, and so made a philosophy from it, but more acutely a
literature, and sold it.

Perhaps in the mysterious ways we do not understand they showed themselves prophets for all of us. But it is not a prophecy we can live by. To begin
with it's a logical impossibility; reflection alone lifts any of us above so basic
a position. Certainly the southern temperament and artistic mind, which is
a believing mind, must reject this school. Critics are saying that the Southern Renascence is over and the horizon bare of anything to succeed it. Well,
renascence is a misnomer. The last half century in our letters, which comprised a large portion of American letters, demonstrates a birth, not a
rebirth. And it comes out of no provincial (in the narrow sense) tradition
but out of the oldest tradition in the world, the *philosophia perennis*, the
perpetual understanding of the nature of things, and the sense that it can
only be imparted formally and that subject and form are combined within
the fierce crucible which is God's tool. I would say that, almost absolutely,
the great, at least lasting, literatures and representative arts are found in
either a pastoral or an agrarian society. The images and references which the
arts find to hand are to things natural and supernatural: to men, animals,
plants, winds, water, and fire, not indiscriminately used but always through
their proper functions and necessities.

What I have been saying presupposes a traditional attitude, one which
cherishes and sustains an inherited way of life, admonishing us about the
necessary functioning without which life could not be. Conventions
change, but the habits of experience, the archetypal patterns of what is
eternal in behavior, persist, and they persist in the very changes which may
seem to destroy a given way of life. It is always the changing convention
against the eternal truth which makes for freshness in the arts, especially in
the arts of literature. Any convention always requires the senses to embody

it. To take the most primitive sense, that of smell: In the sixteenth century you could smell the city of Paris twenty leagues away. No doubt this was not unique among the cities of the time. It was the rich and powerful scent of man and excrement. I suppose a sixteenth-century nose would scarcely recognize man today. And yet, despite the varying strength of smell, there remains all about us the odor of mortality.

Keeping all this in mind, we should recollect that mankind can no more do without the arts than it can do without divine aid. And comfort. It was never clearer than now, when our eyes and ears are overwhelmed by mass media, by ornament which is mistaken for that which it adorns. Experience reminds us that the perpetual truth of the human predicament is always with us and will remain so. If we seem to be consigned to the underground, we can say that this is only the present convention, which is distorting experience to a, not fresher, but too private and special end. This is no new complaint against the arts. In the 1920s and later it was raised against the best poets of the time that they were too private in their appeal. If this is so, the complaint should have been addressed to our immersion in an unbalanced society. To find poets whose imaginations and spirit keep alive the word by their vision and craft is the hope of our time, comparable with the hope of those priests who withdrew to monasteries and cultivated language and the fruits of the earth, while all about them wastelands, because of their belief and discipline, gradually began to resume the season's changes.

I really do not mean that the sensibility as an end or its formless presentation can be a convention. The sensibility merely supplants a convention, for a convention has to be generally accepted. The question arises: Can we by will change an attitude which represents not only the artistic temperament but almost everything else? Nobody can quite answer this, but we can say that a secular society and its partial understanding of experience is not enough, and that the present plight of the arts shows it is not enough. At the same time, certain truths persist, even if they seem ignored or neglected. The ugly fact is that, insofar as histories record (just look into the Anglo-Saxon chronicles after the Norman Conquest), the world has never, except for certain halcyon decades, been anything but violent, brutal, full of sorrow and disorder. And that the great souls were too often martyred. Perhaps there is some confort that in one of the most oppressive and disorderly periods the great cathedrals were being erected. But a better comfort instructs us that our society is still Christian (it is not Muslim) and that we must believe that Jesus Christ is the Son of the only living God. Not to believe this does not change the necessity for belief. It merely obscures the truth and elicits the memory of that universal gray fog encompassing chaos and its silent lull or of its symbols, such as the alchemical *uroboros* or hermaphroditic Adam before Eve was lifted from his side. This stasis preceded the Fall of Man into the divine paradox of the cooperating opposites of good and evil. Chaos can return no more, for Christ, the second Adam, was born. But its shadow can darken the mind.

As human beings we are caught in the tension between these opposites. The increase and decrease of such a tension comprehend the habits and wants and hopes and sorrows of living. As men and women we are bound to this spiral. I say spiral, either up or down, because life is not a straight line. In life we are always circling about our predicament. We are always in the process of resolving something, some ambition or some betrayal, some pursuit of love or some refusal of it. All our multifarious engagements or thoughts imply action. These actions will succeed one another so rapidly as to lose us in the discretion of the profane world, unless we can believe and pause long enough to explore that belief. The arts have always helped in this, because they free us from our separate actions and give us the necessary distance to look at these actions and find what is essential and lasting—not just man finding himself, but finding what in man is humanity. Only this freedom removes us from sensation and the topical moment.

But it takes the traditional artist to do it, because he knows that the world is a part of the divine order. This *philosophia perennis* is universal. This is Coomaraswamy's term. (Much of the succeeding argument is a paraphase of his. As he says, I make it mine out of belief in it.) The Indian architect was said to go to Heaven for his designs. Neolithic man did not consider his house just a machine to live in but a structure which stood for a cosmology: the column of smoke which rose through the hole in his roof informed him of the axis of the universe; he saw in this hole the image of the heavenly door, through which the sun came. So it is that Santa Claus, symbolic of the sun bringing the gifts of life, dressed in its color, descends through the chimney and not through our kind of door. Primitive man made no active distinction between sacred and secular. The supernatural informed both necessities pertaining to both worlds, the physical and the metaphysical.

We are far from this, but up to now we have presumed upon a common inheritance which depended upon a Christendom divinely ordered. Obviously this order no longer exists. The artist today is a special kind of man. That is, he is so considered by the sentimentalists, the positivists, the aestheticians (*aesthesis* literally means that which deals with feeling or sensation). But in the Middle Ages and as late as the sixteenth century every man was a special kind of artist. He made things, not for profit, but for utility and for the greater glory of God. And also for a reasonable return on his work. There was no distinction between the fine and the servile arts. All were needed for the use of man, and each was judged in terms of what was to be made. A pair of breeches was as essential as a poem, a cathedral as essential as a barn. The whole economy saw itself working through these crafts; so it is we still hear, though faintly, words like *priestcraft, kingcraft. Craftsman* then was a noble word, as *craft* was a common word for work done.

Behind this, of course, was the art of God, who was the Son through whom all things were made, "the perfect Word, not wanting in anything, and, so to speak, the art of God." This is St. Augustine. It follows that art imitates nature in her manner of operation, not as the superficial mirror reflecting surfaces. And so art, in the traditional sense, is nothing tangible. A book is not art: it is a work of art, just as a painting or statuary is the artifact. The art remains in the artist and is the knowledge by which things are made, and so in all respects the traditional craftsman devotes himself to the good of the work to be done and not to the display of his ego. Mind you, that display of the ego, called self-expression by today's aesthetic standards, defines what the artist now does. And it defines what he is himself as ego: the display of time passing and with it what it takes away—that is, what is impermanent. The sacred and traditional art tries to embody what is eternal, and so we scarcely know any names for individual artists of our middle period. What was individual seemed less important; what bound all together, in all walks of life, was the thing to strive for. The ego as artist is continually disappointing. By making his work praise of himself as individual, not maker, he hopes to make time pause forever at his most persuasive and charming moment. What happens is unsatisfactory. An actress making a reputation in a certain role often finds herself forever fixed by that role, even though she feels her ability would allow a greater range.

Man has two activities: the making of things and the doing of deeds. (I am assuming that reflection is an action.) The making of things is governed by art; the doing of deeds by prudence. You will recognize that I am para-phrasing St. Thomas, from very necessity in dealing with the subject. To quote him directly, "Art does not require of the artist that his act be a good act, but that his work be good." In other words, art does not presuppose rectitude of appetite but only aims to serve it, whether for good or ill. There is a very practical reason for this. Immersed in making the idea into a concrete action, the artist cannot be diverted by any thought or concern of his as a man. He cannot allow himself to think, if he is writing a book, how great the book will make his reputation or how it will make enough money to pay off the mortgage; if he is a priest preparing a sermon, he cannot think of the parish he wants and may get if his sermon is good enough. If he does, the book will never get written nor the sermon composed, for the simple reason that he will be confusing two worlds in which the artist moves: his private world of the life with other human beings and the world of the imagination and of his calling. It takes a long time in the morning to put away your carnal nature, or this private world, to build a metaphorical wall around the imagination into which you have entered to be inspired by its pictures and receive there the form by means of which you will make the subject flesh; because an art has fixed ends and fixed means to reach that end, never the expression of the passing ego. To maintain the illusion of life in a book, say, is a most delicate thing. It has its life, of course; but an urgent demand of life will always intrude. But more forcibly, to quote that wise man Coomaraswamy directly, "It will be obvious that there can be no moral judgment of art itself, since it is not an act but a kind of knowledge or power by which things can be well made, whether for good or evil use." If the artist has agreed to make an instrument that will blow up the world, he will have failed as an artist if it merely explodes like a Roman candle. But behind the artist is the moral man. This brings up the ethical question: Should the instrument be made at all? What a society needs and wants must be agreed upon beforehand. But once it is agreed upon, the artist will fail and miss the mark if what he makes does not work. He will make nothing if he carries on an endless debate with himself as to whether it will do good or ill. This difference between moral and artistic sin is universal. Confucius speaks of the succession dance as being "at the same time perfect beauty and perfect goodness," but of the war dance as being "perfect beauty but not perfect goodness."

The *philosophia perennis* seems remote to us now, but it persists, for it is the only way that the craftsman, as apart from the machine, turns out his work. It is not today in fashion, but since a traditional art has fixed ends and ascertained means of operation and descends from an immemorial past, it will survive the antitraditional, personal, profane, and aesthetic kind. The question is when. When does belief return? Belief is never altogether absent. In the times of false luxury there is that complex and difficult prophet Isaiah, whose prophecies pale before his poetic language. He is one of the four great poets in our inheritance. Let me name them: Isaiah, Homer, Dante, and Shakespeare. All of these great artists came at the end of something; if you will, they were at the time of great transitions, transitions comforting as renewals and promises. It is in the times of folly and corruption and madness, such as ours, that those who believe, who are beyond time, whose imaginations are saturated with the divine effluvium emanating from the godhead, promise renewal of that mystery of the cooperating opposites.

I don't want to seem to blame the Puritans—that is, the satanists—for everything, for obviously Satan has a larger court. His followers are not the only ones who have fallen, are falling, and will fall. But we must recognize that it was the Puritans who disrupted the understanding of what a craft is and does, in their greed and hatred substituting profit for utility, Mammon for God. Greed is a mortal sin, and profit powerfully tempts this sin. But universally among us it introduced or represented the secular and profane as the final guides to conduct and manufacture; that is, it was a falling away from a divine sense of the universe. Without pursuing this argument further, let me juxtapose the descent through the intention and habit of an art, not this time the literary arts, but the visual ones of painting and sculpture. Before the thirteenth century the effigy on top of the tomb did not try to portray the personality of the dead as he had been in life. The effigy showed one of two things and often the two together. It showed the man as he would like to be considered at the moment of resurrection—that is, in the embodiment of his spiritual essence and aspiration; or it showed him as the prototype of the office he had served, in the ideal of what that should have been. As we enter the Renaissance, we find that the subject has become the Court of Heaven, but already brought to earth. There is a striking observation to be made. Christ on the cross, or being taken down from the cross, is a dead man, and the grief is mortal. In the Orthodox icon the eyes of saints and angels and the Heavenly Family all shine with the light of eternity. Growing out of the Western earthiness and mortality, the subject became the natural man, but a man full of vitality: vitality versus spirit. You may remember that W. B. Yeats said that a Renaissance portrait showed a man all alive, even to his skin, whereas Sargent's portrait of Woodrow Wilson brought only the eyes alive. Even this energy, this fifteenth- and sixteenth-century vitality, was a waning. These centuries were wastrels squandering their Christian inheritance; they were spending, not making. It took us only four centuries to reduce the natural man to the naked man; indeed, as a recent popular book on biology states, not the naked man but the naked ape.

This, I suppose, is evolution in reverse. At what future moment, then, will science and theology converge? That is, at what moment shall our descendants cover themselves with the leaf and so know they are no longer apes, but men? And what will be the shape and size and color of this leaf? Its fruit? Will it be as once it was—the fig, the succulent, the hermaphroditic fig? Or will it be carbon turned to cloth, no symbol of the natural or divine order of things? Whatever it may be, after it follows again the long wastes of time, how many wanderings of generations will it take before men settle and the community returns? Who knows the long gap between ape and man? We all know the expense of beginning again.

The Hero with the Private Parts

THE WRITERS WHO WILL AP-
pear in these pages may all in some
way be called impressionists, but it
will be the burden of this piece to
show how little is the help, in reading, of the large definitions. Realism, naturalism, impressionism, ex-
istentialism—all these derive from
philosophy. They are pseudophilo-
sophical terms, and they are of some
help. There are times when discourse needs comparisons, needs
formulae. Such terms discriminate
the larger areas of learning; but they
remain signposts, showing the way
only towards the discovery of the individual talent, which is there to be
read for itself, for its unique contribution, not as evidence of a school.
Yet the terms are honorable, of long
standing, and for the critic, when
he is not deliberately trying to be
scientific, useful. But they must be
remade in sympathy and understanding to serve the arts.

And this latest of the arts in language, fiction, has suffered most
from inadequate critical tools. Verse
has inherited numerous formal aids;
fiction—this itself is a bad enough
word for what it represents—depends for its formal control upon the
point of view. The view or post of

observation, to use James's definition, orders the structure which in an impressionist novel leaves nothing inert. This structure is composed of two actions: the enveloping action, which contains a universal truth or some one of the complications which forever recur upon the human scene; and secondly, the action itself, which is one instance of such a truth or complication. These actions fall into two parts, the scene and the pictorial or panoramic summary. The play, of course, is composed of scenes. Fiction's peculiar distinction lies in the summary. It is of the very essence of fiction, and when the writer relies too largely upon scenes and dialogue, he diminishes his art and possibly should write for the theater.

On the stage, dialogue is supported by the living presence of the actor, his gesture, magnetism, intonation of voice. Under a good director all of the actors make the structure of the play "work." Since all of this living presence is lacking in a story or novel, the pictorial summary must take its place: it does more than this, and also less. Nothing can substitute for the living presence of the actor. However, there are areas of the mind and imagination which the spoken word neither reaches nor reveals. The extreme artificiality of the soliloquy shows what an advantage fiction has in the exploration of any part of consciousness, even to the extent of suggesting the supernatural.

It was Henry James's mastery of the panorama, perhaps, which made his plays theatrical failures. In impressionism the scene is usually limited by the restrictions of a mind seeing as well as interpreting the action, whether this mind uses the first person or the "central intelligence." There are two kinds of scenes, the objective scene, which stands by itself, and the scene depending upon this mind (such as the marquis' ball viewed by Emma Bovary). Although fiction can use both kinds of scenes, this last is particularly the impressionist scene. Nobody does a better scene than James; it depends upon, and fulfills, with the immediacy of sensible action, the panoramic summary which has gone before it. James, who is recognized as the first master of this method, defined it as a direct impression of life; and nothing can be more direct than a mind involved in a crisis receiving impressions of others as this crisis is taking place. James learned from Turgenev not to use a contrived plot, but to control the action as it grows out of the complication. It follows that whatever sets the action in motion does so by entering and freeing the author's imagination (James took from an anecdote only what would release his own mind and story); but chiefly impressionism seems to be dependent upon the point of view or post, substituting a central intelligence or a first person for the old reportorial omniscience. And this required an intrusion into areas of the mind only crudely used before, giving the critic the inadequate terms *stream of consciousness* and *interior monologue*. I hope I may be excused for stating the obvious, but no critical nomenclature exists for fiction upon which all may agree.

There may be millions of views or posts of observation, but the central intelligence can take them only one at a time; and each time there is a twofold operation. The level of experience will be restricted by the view, but to it the author adds his own vision. Sight into the world and insight into the psyche, fused by the shock of recognition at the post, gives to the vision its proper form. An element of the form is generally some degree of the stream of consciousness, in which it is possible to explore the mind in all its mystery and properties as the grounds for action. One might ask why the omnisicient view cannot do the same. It can, but the delusive freedom of all knowledge is generally too seductive for most writers. It tempts them to intrude their opinions; too often they report where they should render. In the impressionist novel, or rather in the novel whose view is restricted, ideally no word is used which does not forward the action. This is rarely so with discursive omniscience.

But a real danger presents itself upon entering a mind so freely. The possibilities for variety of experience are enormous, and so only the strictest view can save the fiction from redundancies, irrelevancies, obscenities more deadly than the reportorial prolixities of omniscience. The best of the impressionists understand the technical necessity for restraint in the plunge within and below consciousness. The clearest image for this act is very old: the labyrinth. The explorer may wind and cross and lose himself, so long as he holds the thread and so long as its terminal is outside the labyrinth. However, many of these writers seem not to understand the dangers of the first person. Since this view is a prejudiced one and since it seems to carry the most authority, it requires of the author all his ingenuity. Nor can they resist the sound of the author's voice. The voice is the swiftest way to set the tone, but too often the writer falls in love with it, so that the action drowns.

I suppose Henry Miller's voice is the most torrential in present-day letters. There is no ism which will quite define him. I would hesitate to call him an impressionist; and yet multifarious impressions of the world pass through his ego and sometimes are given form by it. He is not really an artist, and yet at times he produces works of art. He is the hero of everything he writes and is as innocent as a child speaking of himself in the third person. He is not actually a fiction writer; he is a prophet without a religion. He is a tremendous sensibility which mixes up all that is current in the world and more often than not makes nonsense of it. For example, "the time will come when they [the poets] will communicate silently, not as poets, but as seers." You can go through almost any page of his and find brilliant assumptions and in the next sentence contradicting sentiments. Too often you feel that all of this goes through him, like a flux, without any reflection, as if he were in a trance. And yet when he really brings it off, as in "Berthe" and in "Reunion in Brooklyn," he manages to make of himself a fictive actor. He "immolates" himself as a person and becomes the protagonist of the story. In "Berthe" the fictional Henry's sympathy, his bleeding heart, reveals the isolation and despair of the whore before she has become reconciled to her plight. This is so managed by the final little scene that it is not sentimental but the best kind of irony. For all his kindness and sympathy merely isolates her the more, revealing to her the hopelessness of her situation and therefore increasing her anguish.

As good as they are, these shorter pieces do not make him a fiction writer; yet all of his work comprises a kind of fictitious autobiography of modern man looking for truth and salvation. His protagonist and his view is that of a superego. This superego is historic man making his last stand. For this reason Miller seemed to me to be a prophet without a religion, for try as you may, you cannot make of the secular world a religious one. In that second Fall of Man, the fall into history (Machiavelli's *The Prince* being the New Testament for this), the individual found himself in a world of endless discretion. This is the obverse of the Christian vision, in which man decried his uniqueness to become more nearly what was common to all believers. As belief in divine authority waned, the ego and its impression, the personality, alone were able to resist anonymity, confront the terror of time imitating eternity. Now the citizen confronts the very abyss itself. There is no longer the historic man to shield him.

From the beginning the impressionist has sensed the gross inadequacy of the secular world as the subject for fictive truth. The technical usage of the consciousness and the strict view is evidence of this. The invisible mind as stage forces the impression beyond external reality, downwards or within the consciousness, that area of the writer's being which is mysterious, where the opposites of good and evil will be encountered. This is not a substitute for religion, but it is a part of the religious feeling. How well the techne performs depends precariously upon the writer himself, since his private vision is no longer supported by either universal faith or the historic man.

For this reason, perhaps, there is such diversity of performance, differing levels of authority among the impressionists. The decline in the method seems to be found among those writers who never get out of the stream of consciousness (Claude Simon) or who use the first person for material it cannot handle. The succession of impressions with brief statements reporting what a person is like, the long, almost abstract comparisons of human beings to natural objects, each impression taking a short chapter, with no transition—such too often is the structure of these novels. You will find exactly this in the opening chapters of Anaïs Nin's *Cities of the Interior*. The first person is so isolated within its uncontrolled reflections and sensations that it cannot withdraw critically in any sense. The married heroine has a husband, children, an incomparable housekeeper, a thriving establishment. But this is not enough for her: her romantic ego must find strange and perverse understanding and experience. This is grounds for a true action. However, to give it meaning, the author should establish the fullest relationship to husband and children, housekeeper and establishment. Instead the author makes the briefest of references to the life she will give up and the house she will set adrift. We are, therefore, not convinced affectively that she ever had a husband, children, or an establishment to sacrifice. We can only accept her in the monstrosity of her ego.

Here we have the ego turned loose, without the thread of direction, in the unconscious, the near conscious, and the consciousness itself. This self-absorption in the accidental part of being, the great I, becomes the more monstrous the greater the sensibility it occupies. Its very monstrosity comes from its isolation from all other parts of self and, in the artist, from the post of objectivity, of critical awareness. Like the Minotaur, that image of man's predicament, it wanders impotently among the corridors of the most intricate work of art, as in a wilderness. This suggests why the acts most real in Miller and Durrell are the sexual ones. Once sex defined male and female. Now it is reduced to the act itself, the act as the only reality left in common understanding. In a world where neither the historic man nor the whole man governs (and therefore where his institutions are either empty hulls or the agencies of the state's arbitrary acts), this cultural and political predicament, as always, is anticipated by the artist. Once you accept sex not as the source of life and human relationship but as the meaning itself, you must accept any and all of its varieties; and you must accept them without restraint of judgment. Since it seems the last vitality, to withdraw and judge is to withdraw from life. In *The Black Book* Durrell's protagonist sums it up: the verb which means *to copulate*, he says, "has become synonymous with the verb *to be*. It is as if this act were the one assurance of existence remaining to us still." The only thing about this truth is: what are you going to do in between times? We have lost so much ground since our mythological world parents lasted out a three-hundred-year embrace.

Durrell's book seems to indicate that death-in-life fills the time not only between but in the act itself. This death has for components a confusion between public and private matters: the four-letter words, acts which once would have seemed pornographic, scatology, the secret dark things exposed to light. The author's intention is to present us with the terrors of this situation. However, his characters are unequal to the occasion, and this is generally true of this kind of impressionism. Instead of being the death of England, as he asserts, they actually represent what has always been about: the vulgarity of easy vice, easy because it has no longer behind it the threat of evil and because vulgarity is the clearest sign of life these people have.

Death in *The Black Book* is, therefore, sentimental. The ego of the first-person protagonist is drawn into but does not control the action. There are comparable scenes between this fiction and *Nightwood* by Djuna Barnes which demonstrate the differences between a work of art and an imaginative book by a young man not yet in control of his medium or of his sense of reality. In *The Black Book* Tarquin, an older man attracted to a gigolo, enters his room.

He takes a few turns around the room, in such precise don's paces that he almost trips in the snowy bits. On the washstand a comb, thick with dirt and grease from Hylas' sable locks; on the pisspot holder a thriller, face down; the book he had lent the boy on the first day of his campaign for higher thinking and purer love is deep in dust. The bed lamp is on. Hylas is afraid to sleep in the dark. On the shelf is a broken enema syringe and carton of crab ointment. Tarquin explores these things with disgust.

The details are precise: they describe a boy whose sin is sloth certainly, but the meaning has been reduced to Tarquin's disgust. It doesn't go beyond the immediate relationship between the two characters, because the first person uses only his eyes to report, not his mind, which might render the total dramatic effect.

In *Nightwood* Nora at a crisis in her life mounts six flights to ask Doctor O'Connor "everything you know about the night." She enters his room to learn from the damned the nature of the dark, evil's atmosphere. What follows is not merely a self-contained impression but the introduction to an action which advances the total action of the book. As the door to the doctor's room opens, she "hesitates" before the incredible disorder that meets her eye. This disorder is the very order of evil. She has entered that domain, Night, where all the dark opposites hold sway. The night, the grave, the prison, the inchoate and criminal needs, the secret impulse for innocence to be ravished—all this is here in the opening scene, and it is all here in revealing images. The room is so small that "it was just possible to walk sideways up to the bed; it was as if being condemned to the grave, the doctor had decided to occupy it with the utmost abandon." There are bars on the one small window, which suggest both the prison and the grave, that ultimate confinement after judgment. The dust and filth is here as in the other scene, but the images are more dramatically exact. The books piled to the ceiling are ruined both by dust and water: the neglect relates to and introduces the rusty forceps, the broken scalpel, odd instruments of a doctor's profession. These are juxtaposed to the twenty-odd bottles of pomades, creams, rouges, etc. In this juxtaposition the images clash and in so doing show the evidence of the doctor's damnation. It is the betrayal of the profession, the trade, which is the masculine betrayal, since a man's work describes and judges him. The pomades follow and show another betrayal. In the scene in *The Black Book*, at the most, we get in the broken syringe neglect or abuse of the body, and the excremental parody of the act of love. The swill pail in *Nightwood* is called by its name.

In *The Black Book* the shock is the surface shock of the four-letter word. The jar "swimming with abominations" in *Nightwood* is a controlling image and hence technically apt.

The doctor is discovered in bed, in a nightgown, rouged, with long, false curls and painted lashes, his appearance that of narcissistic innocence, not transformed in the instant of self-love but continuing into middle age. This is the innocence never truly lost, and thus a perversion of both innocence and knowledge, the suggestion of both and the actuality of neither. It flashed through Nora's head as she looked: "God, children know something they can't tell; they like Red Riding Hood and the wolf in bed!"

The true terror of his situation is that he evacuates custom only at night; the agony is that he can live only at night, that the opposites of day and night, comprising the conflict which is life, do not serve in the doctor's case. To him the day is a prison; he tries to drink it away. The night is a prison as well; it confines him in the distortion of his love, since it reduces love to the act of darkness. This is a denial of light and therefore a kind of hell. So it is that the coffinlike room, the little scene there, "is as mauled as the last agony." This becomes the reality of his being; it obliterates time in its suspension; it persists like but is not eternity. His final drunken scene protests his predicament, in the horror of self-knowledge which comes only from knowledge of the world as it afflicts and, in afflicting, shows the self. "Now," he said, "the end—mark my words—now *nothing, but wrath and weeping!*" Wrath and weeping suggest the Four Last Things and the inexplicable mystery of faith.

In *The Black Book,* God is reduced to man and even less than the full man. Durrell's relativism, consciously got from Einstein and Freud, becomes the structure for *The Alexandria Quartet.* There is a good deal of tiresome lecturing on relativity, not only tiresome but stale, since it is repeating at second hand the discoveries of first-rate minds. The legitimate method is to let the actors perform in such a way as to show the theory embodied: to make it flesh, as fiction must. And to a certain extent this is done, but Darley as the first-person narrator never resolves the meaning of all the action in the four books. He is the first-person observer (who sometimes acts) whose mind receives images and sensations without reflection. When he becomes actor, he does reflect and report, but altogether within the immediate situation he finds himself involved in. Justine remains, at the end, disconnected shapes and images. So does Nessim. The relativity begets one illusion after another, but finally the reader surely can ask, What is the reality of this large and complex action?

Darley and Clea at the end of the fourth book find some solution, if not salvation; she as a painter and he as a writer, they hope. This is no more than some kind of ending of their personal involvement, not an intelligence resolving the complex matters of the action in all four books. The author no doubt meant it all to be relative. Whatever he meant, he asks the reader to do his final work for him, the pulling together of the separate parts into the one meaning. The author in the end should "know," as any creator knows, the entire truth about his creations. He as creator cannot be a relativist, even if he deals in relativity.

A writer who started out well, William Styron, has a book, *Set This House on Fire,* which could serve as an example for the failure of the first-person view. It is a long, discursive book, and in the two hundred thousand words of impressions, much does not bear directly upon the action. The book's mechanical and formal structure is in two parts. The first person, Peter Leveret, a lawyer and youthful companion of the antagonist, Mason Flagg, should be the principal actor, since it presumably is his story; but actively it is only his story in the first part, and even here he is more of a commentator than actor. Cass Kinsolving, the painter who can't or won't paint, takes over in the second part; that is, he becomes the protagonist who acts and is changed by his acts. The only way the reader can accept the lawyer, Peter Leveret, as the protagonist is by restricting the author's meaning in the book to the legal curiosity of solving a murder mystery.

But the author's intention is obviously more than this. The action seems to arise from the constant struggle the artist suffers—the conflict between his work and his "life." Cass Kinsolving, who enters the action addicted to drink, falls into bondage to Flagg, whose person and possessions threaten the integrity of the painter as artist and man. To free himself and recover his self-respect, he murders Flagg, who has raped a girl to whom Kinsolving is sentimentally attached and whom he thinks, mistakenly, Flagg has also murdered. This act of violence miraculously returns him to his manhood and profession, since Flagg had used his power to reduce the real artist to his own spurious level. So the murder becomes symbolic of self and artistic recovery in a literal sense: for drink, Kinsolving has painted a pornographic picture of the act of love, which he regrets and which he tears up as a sign of his release. Any violation of viewpoint or drifting of it causes confusion in the reader's knowledge and sympathy. As well, it is often a sign that the author is backing away from a seemingly insoluble problem. Such problems, if confronted, are the way into the true subject. Anybody with a narrative gift can tell some kind of a story; the successful artist tells the one story the circumstances and actors demand.

There are several technical failures which come from the shift of view when, in the second part, Leveret is not close enough to the action and Kinsolving has to take over. To begin with, it is never clear why Kinsolving is addicted to drink. Nor can we believe his wife in the role she has to play. She appears like one of those characters a playwright leaves on the stage, mesmerized, until needed for a too-plotted appearance. At the height of the crisis, in a crowded house, she remains curiously hidden. As if the author felt her lack, he does earlier let her come to Flagg's apartment and protest, but it is a protest we do not believe, because we do not believe in her as a human being. And we must believe in her, because by not answering a letter, she loses the money, which puts her husband into Flagg's hands. Such irresponsibility is known to exist, but the miraculous recovery from it which follows her husband's miraculous recovery of himself is hard to believe. Certainly murder takes on virtues we never dreamed of. But the great flaw in the book is Mason Flagg. He is another hero whose slogan is SEX, THE LAST FRONTIER. It is never clear what power he has over men and women; he is so easily triumphant that it is no wonder he has a spoiled, vicious nature and is a leader of the movie set, the choral representative of spurious art. He is in both parts of the novel, but he is treated from the outside and superficially. Probably Peter Leveret should have been dropped and the view put with Flagg, the antagonist. At any rate it is the author's failure to bring him alive in the full necessity of an evil, rather than vicious, force at work which is the failure of the book.

As this investigation continues, it is becoming clearer that the impressionism of the ego makes of the first person not an aesthetic procedure but a subjective fusion of subject and method, a kind of autobiography of the author's stream of consciousness, with little critical examination or restraint on his part. It is a cultural phenomenon and an artistic regression. An art is first of all selective, and that means frequent withdrawal for critical appraisal and revision from the stream of creating which holds tangential and diverting material that has to be thrown out. The impressionist of the ego seems to want to keep everything, whether it advances the action or not, keeping it worshipfully because it is a part of him. It follows that in this kind of fiction the author may dispense with decorum, convention, all the formal restraints and institutions by means of which society governs and recognizes itself. Even when institutions and manners are recognized, they are treated frivolously or ridiculed, as limitations upon self-expression, the only truth. These writers make a grievous error, for there is in art no action without its proper form; nor is there, as norm, any uninhibited man in society. These writers rarely go to such extremes, but they go far enough to fall short of committing themselves absolutely to their material, and in treating it, they never risk failure in the adventure of the one comprehensive meaning for the action.

The first person can be skillfully used when it conforms to a traditional attitude towards nature and society. A good example of this is a book by Albert Guerard which came out in 1950: *Night Journey*. Whereas Styron divides his novel mechanically into two parts, neither of which receives the control of a view (and this means the reader does not know quite with whom his sympathy should lie or in which part the meaning more nearly may be discovered), the action of *Night Journey* takes place between two first persons, each one carrying on an interior monologue—the hero and his choral interpreter—who in alternating their voices make a dramatic dialogue which clearly advances the action toward its resolution. The resolution unites as it should the action and the enveloping action, giving the hero, Paul Haldan, a universal meaning as well as the meaning of his particular fate. As much as the other writers so far considered, Guerard confronts a shattered and changing society. But behind *Night Journey* is a civilized intelligence which renders the terror of Europe when the controls for action are no longer interrelated and abstract ideas are the last expression of organized government. Ideas become propaganda, propaganda deliberate lies, out of which rises the hopeless cynicism which describes the condition of the state. This is the enveloping action: nothing is as it seems; the thread of belief has snapped; man wanders without direction over a terrain where war never stops, with the fog of war now the fog of all human action. When peace is war and war is peace, every institution and convention is distorted.

The controlling image for the action is a civilian who is more military than the soldiers. He dresses as a civilian but carries himself like a Prussian. He comes into an army with orders from the highest command and so moves about out of any control from either the military or the civil authority. This is the ultimate confusion. To this has the state been reduced.

Paul Haldan, thrust into this situation with youthful hope of purpose, is attached to this concrete symbol of disorder and betrayal; he represents the night journey mankind must now take. Since Haldan remembers Europe in its civilized era, both the action and the enveloping action are united in his dilemma and in his relationship to the controlling image. Not sex but the nullity of all desire threatens Europe. The first person operates both on the literal and symbolic level, and it delivers its meaning, which is not an autobiography of a consciousness but a consciously controlled rendition of the subject's complication, established upon an individual's conflict and illuminated by a choral effect, also concentrated upon an individual. If at times the monotony which describes the edge of the abyss affects the reader as well as the actors, it is the trap of the first person, even traditionally used.

If *Night Journey* suggests the true desolation which must follow the breaking of all forms and rules, annihilating the human capacity to be, making the egos in life as shadowy as the ghosts in the classical underworld, then *Under the Volcano* by Malcolm Lowry renders hell in the mind of one man, the Consul, as a condition of such exquisite agony that society impinges upon the struggling psyche of the hero with no more certainty than images seen through the poisoned vapors of the volcano. It does not matter whether this society is shattered or alien; the Consul is in exile and alone. His aloneness is the result of and the punishment for a mortal crime; it is Satan's condition when he was cast forth from the mind of God, that is, from love, to the isolation of his own thoughts, which is hell. What is lacking in Miller and Durrell and Styron is a sense of evil. None of their characters suffer the consequences of their acts. Cass Kinsolving commits murder; yet, instead of being made to suffer either in his conscience or by the state, he is regenerated by murder. This is surely heresy. He remains perpetually drunk throughout the action; yet he acts more or less in control of himself. The only indication of drunkenness is in his sentimental relationship to the peasant girl and her father. We do not believe the depraved acts Flagg makes him perform before his guests, because he never seems drunk enough either before or after. This is again evidence of the failure of the chosen view. We are never close enough to the hero's inward plight.

I take Kinsolving for comparison, because both he and the Consul commit murder and remain drunk throughout the action. Kinsolving commits murder towards the end of the action; the Consul, before it begins. In other words the Consul's story depends upon what effect the murder has had upon him. We watch the process by which sin destroys a soul and how it suffers in hell. We don't know why the Consul put three German officers in the ship furnace; we are not quite sure he did it, but certainly he feels responsible, for there is no other explanation for the loss of love and his decline and self-damnation. His marriage failed, we must assume, because of his conscience and his pride and not as a result of his wife's adultery, which he drove her to; for it is she who loves, who comes back to him, and it is he who cannot repent and ask forgiveness, either of God or of man, which brings them both to their deaths. This is the action of the novel: the vestige of love which the Consul has for his wife struggles for, but does not achieve, atonement. Pride triumphs. "The will of man," he says, "is unconquerable. Even God cannot conquer it." They both literally and symbolically die for their sins, wandering in the literal and metaphorical dark of the jungle path: he for murder, she for adultery. The horse is the occasion for his death; its flight actually kills her, the agency which his hand literally sent. The horse stands for the masculine intuition and instincts which may save but, out of control, destroy. It was this instinctive sense of their need for each other which brought Yvonne back to him, but it was too late. He was too far gone in drink and remorse and illusion and hatred. Salvation in the spasmodic rise of his need for love offered itself until he took to mescal, that drink which destroys the reason and with it reality.

As is often the case, that which saves can destroy. Yvonne, returning to reoffer her love, brings death instead. Her husband, the Consul, struggles to reunite with her, but as he says, he loves hell now, simply because in the state of his conscience he is no longer free to love elsewhere. His sins have so isolated him that his communion can only be with his damnation. He has committed every mortal sin, and each is the doorway to hell, although he enters it first by the gluttony of drink, which he says is also food. Never crying *mea culpa* for his initial affront to God (that is, his taking of a life,

THE HERO WITH THE PRIVATE PARTS

which only God may do), he substitutes for the actual world a state of continual and extreme intoxication, whose delirium is filled by the voices of his "familiars." This is his hell. His conscience intrudes but in an inverted way, so that all his acts show the double betrayal of self and love. In moments of clarity he "flees for his life" not to a church but to a pulcheria. Everywhere he looks he finds another aspect of hell.

Nobody has shown so well the hell which is the flight from self, even to the quality of the style, which is heavy and overweighted, as if to draw the reader there, too. All the controlling images contain the pains and degradation of hell. The volcanoes give the physical sense of it. And they stand, also, for a mythical separation in marriage, as does Maximilian's broken palace, turned into an outdoor privy, among the ruins of which insects and mongrel dogs wander. Betrayal, the failure of marriage, madness find in the ruins the proper images. The Consul prays to the Virgin who describes his condition: "She is the Virgin for those who have nobody with." He asks to truly suffer; he asks for the return of his purity, the knowledge of the Mysteries that he has betrayed and lost. He asks that he may be truly lonely, so that he may *honestly* pray. Then he asks, "Let us [he and Yvonne] be happy again . . . if it's only out of this terrible world. 'Destroy the world,' he said in his heart." The only thing that will destroy the world is love, and that means the giving of self, which the Consul is no longer able to do. "No se puede vivir sin amar" is repeated, and again at the very end. All of the images match or suggest his betrayal and damnation. He alternately sips strychnine and whiskey, a way to sober up; but it fails because he takes it in excess, as he doesn't want to sober up. They are both aphrodisiacs which cancel each other out and contain, in excess, death. This symbolizes his plight and the end, as does the picture show where "dark shapes of pariah dogs prowled in and out of the stalls. The lights were not entirely dead: they glimmered, a dim reddish orange, flickering" (like hell). The picture is a horror story with Peter Lorre, presenting a murderer who has an artist's hands. So has the Consul, who never finishes his book; his crime thwarts his true profession and hence his manhood. The action takes place on the day of the feast of the dead, whose meaning as ceremony and private grief divulges, by antithesis, the double nature of the Consul's crime: the betrayal of the state and of his marriage.

He and his wife and his brother Hugh (who has loved Yvonne) hold what is, unwittingly but pertinently, a last supper in a pulcheria, in which love is travestied and addressed obscenely and subverted by salacious and vulgar punning. The main dish is "the spectral chicken of the house." This is the beginning of the end, and the end comes with the literal and figurative diverging of the paths, in the Consul's last flight. If Yvonne and Hugh had taken the right instead of the left fork, they would have overtaken him. They might have rescued him, but it is more likely that they would have only postponed to another occasion his death and the final damnation, for the action of this story is the perpetual relosing of the earthly paradise. I suppose the action hangs upon betrayal, the enveloping action, the death which came into the world at the original Fall. Death's images match the images of life which struggle to oppose it, but the dead ones predominate, as drink in the Consul's mind turns into the fumes of hell and the loss of hope. "How indeed could he hope to find himself, to begin again when, some-where, in one of those lost or broken bottles, in one of those glasses, lay, forever, the solitary clue to his identity?" The nature of his original crime is lost in the severity of the punishment for it.

At Parián his spiritual and moral crimes create their physical counterparts in the actual world. Here he recovers Yvonne's lost love letters (lost when drunk, drunkenness, however, being the mere occasion). These letters in all humility and grace and longing offer the solace of love and life and salvation to them both. His first thought is that she has been reading some good stylist. The last chapter opens with his order for mescal. This gives the image and direction of the final act. He allows himself to be manhandled, his person to be rifled (her letters are taken from him). His money is stolen; he is mocked; he is covered with the slime of pimps, criminal police, subversives, since it is they who should keep order. His will, which he boasted even God could not conquer, is now at the mercy of criminals and criminal suggestion. He is led off by, and commits the act of lust with, a whore, while the pimp watches. He looks up, and a picture of Canada on a calendar confronts him. Yvonne had planned that their new life would be there, in a kind of physical paradise. To see it on a calendar marking time makes the final twist of irony. He knows now all is lost, that he can never return to his wife, because the act he has committed is the final affront to and denial of love, without which one cannot live. After this he quickly comes to his physical death, but not until the hell where all the deadly sins take shape among the various criminals, hags, and subhuman individuals who surround and taunt him or try to warn of what will follow. He is now beyond shame, dignity, feeling, even beyond all that is done to him. He is already dead when the representative of law and order, now a murderer and outlaw, shoots him down with malice. His death repeats in parody his own act with the German prisoners, the public and private violation which cast him out of the world into the symbolic volcano, a ravine into which a dead dog is thrown after him. At the end, from the third person of a roving narrator, the author steps forward and prints on the page opposite:

> Le Gusta este Jardin
> Que es suyo?
> Evite que sus hijos lo Destruyan!

The excellencies and native talents of these writers must be taken for granted—these writers whose performance has been impaired by the ego. This ego represents a cultural disorder which should be used by, instead of using, the first-person point of view. The material is incompletely controlled, therefore, and the decline of impressionism is witnessed. The invisible form which resides within the mind does not realize itself substantially at the post; nor, in Percy Lubbock's words, do the form and content mutually use each other up. The third person, James's central intelligence, promises to the reader the author's self-containment, his artificial presence instead of his personal being. Specifically in the light of the argument here, it means that when the author has to intrude, he should do so invisibly and exit the same way, leaving no evidence of himself except in the changes he has wrought and in his irony.

There is one other thing. The stream of consciousness, when used by this imperfect ego masquerading as a point of view, makes the action more imperfect by the intensity this use of consciousness gives to the action. There must be some hone, some point of objective reference, some measure for this interior flow; usually this is the secular world. But it need not be just this. Without objectivity the consciousness reveals itself as too private. To the Lighthouse is an example. Claude Simon, who has been influenced by Faulkner, keeps his sentences vital and clear for pages, with an astute handling of punctuation; however, the affective intensities of his heroes and heroines make them incomplete. This is because of a disproportion of feeling and reflection to what is actually happening. Again it is the first person, but this time the first person lost in the stream of consciousness. Faulkner used this view, but only as one tool among many which the fictive inheritance offered. Of course we must never forget that execution shares in the imperfections of our mortality; but the post must achieve a disentanglement, so sight and insight can be distinguished and measured and fused.

Fiction and the Essence of Things: Stephen Crane's "The Open Boat"

THE SINKING OF THE *COMMO-dore* is the only instance I know which allows for a strict comparison between journalism (even in Eliot's sense) and fiction. After his rescue Crane, along with the captain and others, wrote for the press his own story of the disaster. It is good; it is the best of journalism. But it is not fiction; nor was it meant to be. This was to come later in "The Open Boat," certainly one of the finest works of its kind in the language. We have, then, the perfect exemplum of reporting and rendition of the fact of disaster at sea. As Crane says beneath the title of "The Open Boat," it is after the fact. All of the difference is in this statement. After the fact there is time for reflection, distance, and out of the act itself the growth of meaning.

The immediate report of disaster is always too sensational and, as journalism, of necessity too hurried, too involved in the moment, too dependent upon clichés and the choice of the obvious in violence and sentiment. For example, in "Stephen Crane's Own Story," written shortly after his rescue, the loading of the ammunition and bundles of rifles is presented in this way: the hatch is like the mouth of a monster, "the feeding time of some legendary beast." This comparison is strained. It blurs the picture and diverts the reader, for no conceit is strong enough to add anything to a function whose literal meaning or performance also contains its symbolic meaning. The rifles and ammunition are themselves the agencies of death, their violence momentarily hidden as they actually are being hidden within the hold. Later we will find that the beast, after the fact, discovered its true relationship in the fiction. In the New York press the hatch as monster is after the fact in the wrong way. Crane is with false artifice giving a foreboding of disaster. There are other incidences of this, such as the cook's feeling in his bones, the helmsman's intention not to go filibustering again in spite of the good pay, the ship's running aground twice. The details which describe the sinking are accurate and theatrical. They all have to do with the report giving the illusion of an act. The report does have the drama of a shipwreck at sea, but the actors lack humanity, since it is the general fright, not the individual responding, which the newspaper reader is meant to receive.

Except in a disaster so great that everybody is forced to feel a personal involvement or threat, the news story insulates the reader from life. The generalized report never gives him the sense of having observed, but rather of receiving a rumor, the details of which are not quite to be believed. The reader's position is always that of the stranger, the uninvolved. Rarely does he feel: There but for the grace of God go I. When the first mate jumps to his death, we see him begin his flight, but we do not feel him hit the water. Crane has to interpret this for us. On the other hand, in fiction there is always a chorus, or what stands for a chorus, the enveloping action. This holds some essential archetypal explanation of experience, of which the action is one example. The sympathy between the reader, then, and the protagonist involves the reader and lifts him from the accidents of life into some phase and understanding of the essence of things. This is why the best of fiction stands to last and the news story disappears with the paper it is printed on.

There is one instance in "Stephen Crane's Own Story" which puts side by side the report and the rendition of fiction. When the crazed Negro stevedore pulls the towing boat towards the raft, we are told he "had turned into a demon. He was wild—wild as a tiger," vague and timeworn figures of speech for the threat of irrational force. But "his eyes were almost white" is fiction. This is not only accurate observation, it is also selection of the one detail which reveals the wild, animal fright of brute strength usurping manhood. The pulling on the rope is the physical and outward sign of this inward chaos. The pupil, which focuses what is rational in man, is closed or lost. And loss of control, the loss of reason before the threat of death, is actual with the stevedore, but it is a surrender possible for all here engaged. Under the strain the yellow eyeball seems or becomes white. It is as unfocused as chaos. It is the concrete instance, physical appearance, and moral and mental loss combined, of that which in man equals the unruly waters.

Journalism in Crane's day was closer to fiction than it is now. The mechanical formulae of platitude as the norm would not come for another generation or so, so that at its best, as in "Stephen Crane's Own Story," the news story has at times the same authority as fiction. But the reader must wait for "The Open Boat" to know what it is to be at sea, to be within six inches of death minute by minute at the height of a storm which lasts for thirty hours. Of course there is the obvious suspense: will the men get ashore? But this is merely the statement of a desired end; it is not the action itself. The shipwrecked, except at intervals, are not involved with rescue (this is their concern, of course); they are involved, to use Arthurian terms, with the dolorous quest, unconsciously, nevertheless truly; and this enforced quest becomes ignorance changed into knowledge and especially self-knowledge before a continuing precarious plight. This is the way in which the ordinary man becomes a hero or fails in manhood. With the frail support of a ten-foot dinghy four men—the injured captain, the cook, the oiler, and the one alien to the sea, the correspondent—confront the ocean (the elemental) at its most destructive phase. Without water there can be no life, but that which is benign and sustaining is merely one part of the dualism which holds in reserve, for its own mysterious reasons, the opposite or destructive power. Such is the course of learning these men are forced to undertake. They are at the mercy of one element, but they are affected by all four; to say four is to say the elements are pagan. The outcome of the action will show whether the cosmos to the shipwrecked is pagan and whether they so view it.

Four elements, four men in the boat who comprise the basic qualities of men acting as men. We begin with this. The captain is the legal and moral authority; he is the sovereign power. The cook is the one who attends to and satisfies appetite. The oiler has all of the craftsmanship and deep knowledge of the sea; he is the one who can make a thing work or go, and it is these qualities as expressions of his character which allow the captain, by ordering them, to bring the men to shore. It is also these qualities which make of him and not the captain the hero-victim. The correspondent is the outsider and so is better able to interpret what takes place. But particularly he is the man of words, and it is by means of words, artfully employed, that actions are most fully known. For these reasons the point of view must lie with him. We have a definite clue. He wonders why he is there, and to wonder is the beginning of knowledge. He enters the minds of all, but he is an actor, too, and finds himself most identified with the oiler. He is the twin and counterpart, but the articulate and imaginative part, of the oiler, who only does.

Each of the men is, in a way, the protagonist, for each by his office (not personally) represents an intrinsic part of man. These parts must be seen not as allegory but as offices. That is, the man of appetite is a cook; sovereignty is specified by what it means to be a captain of a ship, not of infantry. But it is the correspondent who is the actual protagonist, for he is changed by the action. The others are there to be interpreted by him in the course of his learning. They are real but in a sense become his creatures. He is writing the story after the fact to understand the experience and what it has done for him, which he cannot know unless he knows the others in their roles. Only fiction can do this, since facts are elusive and require a point of view and an imagination to fit them together. "The Open Boat" being fiction, Crane is not himself either but his own creature, along with the companions in sorrow.

The action opens not with the melodramatic incident of the crazed stevedore but with the now famous sentence "None of them knew the color of the sky." Here is a simple sentence; yet it is mysterious. What it holds is the essence of the action: the kernel. It is the felt weight of this which induces the mystery and establishes in the first sentence the suspense and tone which will be maintained. This sense of the conflict can only be felt, because it takes the long middle and the shock at the end to fuse together the entire meaning at a specific moment. And this moment of course closes the action. A story whose opening lacks this feeling of weight, of a revelation about to be illumined, will be discursive and suggestive rather than intrinsic and absolute. The shipwrecked do not know the color of the sky, because to remove their eyes for an instant from the mountainous waves will swamp the boat. Their eyes are fixed by the threat and object of death. As in any crisis of violence, man, by being immersed, can act only out of his instincts and reflexes. These men, we are told, know all the colors of the sea; that is, they have the particular knowledge of the ways of the sea. But being so caught up, they cannot use it. They are in this beginning virtually in a state of ignorance. Meaning develops as they suffer and learn.

The author's most urgent technical problem must have been the kind of comparisons to make. To use only pictures of the sea and its effects upon them would have produced monotony. No element in the natural world is finally isolated. Where there is the sea, there is the sky above, which holds the breath of life and, as the winds blow it, the threat of death. Fire at sea is a harder matter, since it is the opposite of water and only in alchemy can conjoin with it. But there are the stars, the lights in the night, the streak of phosphorus. Once water is a spread of white flames. But the images most used are from the land. The sea and the land contain the conflict, the threat of annihilation and the hope of salvation. It is towards the land their desperate eyes most often turn. Can they free themselves of the waves and safely come to shore? In "Stephen Crane's Own Story," when they try to launch a lifeboat, he compares their effort with that of moving a brick schoolhouse. Either instinctively or consciously, here he got the substance of his structure. In their peril the land could only seem safe, kind, and longed for, but this is only half its meaning. In their desperation they, at first, ignore what is hidden.

Because the eye is in the moving boat, the horizon narrows and widens, dips and rises, in fact refuses to make of the landfall a fixed and stable place. The motion of the sea dominates. All things, including the land, are liquid and threatening. Nowhere in the universe does there seem to be a firm place to stand. The waves are thrust up in points like rocks. To be tossed upon rocks is to be spitted; to be rolled in the breakers may be to drown. The threat of the waves is thus reinforced by something equally dangerous on the land. The entire paragraph gives us the shipwrecked in an almost hopeless condition, just after the ship goes down. The next paragraph says that a man ought to have a bathtub larger than the boat which here rides upon the sea. The tub, misplaced in the ocean, because of its misplacement makes visual

the immensity of the ocean, the fragility of the dinghy, and the slight
chance of survival. And what could be more opposite to what is happening
to them than the safe luxury of a warm tub behind a locked door?

These seemingly contradictory effects follow throughout, but particularly
in the first two parts. The boat is a bucking bronco. As the wave approaches, the little boat rises for it like a horse taking a fence outrageously
high. It rides down the slaty wall of water, which seems the final outburst of
the ocean. The waves have a terrible grace, and they come in silence, "save
for the snarling of the crests." Silence against the sound of the crests makes
the reader both see and hear in the wave the threat of the ocean. Not only
has Crane here in a way no one can doubt brought together sound and
silence, exact opposites; but he further enlarges the effect by yoking together things ordinarily never compared, and he does this by what they
have in common, terror. The slaty wall is an actual terror in itself, but the
terrible grace and the snarling imply the beast crouching or springing. The
tiger of the news story takes on now its proper effect. And further, the land is
no longer the simple hope for refuge. The men are still caught up. They do
not notice the changing of the hours; their faces are gray in the wan light of
breaking day; they are still unable to be aware of anything more than the sea
colors changing from slate to emerald green (the foam tumbles like snow).
Against the elemental forces, to view the men at dawn, the author makes a
violent shift of view. He puts it in a balcony, as if the spectator were
comfortably watching a melodrama, something "weirdly picturesque." This
is so removed from the actual predicament as to imply an indifference to
their fate, to make it unreal. It is almost as if they were already dead. At
least the unreality of a view from a balcony makes of the land, their hope of
refuge, a place not to be believed in. Now, against the sea and those threats
from the land similar both in kind and appearance to the sea, the author
places a short dialogue between the cook and the correspondent. In spite of
the fuller knowledge of what the land holds for these shipwrecked men, for
the moment hidden in the enveloping comparisons, they can only see the
shore as a good. The cook speaks hopefully of a house of refuge as being near.
In his anxiety he confuses it with a life-saving station. The correspondent
corrects him. They contradict each other; that is, they argue about a hypothetical situation. The oiler, the seaman, returns them to reality. "We're
not there yet," he says.

These sea-land comparisons contain both the enveloping action, or the conditions forever constant upon the human and natural scene, and the action itself. In this short dialogue the action begins to withdraw from that which envelops it, begins to specify, although it does not yet make clear the fullness of what is amorphous. This withdrawal is never a severance. It merely gives shape to that which is hidden but ever present. It is as old as the Fall of Man, since man falling into his predicament always falls into his original plight, a plight, though unique, common to all. The individual conflict is the only way to show their common predicament. The fear of death is an abstraction until it withdraws from the general into a particular affect. The sense of fear may be in a group, but each member will feel it according to his capacity. The artist manages to make this apparent by the use of his various tools, the most important of which is the sensibility. Its five parts make the word flesh.

Parts 2 and 3 continue and emphasize the ambiguity which relates land to sea; only now the action begins more and more to show it. The crest of the waves suggests not mountains but a hill of water, high and formidable but not impossible to mount. The danger seems less present than the snarling beast, although the situation remains precarious. Canton flannel (soft for babies and croup) gulls fly about them. They sit down upon the water, in front of the men, as at home as prairie chickens a thousand miles inland. They sit near patches of seaweed which undulate like carpets in a gale. All these domestic comparisons of comfort and safety converge through the gulls and then through one gull into the action itself. They make a particular effect. They stare at the men with black, beadlike eyes. Their unblinking scrutiny seems uncanny and sinister. The occupants of the boat hoot at them. Then one gull threatens by sidelong jumps in the air, "chicken-fashion," to roost upon the captain's head. The captain would like to knock it in the head with a painter, but he waves it gently away and carefully. This enforced restraint brings to a point the six inches of gunwale and the turbulent waters, immediate and threatening.

The overwhelming, absolute threat of death which the mountains of water pose in the beginning remains, but in a state of suspension. It becomes the shape of their predicament. The senses begin to work and make the feelings of the four, their responses to particular objects, carry the increasing tensions of the conflict as it moves inevitably toward the climax. The cook bails, the captain directs, the correspondent and the oiler row, sometimes together, sometimes separately, and the care with which the rowers change places compares them to Dresden figurines. And then he who is relieved is no longer china. He drops into the cold water of the boat and is instantly asleep. Touch and sight show the menace of growing fatigue. Their waning strength is thus opposed to the tireless waves. In the beginning the oars seem too frail. Any moment the weight of water may snap them in two and thus doom the boat, but towards the end they are as heavy as lead. This different use of touch measures the time at sea and the mounting fatigue which diminishes their chances of escape. To say that men are tired does not show them so, but the changing weight of the oars does. Nor can statement make time pass either. But time is very important. It is another measure of the men's resistance. It is rendered in various ways, but sight, the sovereign sense, is sharpened upon a small, still thing in the moving horizon. This is the lighthouse at Mosquito Inlet, and nobody can see it at first but the captain, he whose attention is ever alert. Indistinctly this grows from a pinpoint, out of a long, black shadow upon the sea, until it is an upright shadow upon the sky: substances of hope but insubstantial to sight, matter yet not matter. The horizon still moves; substance cannot be relied upon. However, seaweed imitating earth tells them they are making progress towards land.

We now approach the long middle. The fury of the sea has decreased, but only so far as to allow the shipwrecked to be consciously aware of the danger, to assess their chances. They have been cast away not in the pink of condition but overworked and hungry, and the captain has a broken arm. The men strain almost to the verge of collapse, but the captain by some stratagem, each time, prolongs the struggle. As he hangs over the water jar, he hears and sees and inwardly interprets the particularities, the quality of the threats, so that in each command quietly given, he speaks with his proper authority and adds to this the great moral force of knowledge they all now begin to acquire. Sometimes he has them hoist his overcoat on an oar for sail, and at times he has the cook make of an oar a rudder so that both the oiler and the correspondent can rest together. Even when the boat capsizes and they are in the surf, he speaks above its roar and instructs the cook and the correspondent.

But as the land slowly rises out of the sea and the lighthouse rears high, the captain himself voices their suppressed fear. Even he confuses the house of refuge (which doesn't exist) with the lifesaving station (which is twenty miles away). Their irrational state of mind, where rescue is concerned, finds its expression in denying the facts. To accept the facts just then would bring them to despair, so great is their stress and so inadequate their means for survival. But there comes a respite. The land continues to rise beautifully out of the sea. Another sense now is used: sound. They hear the low thunder of the surf: the threat of death and the hope of salvation, just where the black line of the sea and the white of sand join, that border they must pass over and which now is fixed in their sight. The wind has changed, but their moment seems to be upon them. They grow cheerful, find cigars and matches. "Everybody took a drink of water."

But it is a false hope. The house the captain has seen as the house of refuge or lifesaving station is just a house in a summer resort. They are forced to abandon the false illusion which unspoken fear established in their minds as fact. The surf though far away sounds thunderous and mighty. The captain is the first to confront the reality again, which is that if they are to be saved, they will have to do it themselves and presently, for "if we stay out here too long, we'll none of us have the strength left to swim after the boat swamps." They willingly face up to the enemy, and with understanding, not complete but sufficient for the moment. They exchange addresses, accepting with constraint the possibility of death. This is a kind of moral triumph before the obvious dangers at that place where land and water meet.

It is at this time that the correspondent, in interpreting for all, uses a rhetorical language which seems to violate the established tone. "If I am going to be drowned—if I am going to be drowned—if I am going to be drowned, why, in the name of the seven mad gods who rule the sea, was I allowed to come thus far and contemplate sand and trees? . . . [Why was] my nose dragged away as I was about to nibble the sacred cheese of life? . . . If this old ninny-woman Fate cannot do better than this, she should be deprived of the management of men's fortunes." And it goes on. Actually there is no violation. This is one of the correspondent's voices. The false rhetoric is a part of the professional cynicism of journalism which views all appearance as false or suspect. It is not even a pretense to belief, for the gods here invoked are pagan gods the correspondent no more believes in than he believes in the Christian order of Heaven. He who was taught to be cynical of men does believe in and knows at the time that the fellowship with the other men in the boat would be the best experience of his life. This feeling of comradeship discovered for the correspondent his own humanity, but he is not yet fully saved, not so long as he uses the falsely pagan figures of speech. To be half-saved on this quest is to ask for further trials. And this is exactly what the ocean and the doubtful shore have yet to give.

As they draw nigh to land, it is seen that the billows will surely swamp the boat. The oiler announces the dinghy won't live three more minutes and asks the captain to let him take it to sea again. It takes supreme skill to execute this. The oiler rows them back into their predicament, towards the desolate orient and a squall marked by clouds "brick-red like smoke from a burning building." Moral fatigue as well as physical shows in the collapse of the rower into the cold seawater sloshing to and fro in the bottom of the boat, being drenched without being awakened, within an inch of the waves, into which, if the boat should capsize, he would have "tumbled comfortably out upon the ocean as if he felt sure it was a great soft mattress." This is a small climax of the ambiguity in the land-sea images. The castaways' bitter retreat is made poignant by seeing a man on shore waving his coat. Other men arrive. But what a distance between those at sea and those on land. All the possibilities of rescue pass before those in the dinghy, but the men on land are as helpless to help as they are to receive it. When the four realize this and also realize that they must spend a night upon the ocean, they revile those on shore and particularly the one waving his coat. The coat is a message of sympathy, but the night closing down makes the land seem hostile. After the land has vanished, but not the low, drear thunder of the surf, the correspondent berates the pagan gods about his possibility of drowning. But this time he speaks only about a third as much. This lessening of his use of such rhetoric is a clue to the meaning of its function.

They now literally enter the night sea journey. The oarsman can barely see the tall, black waves. The rest lie heavily and listlessly in the boat. The captain droops over the water jar, but he still commands, saying, "Keep her head up" when the oarsman falters. The long strain has made the cook indifferent to danger. He withdraws into a dream of food. He asks what kind of pie the oiler likes best. The man whose office it is to attend to the appetite of others now expresses his longing for shore in dreams of his own. This is the only time the oiler becomes agitated. To the correspondent the mention of food brings to mind no "cheese" of life but its very bread. They are made to suffer twice over, in their physical need and in their longing for the land's comforts, which the mention of food makes them so keenly aware of.

Throughout the night the oiler and the correspondent exchange places, each rowing after he is no longer able to row. And then in the deep reaches of the night the correspondent is left alone with the full responsibility of his office, for even the captain, he thinks, is asleep. We now approach the climax for all, and for the protagonist the long dark night at sea becomes the dark night of the soul. The correspondent is to be isolated, until he feels himself the one man afloat upon all the oceans, so that the "wind's voice is sadder than the end." There remains this night nothing to sustain him but himself. Before the complex mystery which surrounds him, he begins to change, finding his cynicism no help for what confronts him. The boat is so small that the men touch, their feet reaching under the sea even to the captain. They exist almost as one body, under the pressures of their predicament. But the correspondent does not share this, for he alone is conscious. Fire is the appropriate element to illuminate his predicament. There are two lights, one to the north and one to the south. "The two lights were the furniture of the world." This expresses his aloneness, but the shark trailing its phosphorus suggests death, although its light is harmless. Then there are the stars. All of these exempla of fire, because they are remote and cannot immediately affect him either for good or ill, represent his confinement to himself. This is his trial, and he accepts it as he leans over the boat and swears softly into the sea.

During the rest of the night, the management of the boat requires the others to take their parts with him. He returns to them changed. Part 6 opens with, "If I am going to be drowned . . ." but the rhetoric fails him. The complaint is very short. The indifference of Fate makes him say but, "I love myself." At once he is presented with the vanity of this. His rebellion, the lack of a temple to pelt with brick, quickly declines into a pathos and knowledge of any man's supreme insignificance. "A high cold star on a winter's night is the word" he feels that she (nature) says to him. This is the point of change for him. The star is so remote it might be the core and shine of eternity, and nothing at this moment could so reduce him or make him suffer the humility without which no man is reborn. To make it concrete, out of his unconscious suddenly he is hearing a verse he had forgotten. As a child it had meant no more to him than a pencil point breaking. Like the ninny-woman Fate, it belongs to a foreign world. Through his changing sense of himself, it now becomes present, no longer foreign but a local instance, as is his suffering, of the universal predicament of mankind, everywhere beset and tried by those forces of nature (for so far does he see) everywhere about, lying in wait to try and judge the spirit and resistance of man.

> A soldier of the Legion lay dying in Algiers;
> There was lack of woman's nursing, there was dearth of woman's tears;
> But a comrade stood beside him, and he took the comrade's hand,
> And he said, "I never more shall see my own, my native land."

Out of the isolation of himself from all living creatures, before the point of eternity and in the presence of death (the shark), the correspondent is able to transform sound into sight (the rhythm of the verse into visual images) and out of this combine all the senses into a belief in and apprehension of a real soldier dying in the sands of Algiers. These sands become more real than the real sands before him by a kind of reversal, as he is purged of false rhetoric. The word becomes itself, and out of sorrow for himself has grown a compassionate sympathy for all. This is the measure of the extremity of his change. But even yet he does not understand it. The danger of the waves and the shut-in night does not allow him time for contemplation. He largely feels as much as exhausted muscle and attention will allow. But when morning breaks and it is clear no help is coming and the captain decides to run the surf, then nature to the correspondent (and he speaks for all) seemed neither cruel, nor wise, nor beneficent, nor treacherous— merely indifferent.

The sense of this represents the purgation of "fine" language and the illusion of false aid. There is nowhere a subterfuge for reality, the approaching crisis which in an instant will be death or salvation. The third great wave swamps the boat, and they tumble into the January water; but the warning of that from which they must turn away, yet, whatever the outcome, must also face, comes to the correspondent as the waters from the second wave tumble into the boat. His hands were on the thwarts. He quickly withdraws them as if he were afraid of wetting his fingers—he who has been sleeping in water, been saturated by it, and from the extremity of his fatigue would have rolled into it as upon a soft mattress. I suppose, in fiction, the sense of touch has never been so well used; nor can one find so rare an example of the authority of rendition over that of statement. The nerves, in prostration, reach that exquisite feeling which brings to touch its euphoria and the falling away from this exquisite feeling into the listlessness of no response. Physically, then, the nerve ends, having reached this condition, a condition where water is felt as fire (one feels this in the quick withdrawal), represent the transcendence of fatigue, the weapon of the sea against the shipwrecked, who will now enter the water with only the resistance their separate persons in the mystery of their spirits may show. Also in this touch is the final concentration of the unspoken fear of death, of hope and despair, also unspoken but revealed in full by this action, a repugnance for their condition and for nature, the four elements, and the final denial of any pathetic fallacy. Once the men are in the water, the shore seems like scenery upon a stage. Although it is almost in reach and touch, to turn at this moment the real shoreline into an artificial setting for entertainment is an irony almost too finely drawn; it also sustains by the imagination what touch has done for the flesh. By now we feel all the false rhetoric has been strained away. The correspondent says simply, in the wonder of an innocent: "I am going to be drowned? Can it be possible? Can it be possible?" His isolation from himself is his conquest over self. He is now ready for the final act and understanding.

The captain in the water, holding on to the boat, still gives directions above the mighty noise of the surf. The cook, in a life preserver, is ordered to turn on his back and use the oar. The oiler needs no direction; he swims rapidly towards land, ahead in the race, as if he had suffered no fatigue. But the correspondent is ordered to come to the boat, when a wave lifts him and carries him completely over it to waters in which he can stand, though only for an instant. So fine a hair is drawn in his fate, which is settled by a man on shore running and shedding his clothes until he is naked as upon the first day, naked as the natural man free of all inhibiting social conventions. He drags the cook ashore; the captain, still in his office of authority, directs him next to the correspondent, whom he pulls by the hand. Suddenly the man cries, "What's that?" The correspondent says, "Go."

It is the oiler, in the shallows, face down. His head touches, between each wave, the sand. The two elements of water and earth are now brought together in their complete meaning. The ambiguity of life-death is resolved in the oiler's body. And in human terms, sustaining the elemental, the dead body of the oiler and the live naked body of the man from the shore, whose charitable love saves some of them, represent life and death, which the shoreline holds, the one aspect the forbidding and the other the hopeful. If the irony, however, becomes final in the oiler's body, the paradox remains to the end: one dies, the others live. The one most knowledgeable of the sea, who has brought the others to safety, cannot save himself. Both life and death are here, but only after a respite does the correspondent, speaking for the survivors and perhaps for the dead, receive the full impact of learning. "When it came night, the white waves paced to and fro in the moonlight, and the wind brought the sound of the great sea's voice to the men on shore, and they felt that they could then be interpreters."

From the ignorance of the first line, "None of them knew the color of the sky," the ignorance of absolute action, they now have graduated into the knowledge of the possibilities of all experience; that is, they can now interpret, at last, what has happened to them and what, therefore, can happen to all men. Like a destructive beast, nature is always lying in wait to undo mankind. The elements may be indifferent, but the mysterious, fateful circumstance, depending upon the supernatural, can save or destroy. Those who escape and those who fall define a mystery. The oiler is there for proof. And from the wind, the sea carries to the men on shore this message. The basic element of life, air, without which we cannot live, is the agency of the final mystery. Earth and water are forever present, the physical grounds for action, but the air in its physical and symbolic meaning carries the final authority of knowledge, the conditions of man in life and in the presence of the supernatural. The shipwrecked understand now the price of things as well as the mystery. They know one does not earn his life once and for all, for the beast remains in ambush, whether at sea or on land or within the human heart, pacing to and fro. Although the natural man, the innocent man (he does not know or care whether he has clothes on or not), loves his neighbor as himself and shines like a saint (angel), the ending does not necessarily show them all turned Christians. They in this knowledge which is experience may still be pagan. Their learning could be in the limits of stoicism. This kind of withdrawal of ignorance could be the answer to the mystery they have suffered. But it seems more likely that the correspondent, who entered this adventure cynically, now crowns his learning and change with a Christian image, even though he may have reached only the threshhold of faith, such as the early Christians knew. Perhaps it is this which makes them all feel, as the correspondent interprets for them, "that they could then be interpreters."

Part II

The Subject of
Southern Fiction

WHENEVER A WRITER TALKS about a story or a novel he has done, he is not speaking in his true voice. That voice has already been heard in the rendition of the action, and once done, the covers of the book enclose it. It is no longer the malleable thing he worked with; it is set to its form, beyond further help or damage from him. If he persists in talking about it, instead of leaving it alone to make its effect, it is generally by way of a paraphrase or an apology. It's why we tend to skip the passages on the historians and the man of destiny in *War and Peace*. Tolstoy is not then speaking as the artist he is; he is using the voice of a Russian theorizing about a segment of Russian history. This is all the more restricted in its appeal, because Tolstoy has already put the man of destiny in the book acting out concretely his theory and thus negating it as theory, since he has brought Napoleon alive. No abstraction can stand before Prince Andrew lying under the blue sky, thinking he is dying, and looking up to see in the flesh his former idol. What he sees in this moment of truth annihilates the argumentative assertions of the essays.

It should be obvious that polemics is one discipline and fiction another. If you are going to preach, get into the pulpit; if you want to bring about political reforms, run for office; social reforms, behave yourself and mind your manners. The professions appear in a novel for technical purposes. A preacher may be needed to save a fictive, not an actual, soul, just as a bore may be put there to bore some other character; but the skilled writer will not bore you with a man of total recall any more than his preacher will save you your soul. Sometimes, though, the sense of damnation in a book may be grounds for spiritual review, as Dickens' *Bleak House* is said to have set about the reforms in the courts of chancery. Such a result, however, is residual, not the essential intention of the writer towards his reader. When a novel obviously makes an appeal other than its proper aesthetic one, you may be sure it has been written with the left hand.

This intention of the writer towards his hypothetical reader involves many delicate and insoluble matters. Ideally the artist creates his reader as well as the book, establishing in his mind that perfect communion of sympathy and understanding which, unfortunately, remains ideal. There are no limits to hope, but there are limits to the artifice, and these are his main concern. Granted that an art is of greater truth than the accidental nature of human affairs which is its source, the artist should never forget how precarious are the grounds of attention he must ask for. The most trivial interference from the actual affairs of life is always a threat. A child falling down the stairs and screaming bloody murder will bring a mother from the very death of Hamlet. This very frailty puts an obligation upon the serious reader; he should bring to a book no preconception which will prevent him from following the action in all its levels. I am taking for granted that the story has found its formal expression. After distinguishing between the simple art of narrative and the comprehensive art of fiction, Percy Lubbock says the critical reader becomes an artist, too. He must re-create what has been done, a greater reward always than some sensational impression of it. The pleasure of illusion is small beside the pleasure of creation, and knowledge better than simple entertainment.

The lack of a critical nomenclature commonly accepted and practiced certainly does not help reading. We hear too often the term *prose fiction*, which seems to make of it a branch of rational discourse and not its true self, an art in its own right, with its own laws and conventions, by means of which it enters the large field of the creative imagination common to all the arts. In academic circles, but not always and not only there, this lack of the proper critical tools fosters the habit of reducing a book or story to its theme or idea, which is to say to an abstraction. This does violence to its singular aesthetic appeal, that illusion of an action imitating men and women caught in some one of the human predicaments forever repeating themselves. The meaning in fiction should always be received actively, in the structural relationships between the parts. Reception is crucial; the reader must be moved affectively, so that his insight will comprise the fullest meaning which lies before him.

There is another approach which misses the mark. Older than fiction, it is the game of discovering sources and influences, which is all very well up to a point. Too much is made of these influences, however, when they pretend to disclose the secrets of the creative act. There are only two ways to learn anything, by actual experience and by imitation. If you are a writer, you partly learn by reading other writers. But the moment comes when, to quote indirectly T. S. Eliot, you steal instead of borrow; that is, you make it your own. At this moment you pass from apprenticeship to the beginning of mastery. Henry James, as we know, never listened to the end of a story. He wanted from it only what would set his own skill to working. Besides, to hear it all would have brought him up against a false sense of the history of it, false because all the facts would seem to be but could not actually be present in the report at second hand. He could not know another's mind, but he could take the risk of his own imagination. It is just this about sources and influences: the scholar can know them only in their raw condition, not how the imagination used them.

One of the influences on "Jericho, Jericho, Jericho" was *The Time of Man* by Elizabeth Madox Roberts. I finished her book and, in the fullness of the catharsis it had given me, sat right down and in less than two minutes wrote the first page. I remember very clearly the feeling that her rhythm had set my own to going. After writing this one page, I set it aside for four years, because I was not sure whether I was beginning a novel or a story. I might have set it aside forever, if the editors of the *Southern Review* had not asked me for a story. Or in the fullness of time, I might have gone back and turned it into a novel. All kinds of accidents play their part, but in the end the writer has only one subject, and he spends his life discovering how to unfold it. And when it lies all before him, he is done for.

To put such store by influences, then, is to make a basic mistake about the nature of an art; it is to reduce it to a rational act. This attitude also falsifies the thing made by confusing what is unique to it, the artist's own way of seeing and doing, with the common grounds of experience any artist of necessity must draw upon. This common ground is the repetitive involvement with himself and his fellows which is man's affliction and his delight, the archetypal experience which forever recurs within the human scene. For example, the loss of innocence, or the initiation of youth into manhood, is an archetypal experience. The young Spartan who did not falter, as the fox was chewing his bowels, discloses his way of undergoing what every youth suffers at a certain time of life. But the young men of differing societies will respond in various ways. Unlike Sparta we do not formally instruct our young men. What there is of it is private and acci-dental. This lack of ritual limited, at the very start, the archetypal conflict in "The Mahogany Frame."* The boy's initiation happens by accident, through the ritual of hunting, itself debased; and the change in him which comes at the end in a shock of illumination is the measure of how he achieves maturity without formal guidance. The way it came out was not the way I saw it when I began it. I began with the wrong enveloping action and had to lay it aside, again, curiously enough, for four years. When a neighbor, Sinclair Buntin, invited me to go on a duck hunt, I accepted and returned not only with duck but with the way to do the story. Any-thing, a mood, an incident, a character, an idea, can set you going; but the end must be not any story but the one story which will deliver the meaning. The process is the advancing discovery, always controlled, of the hidden meaning. Michelangelo spoke of releasing the image in the stone. Material, any material, produces a kinetic change in the psyche of the artist. The subject matter is never inert, a thing merely to be observed and used. An interaction takes place between the writer and what moves him to write. Any kind of reading which ignores this is committing a kind of aesthetic crime by taking away from the author what is rightly his.

*The story was originally called "The Guide." Allen Tate suggested "The Mahogany Frame," which now seems to me much better.

Fiction is an action, then, and an action which tells the only story which makes of the form and subject a single whole. This is the first limitation which the writer as artist confronts. So conscious was Flaubert of this wholeness that when he was asked to take away a line in "A Simple Heart," he protested that to do so would cause the structure to fall apart. The action must have a beginning, a middle, and an end; and the end is in the beginning, as the plant is organically found in the seed. An art is a craft confronting the mystery of the imagination and an even more private impulse; so the artist warily but persistently tries to discover the proper environment for its singular growth. It becomes apparent, then, that there is not one action but two: the action proper, which is the conflict, and the enveloping action, sometimes miscalled background (a borrowing from painting), miscalled because background implies a static condition. Since fiction is an action, nothing should be left inert. The two actions take place simultaneously in fiction as they do in life, just as a man must be made convincing as man before he can become an individual man. Let us say that it is his masculinity which more nearly represents the enveloping action, and his unique response to a conflict the action proper. However, this is not quite adequate. The enveloping action is that universal quality, some constant, forever true aspect of experience. The action proper is its concrete showing; or the action proper may be the very obverse and so show it by contradiction or contrast.

The action has two main parts: the pictorial or panoramic summary and the scene. That's all it is, reduced to its basic structural components and controlled by a point of view. Of course, such does not describe the conscious or intuitive arrangement of these two kinds of effects, or the special attention to the use of the five senses to evoke the illusion of flesh. No matter how well you write in fiction, or what profound meaning you feel suffuses the action, unless you can imitate men and women caught in some one of the tensions we all know, you fail. And it is by means of the senses, more than anything else, that the word in fiction delivers the immediate sense of life. It is by and through them that we receive the world, know we are alive; they are the avenues, the nervous cords, which unite the physical and spiritual parts of being. They are the invisible, in a way servile aids upon which the more crucial matters depend and without which the archetypes would hover in the distance like ideal concepts. At this point the artist discovers a restraint as conventional as blank verse. And this is location. People do not live in a vacuum. They live somewhere. Mention of this has already been made, but too much emphasis cannot be given to the varying artificial distinctions of a culture's polity through which the archetype repeats itself. The natural man is an abstraction. He has never been seen, but what is natural to men always shows itself shaped by the manners and mores, the institutional restraints, of a given time and place. Underneath, as the impulse to action, is the degree of strength or weakness of religious vision; for without belief there would be no coherent incentive to any kind of performance, good or bad. To say this would once have been a platitude; it is no longer.

We used to have hopes, and there are occasional echoes now, of somebody writing The Great American Novel, as if it could be some agglomerate concretion of the American spirit. This is a naïve expectation, which will become clear when it is asked, Did Tolstoy or Dostoevsky write The Great Russian Novel? Or even here at home, which is The Great American Novel, *Moby-Dick* or *The Ambassadors*? They are both great and both American certainly, and yet how they differ in style and meaning, as they differ in location: New England confronted by Paris, New England confronted by the sea. From the beginning the cultural, certainly the political, stresses have in this country been local and sectional. Whatever novels we have, good or bad, will show this, no matter how disguised the sectional attitude. The very assumption that there can be a melting pot is an unrealistic belief, all the more for the pretense that it is universally American. This is not to say that the great divisions of this country do not have in common something aside from their local awareness of themselves, or even that the sectional differences can be so marked as in older cultures, let us say Normandy and Provence. But the diversity of difference goes beyond political attitudes. It is even found within the sections themselves, and certainly as the sections are changed by historic accident: New England before the War of 1812 and New England now. What there is in common we might call the diminished vision of the Christian inheritance. *Liberty* and *freedom*, as we understand the words, and that understanding is growing vaguer and more confused, are secular interpretations of a more complete Christian polity now lost to us. The westward movement of Europeans, beginning with Columbus, not only shattered the narrow physical boundaries of Christendom but, like all extension, weakened it by reducing a union composite of spiritual and temporal parts to the predominance of material ends. With us it is called pioneering, and every part of the country was involved in it; but even in this common inheritance we find distinct local differences. The New England theocratic shift of the Mormons was unlike the southern cattleman's gradual advance from a semipastoral stage to an agrarian society. And there were those individuals, the hunters, who went alone or in small parties, following an even more ancient impulse. The general is always defined by the particular; so even what we share together cannot escape expression in terms of local history and culture.

Of the South, and *the South* is a more complex term than is generally recognized, too much is made of ethnic complications as its distinguishing feature, although of course this can in no way be ignored. But it is the family which best describes the nature of this society. And by family I mean the total sense of it, the large "connections of kin" amplifying the individual unit. There are the geographic limits which allowed the family in this larger meaning (it was the community) to spread itself in a mild climate and over alluvial soils to give to the institution its predominance as not just one but *the* institution of southern life. In New England, at least the coastal areas, there was always the sea to intervene, holding up a distant image and not the familiar, seasonal one such as land allows. Of course there was a seaboard in the South and farms in New England, but the county and township represented the difference. Both the sea and land are feminine images; but the sea takes only men, and so the communion between husband and wife was interrupted and for long periods of time. Relate this seafaring to the theocratic oligarchies, and we discover the cultural forms acting upon man's relation to woman, which at one time made witches. What is a woman deprived but a witch, especially under the discipline of a Puritan distortion of the senses?

Man's attitude to woman is the foundation of society under God. In the South, because of the prevailing sense of the family, the matriarch becomes the defining image. The earlier insistence on purity, an ideal not always a fact, was not chivalric romanticism but a matter of family integrity, with the very practical aim of keeping the bloodlines sure and the inheritance meaningful. Before machinery was made which lessened the need for the whole family to do its part on the farm, husband, wife, children, cousins, dependents, and servants all served the land and were kept by it, according to their various demands and capacities. The parts of the family made a whole by their diversity. People lived fairly close together without losing their privacy or their family distinctions. The radius of visiting and trading and marrying was generally not more than seven miles, but seven miles at a walk or even in a buggy takes time. You just didn't drop in for a chat. You spent the day at least. And the railroads did not disrupt these communities; they merely connected them. Conversation reached a high art, and it generally talked about what most interested itself, and this was the endless complications within the family and what gossip or rumor hinted at in the neighbors. Every human possibility was involved, including politics, but the bloodlines were the measure of behavior. There was never any doubt about the argument between environment and heredity. Environment was what heredity inherited. At a family gathering, when people were not working but celebrating, there would always be one voice more capable than the others of dominating the conversation. It was a kind of bardic voice. This opened my eyes to a technical device about the point of view, what might be called the Hovering Bard. Everybody in a country community knows something about a happening, but nobody knows it all. The bard, by hovering above the action, to see it all, collects the segments. In the end, in the way he fits the parts together, the one story will finally get told.

This is not to say that the subject of southern fiction is limited to what goes on within the family circle or even that the family is always the enveloping action. But this larger sense of it must always be taken into account. It is the structure through which the cultural image, with its temporal and spiritual rituals, complicates the human drama, receives and modifies by its conventions the archetypal happenings which forever recur between birth and death. There are societies where the family as institution is subordinated to some abstract idea of the state. At one time such was Sparta, as now it is with Russia or the welfare state anywhere. But in the great days of Greek drama what would the dramatists have done without the House of Atreus? Or would we have had the fall of Troy if Paris had merely run away with one of Citizen Menelaus' women? Or the classical idea of Fate, which both men and gods had to reckon with—how would that have been diminished if a tyranny based on abstract economics had held the total meaning of life? There would have been no Sophocles or Aeschylus; there might have been some kind of Euripides. There certainly would have been no Homer.

To repeat a platitude, we are caught between two conflicting world views which operate within and without our society, but most acutely in the South, because the South has been the losing cause. The prevailing Faustian view, to borrow from Spengler, has until recently seemed invincible. Relying entirely on the material ends as the only proper reward for action (the delusion that man can know the final secrets of matter), it defines itself as laissez-faire in economics (the shift from the individual to the state does not alter this), faction in politics, social welfare in religion, relativism in history, pragmatism in philosophy. The older belief in the City of God as the end of the drama has persisted, if defensively, in the South. But it is the fractured view of this Christian drama, the loss of its inner meaning, which has confused southern institutions and required of the family more meaning than it can sustain. Yet this very situation focuses the artist's approach to his material. If he tries to free himself from it, he can do so only by betrayal, which is not infrequent.

The Working
Novelist and the
Mythmaking
Process

WHEN I FIRST BEGAN THINK-
ing about the book which was to become *The Velvet Horn,* * I was
thinking consciously: that is, rationally. I could almost say falsely,
except that the creative act uses all
the mind's faculties. I thought I
wanted to do a long piece of fiction
on a society that was dead. At the
time I saw the scene as the kind of
life which was the southern version
of a life that, discounting the sectional differences, had been common everywhere east of the Mississippi and east of the mountains.
That life seemed to me to be what
was left of the older and more civilized America, which as well re-
tained the pattern of its European
inheritance. The Civil War had destroyed that life, but memory and
habit, manners and mores are slow
to die.

As a boy I had witnessed its
ghostly presence, and yet the people which this presence inhabited
were substantial enough. They
were alive in their entire being.
They seemed all the more alive because their culture was stricken.
The last active expression of this

---

* *The Velvet Horn* (New York: McDowell, Obolensky Inc., 1957) is set in Middle Tennessee
and in the Cumberland hill country in the nineteenth century and revolves round the passion-
ate-natured Cropleigh family.

society seemed to fall somewhere between 1880 and 1910. Those decades seemed the effective turning point of the great revolution which was to diminish a Christian inheritance. The mechanics of the change are obvious to all; through its means, the family was uprooted by destroying its attachment to place. In the South, certainly, family was the one institution common to all its parts. There was great variety to the South's homogeneity, which the false myths about it never understood. There has been no part of this country so afflicted with "galvanized" myths which presumed to interpret it, but it was family as institution which best expressed its culture. By family, I mean all the complex interrelationships of blood and kin, the large "connections" which extended to the county lines and by sympathy overlapped the states.

I take the automobile as the supreme agency in the destruction of attachment to place, since the railroads did not destroy the communities; they merely connected them more readily. Family and place, as I said, go together. It was the sense of both which set the South apart in this country, but too much was asked of the family as institution. It should have been one among many institutional expressions of culture; it was called upon to do more than its form allowed. But the artist works by means of such limitations. So it seemed to me as I began. I had no intention, no sense of dealing with a myth which forever recurs within the human scene.

This conscious approach is merely one way in, or down. The writer may begin with anything—a mood, a scene, an idea, a character, a situation. Whatever sets him going generally appears suddenly in that suspension of attention which is like the aftereffect of shock. It is a condition of the psyche when it finds itself outside time. This condition may be the occasion for vision or dream. In the Middle Ages any man might know it. Today dreams remain, but vision commonly fails us. We are helpless before the condition in which dreams appear, but vision strikes the state of consciousness. This stroke and that mysterious sense of being possessed largely remain for the artist, the point being that presumably he suffers this intrusion when he is conscious. Presumably, because the aftereffect of shock allows for a certain awareness of what is going on around outside, but the consciousness does not respond in action. It is suspended before the intuitive and instinctive action taking place within the mind. Somehow, through a fissure, the unconscious pierces the consciousness, and from below streams the image, or whatever it is, that sets the artist to work. The shock is a true shock. It paralyzes the rational mind momentarily. It is mysterious. The cause, the source, can in no way be discovered by natural or positive means. But the experience is true and forever denies to mere formula a rendition of the knowledge which is experience.

The creative act is, then, both a rational and an intuitive performance. What comes up from below through this fissure generally relates to the subject, but for me at least it always seems at first to be the essence of the subject. It can be this, but it rarely is. It must contain the essence, however, and it is just here that the conscious use of the craft of fiction comes in. The craft is the lesser part, but nevertheless crucial. Without its procedure of arranging, finding relationships between structural parts, and all such matters, as well as the tedious search for the right word or phrase, there would be no art of language as fiction.

It is curious, but for as long as I have written, I am always surprised afresh, after much sorrow and trouble to get a story going, that the idea may merely be related to, not be, the subject. Each time I have to learn afresh that, as it shows itself, it is either a segment of a larger idea or an idea too big for the action. The resistance to its dissolution in the action is enormous, partly because it retains the excitement of the moment of inspiration. This inspiration is a momentary vision of the whole. It quickly sinks into the abyss from which it arose, leaving the idea as a kind of clue, the end of the thread which leads into the labyrinth. No matter how firmly the critical sense has explored the idea's limitations, the moment the artist engages himself, he cannot but take it to mean more than it does. An idea is so inflexible; it tends so easily toward the conceptual. It *must* turn flesh before it is fiction. Fiction above all should give the illusion of life, of men and women acting out some one of the eternal involvements we all know, resolving, not solving. Only God may solve. A character or a situation would be the simpler way to begin. It would lead more directly into the conflict. It is rarely my way.

I feel there is an advantage to beginning with an idea rather than a situation or a mood. This advantage is suggested by its very irrefrangibility. If the idea is universal, in action it becomes archetypal. Therefore, to render it describes more nearly a whole action, and the artist must not tell any story but the *one* story which the people and situation demand. I would like to distinguish at this point between an opinion about behavior and archetypal representation. Opinion is the vulgarity of taste. It is never a true idea, because it is either topical or partial. It distorts any action, since it is blind to the fullest complexity of that action. No matter how disguised, opinion always has a "message," always wants to prove something instead of making experience show itself. Its selection of incidents, therefore, is often obviously arbitrary. This is the failure of the realistic school of fiction, if a school it is.

To begin by wanting to resuscitate a dead society, it seems to follow, involves the writer in a great risk. It gets in the way of bringing his people alive. For the first hundred pages or so he is in danger of being misled by opinion. He is saved by the creative act; that is, he is saved by his people showing life. The moment comes when the actors in the stress of the situation will "come alive," will make a response that reveals them. In the light of this response the writer can go back and rectify, revise, remove the scaffolding. Then he is able to examine, to criticize the impulse which set him going. He can do this without impairing the life evoked. He can do it because life is there. It is at this point that the conscious and the intuitive practice of the craft work most easily together. The mechanics for this is cleaning up as you go along. Ford Madox Ford taught me this method. Many practice it, but not all. You do the day's stint, let it set, and next morning look at it again. Tighten it up, change things about, and then proceed. As the action grows, each day's work moves closely out of what has gone before. In the beginning it is not always clear which of the threads of complication holds the center. Cleaning up at last shows it. This is a decisive moment. Such a process simulates natural growth most unnaturally: that is, it has about it the mystery of all growth and yet is artificial. The common miracle of life is the seasonal change. It is so common, and of necessity must be so; else we would be too aware of living in a state of constant miracle. This would strain the amenities. So it is in the practice of a craft. But there are moments when the craft is overborne by the stroke of life. This is the flash of miracle. This is the artist's reward, almost the only lasting reward, for it is an assurance that the work is moving as it should. Perhaps it was of this that Blake was thinking when he said the artist continues the act of God.

How gradually does this bemusement with the strict idea lift. I do not now remember at what stage it became clear again that you do not write about a society living or dead. You write about people who live within the constraint of some inherited social agreement. They are already involved when you take them up, for there is no natural man. He has never anywhere been seen, certainly not within historic time. But what is natural or common to all men has been changed from birth by manners and mores, institutions, all the conventions and laws of a given society. It is the restraint of decorum, propriety, taste, the limits of estates and classes—all such which distort, repress, guide the instincts, impulses, passions, the unruly demands of the blood toward the multifold kinds of behavior. All forms of intercourse rely upon faith and belief. This is a platitude of statement, but as working knowledge for the author, it shows itself with the fresh light of truth.

And this working knowledge was already informing, changing from a concept to the movements of life, the idea of a dead society. I was not only rationally seeing fuller implications; that is, I was not only seeing of what this society was composed as action, which had already taken it out of a conceptual stage; I was also comparing it with the cycles which other societies go through. The decline of civilizations, for example, of necessity follows the failure of belief, the cultural forces gradually withdrawing made manifest in the hardening of traditional laws and forms, foreshadowing rigidity, that is, death. But out of death comes life, as appositely death is the conclusion to life. Within the circling spiral of such change lies the belief in immortality and continuance. At some point it came to me that it is the archetypes which forever recur, are immortal, timeless; it is only the shapes in which these appear that seem to harden and die, that is, the manners and mores that are unique to a given society; and these shapes are the appearances of reality, the world's illusion moving within the illusion of time. What a shock this was to my partial and emotional view of the South!

Now the South was a mixed society, and it was a defeated society; and the defeated are self-conscious. They hold to the traditional ways, since these ways not only tell them what they are but tell them with a fresh sense of themselves. Only defeat can do this. It is this very self-consciousness which makes for the sharpened contemplation of self. It is comparable to euphoria. The sudden illumination made life fuller and keener, as it made life tragic. But it stopped action. The very heightening of self-awareness made for a sudden withdrawal of the life-force. What was left of it remained in the surface forms. The forms were shattered, but because of this force they held their shape briefly. The shed skin for a while shines with life, but the force of life is already on its night sea journey. I did not know how to define this force at the time; I only felt it vaguely, as I felt the vacuum beneath, which is the atmosphere of chaos. I was slow to connect this basic energy with the repetitive thrust out of chaos into the surrounding void, but I felt I knew that chaos is the underlying condition of any artifice, whether it was the state or the family or a work of art. Mythically, for so far only did I read the myth, it seemed the state Adam and Eve found themselves in after Eve had been taken from Adam's side. Their expulsion from the earthly paradise seemed to put them into the disorder of chaos. Actually, they were confronted by a natural order which was a multiplicity of the conflicts of opposites. This is not chaos but life as we suffer it, and we fall into it as the child falls into the world. Continuance depended upon the exercise of the will and especially the crafts, not only to survive but to try to restore, to bring together the two halves which make a whole. Together, man and woman serve as the basic symbol for the life drama. How old is the sentence we hear every day, "This is my better half."

It was some years after I had been working on the as-yet-unnamed *The Velvet Horn* that I realized I was treating an aspect of this ancient drama. The brothers and sister, under the guidance of the eldest, withdrew from the stresses of formal society in an effort to return to the prenatural equilibrium of innocence and wholeness. This is an habitual impulse, the refusal to engage in the cooperating opposites that make life. It is also as illusory as any Golden Age, and forbidden by divine and human law. Therefore, it is the grounds for one of the oldest forms of search and conflict. The symbol for this is incest. It need not be fact, but it is symbol, one having a literal counterpart; in one instance in the story it happened as fact as well.

For many years it has seemed to me that incest was a constant upon the southern scene. There was plenty of circumstantial evidence. The boys' and girls' rooms seemed too obviously separated. I remember in old houses the back stairs with solid paneling to hide ankles and lower legs as the girls came down. Call it prudery, but what is prudery? The fear of incest, if incest it was, was perhaps not overt, but I knew of whorehouses where too many of the girls had been ravished by fathers and brothers. Even if these were extreme instances—I had no way to know how general they may have been—still they were indicative. But the actual union between close kin was not my interest. It was the incest of the spirit which seemed my subject, a spiritual condition which inhered within the family itself. I did not have to look very far, no farther than both sides of my own house, to know this. It was clearest in the county family, where the partial isolation meant an intimacy and constancy of association in work and play, which induced excessive jealousy against intrusion from the outside. Often enough a partiality for one child went beyond the needs of parental care, bringing about all kinds of internal stresses within the family circle. This jealousy, this love, extended to the land and to natural objects with a possessiveness lasting even generations. I know of a family that today will engage in ritualized quarrels for hours on end over whether a field has been let grow up in sprouts, while the guests sit as at a play. These are all love quarrels, and the land is as much subject as object.

But to return: once I had got well into the first section of the novel, I had completely forgotten that I had wanted to bring a dead society to life. What part incest would play had, as well, moved to the edge of my attention. I was involved in the first pressures of making a world, peopling this world into which the young nephew, Lucius, would be guided by his uncle. The surface action seemed to be the initiation of the boy, culminating in his first sexual experience, although this was by no means his only adventure. The world he was entering, I felt, must seem out of the world, withdrawn, mysterious, of a strange look to him and refreshing, since in climbing the Peaks of Laurel, he left behind a dry and sterile place, burning under excessive drought. Of course he was climbing into his entanglement with life, which his father's suicide would rebegin. The seemingly accidental reason for the climb was to witch a well, to find water. It bore a literal as well as symbolical meaning.

Gradually I became aware of the need for this double usage as far as fiction is concerned. The symbol should always have its literal or natural counterpart. It should never rely upon the Platonic ideal image; this is a concept. Since fiction is an action in which nothing must be left inert, a concept of perfection, say, cannot be known actively. Perfection can only be sought out of imperfection, out of the fallen state of man represented by the cooperating forces of good and evil. The reinterpretation of myth by such people as Jung and Heinrich Zimmer has done much to make this clear, but I think it has always been known by a certain kind of artist, if only intuitively. It was the yeast which worked the dough. An image seemed, then, not an imperfect reflection of perfection, but an action derived from the shattering of a whole into parts, which in all myths of origin begins the world drama. The end of this would be a reunion of the parts into a whole, but a whole no longer innocent. But this reunion never takes place in the world; else the drama would end. Here was the clue to the end of my novel, however, although I in no way saw it. The action had not moved sufficiently to inform me.

Anyway, the action itself must be symbolic of the archetypal experience. This, I consider, was the most important thing *The Velvet Horn* taught me. The symbol must be more than an inert sign or emblem. Where symbols appear—and there will be one to contain them all in their relationships— they represent the entire action by compressing into a sharp image or succession of images the essence of meaning. For example, in animal nature, the horn stands for both the masculine and feminine parts of being, the two aspects of the apposites which make a whole: the two in one contained by a single form. Add the velvet to this and you posit the state of innocence, that suspension before the act which continues the cycle of creation. At a certain moment the buck, out of the mystery of instinct, rubs the velvet off against the tree, and then he is ready for the rutting season. The velvet grows about the feminine end of the horn, and it bleeds as it is rubbed away. The blood is real, but the act symbolizes what the other end of the horn will do. In human nature the horn's counterpart would be the hermaphrodite, Hermes and Aphrodite contained within the one form. Their separation, Eve taken from Adam's side, at another level continues the cycle of creation. Both forms exist within the constancy of the seasonal turn of nature. The entire range of imagery relates to these.

So used, the image as symbol becomes the clue to reading, the means by which all the parts are related to the structure. It is not inert but active, being both root and crown of a particular living experience. This is technically called the controlling image; and once discovered, it allows the reader to read, not read *into* a book his own preconceptions and preoccupations. It also guides the judgment as it analyzes the rendition. When an action eschews the partial or topical, it is always symbolic, that is, archetypal, whether the author knows it or not. To see a fiction as either so-called realism or symbolism is to commit the literal error, either in writing or

reading. Realism distorts or diminishes the full action by plotting beforehand a beginning, middle, and end. How can this be done without
inhibiting the creative act? How can a writer know beforehand what his
people will do? How can he know until he has put them into action and so
let the kind of thing they do show them for what they are, and upon this
ground proceed partly creatively and partly deliberately? I rather imagine
that when such fiction is successful, the author allows his creative sense to
abandon the rigid plotting or the parts of it which get in the way. On the
other hand you find the symbol misused as sign. Sign as symbol will be
inserted in place of the concretion, the motion of action. It will be made to
stand for the action instead of the actors in conflict showing the action. To
let the bare boards of the Cross stand for the Crucifixion is one thing; the
Cross as image releasing the action of the Passion in the mind and heart is
the other, the fictive way.

The writer working out of some form of myth will accept the supernatural
as operating within nature. He does not take the world as the end in itself.
His form will be some form of myth. Myth, symbol, archetype—the structure, the image, the conflict of the ever recurring human experience. In the
Garden of Eden section of The Velvet Horn ("The Water Witch") there are
three parts that represent the three stages of Eden as symbol of the world
drama. Adam alone, the hermaphrodite, is the entire creature isolated
within himself, the stasis of innocence, the loss of which is the beginning of
action. When the woman is taken out of his side (this is symbolic, not
according to nature as we know it), the separation begins the perpetual
conflict. Incest is the symbol for this next stage. The third is the continuing
action of the drama, the effort to fuse the parts into a wholeness which is
complete knowledge. The symbol for this is the serpent, the old intruder.
But there is another symbol for wholeness, the *uroboros*, the serpent eating
its tail, lying about the waters of chaos. This is one of the oldest symbols,
and out of it comes the only perfect figure, the circle. You will find it all over
the world. In our hemisphere it encircles the Mexican calendar stone. To
shift the image, Adam within his form contains the *uroboros*, both the
masculine and feminine parts. Once separated, the feminine in Adam
becomes Eve, and the masculine becomes the serpent. All the goods and
evils grow out of this separation, and one of the images of it is the caduceus,
the two serpents entwining sickness and health. There are numerous forms

of the separation—the dragon fight, where destructive nature takes its fire-breathing, scaly shape without the human creature; the Medusa; and Moses' staff. This, I should think, is repeated endlessly in myth.

Of course reading has helped me tremendously, but I read not as a scholar but as an artist. The wonder of it is its accidental nature. I did not look to books for help. I happened to be reading certain authors at the time of writing, some even before I began—Frazer, years ago; more recently, Zimmer; Jung, particularly his *Psychology and Alchemy*; and Erich Neumann's *Origin and History of Consciousness*. This accidental reading comes close to mystery, but anyway the first real surge of conscious direction and awareness came out of it. The curious part is that, as I looked back over what already had been done, I found little to change. The action was doing its own work. Whether it would have continued or not I cannot say. Of course there was rearrangement, but the intrusion from the depths, where the subject lay, had already painfully and haltingly been moving in its own direction, its own autonomous way. The conscious help from me was ambiguous. I thought I was helping another kind of story; then at a certain moment I took hold consciously. The invisible form showed only streaks of substance, but I was able to *feel* the subject shaping its form. And I had my controlling image well fixed in the top part of my head: incest, the act symbolic of wholeness, not the wholeness of innocence but the strain toward a return to this state of being. Was not the brotherhood of man most supremely defined by the love of brother and sister, at least in symbolic terms? If they represented the two parts of the whole of experience, the effort to become one again must contain every kind of love which the separation had scattered throughout the world as man struggled to escape his fallen condition. Through love and the act of will he could escape it, but only temporarily, as far as the flesh was concerned. The irony of the central conflict lay just here. It is most surely known in the act of love, when flesh and spirit surcharge each other, in that brief annihilation of every separate faculty, the annihilation being the act of fusion, the disembodiment within the body, which was the suspension in chaos before the Fall. The moment in which this could be felt had nothing to do with time, but with its opposite, the knowing of eternity which understands, that is stands under or outside time, the brief insight into the unmoving Mover.

I now saw my two working parts of the structure: the moving present

tense, which is the world's illusion, and the eternal present tense, which
knows nothing of past or future but always is. We know it best in the images
of dreams. But the myth and fairy tale all operate through and represent this
sense of the eternal. "Once upon a time . . . Long, long ago in a far
kingdom . . ."—these beginnings by their tone and meaning speak of no
time, no country. They are outside time; they are always and forever about
what is constant in human experience. The seeming tone of the far past is
the announcement of the timeless held within the point of a moment. To
emphasize this, there is little or no natural landscape, no recognizable
cities, in myth or fairy tale. This is a crucial distinguishing feature between
myth and fiction which deals with myth. They have the archetypes in
common, but in fiction the action must be put in a recognizable place and
society. The moment I say this, Kafka appears. Except for the intrusion of
his moral rage, he more nearly approaches the ideal form of myth. But
morality as we know it has little to do with myth.

As soon as I began to feel the right limits of the structure, I could deal
with its formalities. Within the various levels and distinctions of the mind,
especially where it oscillates between conscious and unconscious, I could
put the sense of eternity, the images of the past which are not past but
forever quivering with immediacy. Opposed to this, by closing the mind and
letting the action take place as upon a stage, I could use the moving present
tense, the action in time. But this last was not to proceed in a continuous
movement of surface beginning, middle, and end. Each of the five sections
was to be nearly complete within itself, the tensions of the action evoked by
eternal knowledge acting against time's knowledge. The movement in time
would allow the sections to be dramatically connected, each showing a
whole, but differently, involving, I hoped, the fullest possibilities of the
central image: incest. Not until the end of the book would the shock of
meaning connect all the parts and the action be complete. There would be
no way to turn to the end of the book and find out what had happened. This
puts a handicap upon reading, this juxtaposition and accumulation rather
than the steady advance of a conflict, which is the way of naturalism and the
oldest form of all, the simple art of narrative.

By now I also had a firm grasp upon the point of view, and I knew who the
protagonist was. Everybody was the hero and heroine, but only Jack
Cropleigh, the brother and uncle, could represent them, for Jack, the

spiritual hermaphrodite, contained them all in his mind. He alone could suffer the entire myth. The point of view would therefore be that of the Roving Narrator, in whom the variety of the action might lie within the levels of his consciousness as it met the unconscious: time and eternity. Having set him apart with no life of his own, other than his entanglement with all life viewed by family and community, he was best suited to control as central intelligence, and his office as victim-savior could bring it all to a focus by his death. The irony I intended, or recognized when it happened, lay in how little his victimage could offer. He could save nobody, not even his beloved nephew, by proxy. He could only save his nephew from running away from life. All he could tell him was that no matter how far you run, you are always there. As archetype of victim-savior, Jack, I'm afraid, denies the efficacy of the Mass. His death implies that for heroes, at any rate, the sacrifice must be forever repeated, actually as well as symbolically. This perhaps is theological heresy but mythical truth, and certainly fictional truth. The feeling and knowledge he suffers throughout pass progressively through the three phases of the Garden's drama, renewing through the nephew, the inheritor, the same perpetual cycle.

The nephew Lucius, the bastard child of incest, is in a sense, then, the youthful counterpart of Jack or, if you like, of all his uncles and of his mother. I think this was the reason I was so long in finding the protagonist. I had begun with Lucius, so the tale opens out of his eyes and mind. Jack takes over in the next section, and the view remains with him throughout for the reasons given, in spite of the fact that it roves again to Lucius and even to Pete Legrand, the old intruder. In the roving point of view it is only necessary, I feel, for one mind to dominate throughout the story, so that no matter where the view shifts, it might seem to belong to one central intelligence, that intelligence and sensibility alone equal to the fullest knowledge. The success of this depends upon how you write it and especially upon the transitions from section to section. (The roving is no good written in chapters.) For example, although the view is with Lucius at the beginning, Jack so fills the pages, especially toward the end, that when he takes over in the next section, the reader should feel no jar and without question follow, as he was now entering a fuller complexity of the complication. If he did not feel that what had gone before was actually in Jack's mind, he could feel that it might have been. This was tricky, I know, but if it could be made to go smoothly, then what follows could also seem an extension of the central intelligence, as every mind is equal to the total experience, the difference being that only one can know the fullest meaning in suffering for all. Anyway, this is how it worked out—how successfully, it is not the author's place to say.

I can only feel that it comes off. My pace of writing is generally very slow, with constant cleaning up and structural revisions. Too often I will spend a day on a paragraph; a page is a good day's work. But as I drew toward the end, the last thirty pages or so, the artifice completely usurped my mind. It possessed me. There is no other word for it, and I had never quite felt it before. I became merely an instrument. I wrote three or four pages a day, scarcely changing a word. It was as if I had divided myself into two persons, one watching and one doing. The physical presence seemed a shadow. I felt disgust for its demands, and appetite had lost its savor. My impulse was to remain at the typewriter and not get up until the book was done, but this would be too long for my strength. Food and sleep were necessary, and the tactical considerations of how much changed from day to day. I could not bear to be touched or noticed. My nerves had drawn into the tissue of the skin. I forced myself to eat as in a dream. I would go to bed at seven or eight o'clock and rise each morning earlier, until I was getting up at two. In a kind of half-awareness I knew that I had to watch this expense of energy or I would give out before the end. I sensed that if I did, I would lose it, that once this possession of me by the actors was broken, it would never return. It was as if there were only so many words left, and each had its place if I could hold out to receive them. The last day my breath was all in the front part of my mouth, and each word had weight. Then in the final hour or so they began to fade, the substance of meaning growing lighter. When it was all done, the final period made a final expulsion of breath. I leaned back in the chair. I felt that all that had gone before was right, or the illusion of the last acts being not fiction but life would not have seized me.

This is the way it was done, to the best of my recollection. There is such cunning in the way the creative part uses the conscious craft that it is hard to follow the twisted windings of the journey. It seems just that. You must act as if it is real and yet know you are acting; but the acting is lost in the act. How it is sustained over so long a time, in this instance over nine years, is a mystery and a cause for shame, as is the setting down of what seems to be the procedure.

This fresh interest in myth derives, perhaps, from a weakening of the formal authority of the Church. Everywhere the satanic acceptance of matter as the only value, the only fulfillment, has been shaken. We sense again that people cannot live, except in some belief outside themselves. The cycles of cultures seem to show that when belief hardens into formalism, leaving the center dry and hollow, it is a time, as Yeats says, of the trembling of the veil of the temple. But before some new faith breaks through, there is a withdrawal into the source. This I believe to be the archetypal conflicts of myth which precede the formalized rituals and dogmas of institutional religion. This is a statement only an artist can make. And he can make it only vaguely, as it affects his work, for the artist is a cannibal of Gargantuan appetite who does not exclude himself, if he is lucky.

Caroline Gordon and the Historical Image

ONE CANNOT HELP THINKING that there is too much open discussion of the mysteries which veil the Muse and too little private performance. Even in the Grove, where all was ritual, where those admitted to the service were chosen with care, even there the pretender slipped in. I take it that the pretender is he who by brutal exposure would get at the secret which, for the sake of our humanity, must remain hidden; must, because the direct gaze sees too discretely, ignoring the representative quality in the object, the mystery of creation in the bare act. If the journeyman artist is diverted and stops making to talk at large, who can distinguish the true tongue in Babel? Witness the serious acceptance in the last decades of the social-science fiction for the real thing. Like all sinners, it looks entirely to the object, society or some part of it, as the cause of the human predicament and so does violence to any given man's historic position, to what he has in common with other men, which can only be rendered through what in him is unique. To assume that society is external to man obscures the actors' humanity and the contingencies which surround and modify action, and so beclouds that clarity of vision without which literary truth may not be plain to the eye. The inner chamber is always dark, because what lies in that darkness are the shreds of raw matter and the dry ligaments of the beast. This is the secret which the initiate approaches ever obliquely, never toward but around, disguising and guarding it by assuming the qualities of the Muse's triple nature: meditation through memory into song (for fiction into rendition). And it is all done with the averted eye but the sure gesture.

The hypothesis of a common mystery and discipline has great value for the artist, especially today, since the secularization of the arts has increased the hazards, making performance depend more and more upon a private discipline and a private vision. But the hazard is lessened for those who understand the practice of the averted eye and the sure gesture. The averted eye allows for an image which focuses the imagination and sustains and controls its vision; the sure gesture predicates the mastery of the tools of the trade, or the necessity for this mastery, and a formal method. Formality depends upon objectivity, which requires the novelist to post himself, whereby sight (of the world, according to his scale of observation) and insight (into himself, through imagination) relate and equate what is seen and so bring the double vision into focus. The end in view is to force the meaning of experience to show beneath appearance, according to the degree of intensity the novelist-as-artist is able to maintain. What results is his ability to deliver up out of any given situation what the tension between the discrete world and the controlling image precipitates. And this more explicitly is a fusion of complexities, or levels of interest, with an emphasis on a particular level which connects all the other levels (in terms always of the controlling image). This emphasis illuminates the point at which sight and insight meet. It becomes the measure of the degree of intensity. It is the center of the circle of incantation. Off center, the writer may include or leave out too much and so distort his vision. If successful, the writer will find that he has made Goldilocks' choice of a gruel neither too hot nor too cold, but just right. This involves not a recovery of innocence but of its quality out of the contamination of experience. This is the strain of creative discipline. Like any strain, it has its limits, is exhausting, and must be continually repeated. Without it vision blurs, since once the state of innocence is lost, we are given over to the flux of the world. Furthermore, in a long piece of work fatigue is progressive, which demands the maintenance of a nice balance between the artist's will and his given physical, moral, and intellectual energy. In the light of these observations it can be seen how great is the risk of judgment required for the writer to post himself. The decision is close to the mystery of an art, for in the end the creative act cannot be explained.

Caroline Gordon, I believe, controls her performance by some such principle of the writer's devotion. If she did not sign her name, it would at first be hard to know her sex. This is a way of pointing out the strictness of her objectivity, and I suppose it to be the last refinement of it. A story of hers, "The Brilliant Leaves," is an example of what I have been saying more generally. It is a story, as is said, that comes off. It may not be her best story, but it is one almost made for demonstration. To begin with, the title is more relevant to the subject than most. It appears merely descriptive, indeed static and as far removed from love and violence as it could be: that is, until we examine it. The quality of brilliant leaves may summon a variety of impressions, according to their numerous associations, but the composite effect has only one representative quality. The leaves stand for autumn, the waning year, that particular moment when nature is at its most intense, and that is the moment before death.

As we begin to read, the title is not likely to mean too much. I doubt that we receive more than a vague sense of intensity, perhaps of color. Our pleasure comes later with the understanding of what the author has done. We have been forewarned, but in such a way that neither the action nor the ending is anticipated. The first three words note the time of day as three o'clock in the afternoon, that last moment when the sun's intensity may be felt. After that hour it turns swiftly downwards, toward darkness. It is the time of day most analogous to the fall of the year. Shifting now from time to setting, we find in the white houses of the summer resort the boy's aunt and mother gossiping about the past, they themselves being at the season of life comparable to autumn. Notice the advance, the triple reinforcement: the fall of the year, the decline of day, the composure before age and death. The setting is not, therefore, simply pictorial. Along with the title, the time, and the human prologue, it contains the larger meaning of the action. Very quickly this becomes specific. Any gossip is out of the memory of action and passion, but it is particularly pertinent to the story about to unfold. The women on the porch mention the death of youth's high hopes, telling of a spirited young woman whose lover fails her, in consequence of which she becomes dead to the world. We do not know it yet, but this young woman is the aunt of the girl who is about to suffer a similar fate. Notice how thickly the strokes of emphasis are laid on, the repetition by analogy but disguised by means of the familiar and casual so that we have a preparation in depth, which, as it prepares, guides what is to take place.

At this point the advance narrows still further. The youth, impatiently listening to his aunt and mother as he waits to set out and meet his girl at their trysting place in the woods, recalls that his aunt has said, "The entrance to the woods is positively spectacular." This must seem to him, in contrast to his romantic longing and to the associations of young love which the place holds for him, the dull and meaningless speech of all elders. But the speech, in the light of what happens, becomes the riddle of an oracular prophecy, technically bearing the surprise of a delayed effect, which exposes the dramatic quality of the natural setting, at once containing and inform-ing the action. The aunt's ignorance of the meaning of her words defines more sharply her part: sibyls never comment; their office makes them the mouthpiece of the mystery and by means of incantation allows them to report without personal entanglements the consequences of fatality. The aunt's time of life has similarly removed her from the involvements of life and passion. The parallel is here suggestively close enough to make the author's intention clear. Beneath the aunt's surface view of the empty pageantry of autumn lies the root connection between spectacular and spectre. The wood, therefore, is more than the empty expanse of nature. This is mere appearance. It has an entrance, and this entrance opens upon a spectral world.

The boy, like all actors caught in the toils of fate, is blinded by his anticipation of what will be denied him. He cannot see behind the familiar marks of nature the mysterious workings of the supernatural, although he feels the change the instant he kisses the girl. Her lips are cold, not warm and clinging as when they parted in June. The intense moment of illusion, which is young love, is dead, but the boy will not accept it. The girl knows it for what it is but hesitates to tell him; refers to the change of the seasons as the thing that is different, without understanding the implication of the seasonal change; and so by her evasion innocently commits herself to her death. The symbols of their plight continue. They move through the dead leaves, kicking them up but without any sense of warning. They stand on the rock overlooking the valley. A black car moves swiftly, in a straight line, and disappears into the secret woods below. It is the distance of vision which transposes the car as matter to the car as symbol; but they do not notice. The girl's aunt is mentioned very casually as a woman disappointed in love. There is no awareness that the girl is already repeating her aunt's history. Her behavior is like one devoted to and done with the world, to be seen through her treatment of the boy, a shift from love to comradeship, the meaning of which is denied her. He is the puzzled follower, the earthbound, the one most suited by nature to mediocrity, and the moment of love's illusion is now vanished, so that she sees his true dullness.

At this point a less skillful workman, with sufficient signposts established, might proceed to the catastrophe. But the author has paused. There is something lacking without which the catastrophe would have no more meaning than any of the violent accidents which clutter life; and that something is crucial: a belief in the love affair. It is already over when the action begins. Up to this point the reader has had to take the affair on faith, and to fulfill the author's intention, more is needed. The problem then becomes the necessity of presenting a dead love as alive. A flashback or interior monologue would violate both the structure and point of view; and yet the love affair must be witnessed. The author is now under the kind of pressure which, accepted, makes for the best kind of writing. Her solution is to continue the seasonal pattern. With the surprise of true invention she takes the lovers down into a cove that has delayed its seasonal advance. The entrance here is choked with dead leaves; they go down a Confederate road, the road of dead hopes, descending into a place that is green like summer, remote, private, made for love. We are allowed for the moment to forget that it is illusory; it recalls the couple to their early love, and by means of the love scene which takes place, although it comes to nothing (the girl brings them back to comradeship before it advances too far), we have seen enough to believe in what has been. The complication of setting is elaborate. Sexual symbols now join seasonal ones: the moss, the fern, the little pines which grow around the pools. But the air of the place is cool and not from autumn chill but with the coolness of a deeper shade; that is, the general symbols of autumn and death now receive a greater and more specific intensity. The illusory quality of the cove leaves the sense of a shadowy place, so that the scene as witnessed might be the ghost of what has been and of what will be. It is as if the girl's spirit has already entered the timeless condition toward which she will soon plunge. The texture is so varied but so singular in its variety and concentration toward one thing that it develops the intensity of a truth which only literary truth can give.

Against this setting which is no mere occasional background, the characters are presented in their fatal entanglement. It is not a story of the death of young love in general (that is, what all the young have in common and beneath which their personalities are for a short while submerged). Both the boy and girl have character and the very character which makes the catastrophe believable. The girl, like her aunt before her, demands the intensity of devotion, the complete denial of self, of love's pure flame. But each has the flaw of choosing men who do not come up to their responsibility either as men or lovers. The aunt, descending the ladder to meet her lover below, while her father holds a shotgun through an adjoining window, descends only to see her lover disappearing through the bushes. She enters the front door and dies to the world. The niece falls to her actual death because her young man's character does not conform to her romantic image of what a lover should be, but more particularly because he refuses the responsibility of his manhood in forbidding her to indulge a dangerous whim.

The complexity of the situation is kept complex. There are no sharp antitheses but a fusion of the forces involved, so that the action becomes on all levels a fated action. It is fated that young love in its pure illusory state cannot last. The temperaments of the lovers are not suited to any affective union. The short intense moment of youth is all they have in common; but while she realizes this, he is attracted by the quality in her which causes her to dismiss him. The sense of his loss, without the recognition of why it is, the love scene in the cove which gives him hope and for which neither is responsible, leads him to acquiesce in the girl's risking a dangerous action (to her, romantic) which he knows he is no longer equal to, but which represents his desperate effort to recover the lost relationship between them. Their characters are set against the fated circumstances. When the boy runs for help, he is running as well from his own fate, not seeing the dead leaves at his feet but looking toward the white houses of the summer resort—another kind of death, but representing to him the secure, stable

world. He is ill-fitted to the tragic mould. The shock of what has happened
is too much for him (he expects the houses any moment to slide off the
mountainside), so that he is now as lost as the girl. The girl's death is a kind
of triumph, his confused terror only pathetic. Each makes its comment on
the ways of the world.

The story of young lovers, one of whom jumps or falls from a high place, is
a legend of all mountain resorts and is continually being told by people with
a gift for storytelling. They make it interesting, but the interest is accidental
and sensational. What it lacks is meaning. No doubt the aunt who has
called the entrance to the woods spectacular will speak of the death as
tragic, which it has been Miss Gordon's intention to show it is not. She
supplies the meaning through the carefully balanced tensions in the structure and composition, forcing from her language connotation as well as
denotation, but restricting both to the representation of what her imagination sees in this particular incident, so that what is unique in it, though
never obscured, relates and refers to an experience so common that the total
fusion of the parts delivers up for meaning an ironic attitude toward all
experience.

To go so fully into one story, and that not her best, may seem dispropor-
tionate to the larger issue of her novels; but it will serve, I hope, as an
introduction to her method of attack. It will be my assumption that writers
of Miss Gordon's vision have but one subject. On one level hers is in the
fullest sense traditional and historic. By this I do not mean what is commonly understood as the "historical novel": that is, the costume piece or
the arbitrary use of certain historic periods dramatized through crucial
events. The costume piece can be dismissed as offering a special kind of
entertainment; dramatized history is often, not always, too eclectic, suffering from a structural split between the scene and the action, obscuring the
poverty of the performance and the actors' inhumanity by its pretensions to
historic truth. Historic personages, when they appear, appear not as men or
women but in a quasi-mythical clothing. It would be a great feat to subdue
the Lincoln myth and present him as a man acting within the limitations of
his private needs and their public expression. The "history" gives a false
authority to the action and a spurious illusion which in retrospect seems
forced and arbitrary. The same objection brought against the sociological
novel repeats itself here: you cannot say what is history and what is fiction,
so that inevitably you get bad history and bad fiction.

The legitimate illusion, on the other hand, once established, will always give the sense of contemporaneity, of happening before the reader's eye. To manage this successfully, the author must first absorb the period of his scene so thoroughly that the accidental restraints of manners and customs become the medium of representation of what is constant in human behavior. The tension between form and subject then becomes right in its strain. But the sense of watching the action as it is taking place, although the primary test, is not enough. There must be for the definition under consideration also some historic image of the whole which will serve as a center of reference and the selective cast to the author's vision. MacKinlay Kantor's *Long Remember* failed, in spite of its splendid rendition of the battle of Gettysburg, for the lack of an image equal to his subject. In spite of Percy Lubbock's well-reasoned contention that *War and Peace* is two books and that the incidents surrounding Natasha begin as the representation of eternal youth only to change into her private destiny, Tolstoy does have a unifying force, and this force is his central image: an image not to be found in his historical argument but at the very core of the dramatic plight resulting from the revolutionary decision to Europeanize Russia. In terms of this, his title has meaning, and so do the waste and confusion of Pierre and the cynicism of Prince Andrew. Prince Andrew's father, Kutúzov, and even the czar clarify themselves more completely when examined in the light of such a referent.

It has always seemed to me unsatisfactory to explain *Madame Bovary* as naturalistic and *Salammbô* as romantic. Flaubert's craftsmanship is equally good in both books and of the same quality. The dimensions of his art and of his imagination are better described by means of a vision which is controlled by a historic concept of society. In *Bovary* it is a special view of bourgeois France; in *Salammbô* it is the fertility rite of Tanit. Naturally cultures of such diversity could not be represented in the media of each other's textures; nor does it follow because of this diversity that an extreme dichotomy exists in his imagination. Félicité and the old count with the napkin about his neck and drooling his food, in the context of the story and the scene of the book, are clues to Flaubert's critical objectivity toward the bourgeois world, which suggests a historical understanding more inclusive than this world.

This historic image of the whole allows for a critical awareness of a long range of vision by equating the given period to the past and future, sometimes explicitly, always implicitly. This makes the period at once the setting and the choral comment. Such a restriction upon the imagination adds another range of objectivity to the post of observation, another level of intensity to the action (as if the actors, while performing, expose to the contemporary witness, the reader, the essential meaning of their time). This is literary irony at a high level. It is the nearest substitute for the religious image. In a time of eclecticism, such as ours, while it will not directly solve the writer's simplest technical problem, it gives him balance and lessens the risk of a faulty vision in that it keeps the scale of observation from being entirely private or of seeming so.

It has allowed Miss Gordon in *Green Centuries* to relegate the usual American interpretation of the frontier to its proper place as evidence of a social phenomenon of the late nineteenth and early twentieth centuries— not an easy thing to do, for, spurious as it is, its pretense as the most common inheritance in the American tradition obstructs at every angle the clear view. As a myth it stands for a vague but persistent belief in a mystical vitality which will overcome nature, whether it be the wilderness, a business opportunity, or through science the very secret of life itself. The vagary of it, I believe, undid Wolfe as an artist, just as his pursuit of it made for the wide cult of his readers. His own true vitality and talent, wasting for lack of critical apprehension or of a historical sense, seemed the regenerating fountain to his spiritually thirsty contemporaries. But in *Green Centuries* the frontier becomes the complex fusion of two attitudes toward the vast expanse of the wilderness in the middle of the eighteenth century: that of the late Stone Age Indian and the European. As I shall try to show, it becomes much more.

These attitudes are never treated didactically but disclose the cultural tempers of the two societies, with the understanding that the source of this temper lies in man's view of himself against nature. And in the background there is enough of English colonial policy to keep the perspective just. The Indian settlements had barely disturbed the endless wastes of forest and plain. A religious people, their behavior was governed by fear of and identity with the power of nature. The supernatural existed as an extension of nature. They took from the wilderness only according to their needs. In their positive identity with the natural world families traced their descent from the beast, the fish, or even the wind. The preservation and continuance of life, therefore, became the center of their religious practice, the dignity of man and the rites of hospitality its corollaries. Their warfare did not evince a destructive instinct. It was a religious rite, and therefore a social rite, which submerged the end of fighting, which is death, beneath the ritual practice of it. The great warrior was he who most skillfully practiced the arts of war, endurance, cunning—the ritual of the warpath. Surprise was the great tactical feat. Fighting to the death was rare. To bring home hair and not lose your own was the measure of the fighter's reputation. To the European the virtues of the Indian, matrilineal in descent, seemed feminine. Their muscles were round, and the texture of their skin was soft like a woman's.

The purity of this feminine culture had already become corrupt by the eighteenth century. By means of the traditionalist faction in the Cherokee nation Miss Gordon was able to use the resulting self-consciousness to bring them alive, as she could not have done if she had had to deal with the Indians in contact only with one another, in the isolation of their own world. In opposition to this society the European presents a masculine principle. He makes a destructive war on nature, and therefore upon himself, setting out to reduce it without measure to his will. He does not want to live at peace with the Indian (the land was large enough for all, as the Indians pointed out). He wants to destroy him as one of the many obstacles to his own restless drive. It was he who used the peace treaties as breathing spells. The Indian's word meant what it said; it was an expression of his integrity, of himself as a whole man, since his behavior at any moment under any condition, whether it was hunting or fighting, making peace or making love, all come from a coherent view of himself in relation to nature. The European, now at the tail end of the Renaissance, suddenly released from the restraint of Christian feudal forms which in Europe were able to disguise the revolutionary change in attitude, was able now for the first time to find his antagonist in the absolute state of wild nature. The axe and gunpowder were instruments as later the technological process and practical science were instruments, but man's obsession that he could force nature to deliver up all its secrets and its goods has never been more clearly seen than in this westward advance.

Each long hunter, each frontiersman became a primitive, homespun Dr. Faustus. Having dismissed the devil along with God (the Protestant belief in a private communion with God is equivalent to man-become-God), man no longer had any defense against his violation of the laws of nature, nor any absolute set of principles to which he might refer the processes of reason. His plight is more terrifying than that of the protagonists of Greek drama, whose fated action achieved the dignity of suffering the inscrutable will of the gods. The unbalance of a purely masculine society, sharpened by the appearance of the Indian feminine society, itself a violation of nature's laws of reproduction and therefore no true opponent to the European (who never doubted his ultimate ascendancy, and because of this, the Indian's opposition drove him to callous acts more brutal than the "savages" could possibly perform), becomes the complication determining the action of *Green Centuries*.

It is useless to inquire whether the author's original interest lay in wondering what really happened on the frontier or whether she began with a historic concept. To know what was happening to men and women as men and women in a frontier society, it was necessary to represent the action in its fullest context. While acting out their private lives, they must perforce present a more public destiny. And the more private in character her actors, the truer the vision.

When she uses historical figures, such as Daniel Boone, it is always as they might appear to their contemporaries, men in some way heightened but always men. Boone is not he who "killed a b'ar." He is the person in young Outlaw's eyes who is exciting because he has been there and has seen actually what the long hunters all see before their eyes—"three, four hundred buffalo grazing in one place, and deer and elk mixed with them—High land and open all around, open and covered with white clover. There had never been anything like it, never would be." It is this dazzling vision, the purely masculine vision of the hunter, of man alone with himself in an elemental trial with nature (that temptation of all the nearest to a return to chaos, chaos being disguised by the purity of the vision, the longed-for land replete in richness, both in ground and game; perhaps it is the hidden nostalgic effort to return to Eden or some state of innocence) which kept the individual of heroic proportions intact but initiated the wandering restlessness that denied ever the occupation of such a land, the irony being that it was everywhere about, sight of it obscured by the brilliancy of the delusion which all suffered.

Any report would cause the hunter to abandon the rough cabin, the cleared space around it, and remove. Daniel Boone thought it time whenever he had to fell a tree whose branches would not drop near the house. This was not so with womankind. Biologically, and not only because of children, her need was to settle somewhere. The hunter's need for women always brings him back, retards him; but he also drags her into danger beyond her strength and will. This stress at one level is the subject, involving the deadening of the sensbility of womankind, reducing her to natural or even to subanimal responses. The moment when this is reached tells the climax to *The Captive* and *Green Centuries*.

The effect on the reader is an almost unbearable irony, not tragedy, because the impact of the wilderness is greater than man can bear. We no longer believe in demigods or in heroes become gods. Rion, the sign of the great hunter, has a personal meaning for Rion Outlaw, not a symbolic meaning for the reader. Nor does Cathy come from the Garden of Eden, but out of a settled and late stage of European civilization, with inherited needs which are denied her in the wilderness. More or less is demanded of her than she can respond to. For a finer shade of the irony we turn to the basic stress between the sexes, clearer in the wilderness than in an ordered society, since there are no institutional restraints to mitigate the biological sexual strain. In the end there is little dignity, no purgation of pity or fear, in Cathy's state or in that of her husband, whose restlessness will never cease nor ever come to rest in the perfect spot of ground. By means of his humanity man is punished for the pride and vanity of his dream. His human needs he can never discard. His punishment in the aimless wandering is a Sisyphean agony, but the victim becomes the woman. Man also becomes the equivalent of Cain, for Rion Outlaw is indirectly responsible for his younger brother's death. Skillfully and very indirectly Miss Gordon has prepared by his softer temperament for young Archy's adoption into the Indian tribe, which is an affront to his older brother in terms of the masculine obsession. Her use of the two brothers sharpens the focus which the feminine culture of the Indians would not alone have allowed.

It must be emphasized that there can be no absolute sense of contemporaneity in the presentation of any age, or segment of an age, anterior to the time in which the author writes. Indeed, if this were so, the principal value of using historical material would be lost, the value being just this illusion of the contemporary within a context of historic perspective, so that while an act takes place it is rendered in terms larger than those of its immediate appearance. This is, I believe, the furthest extension, and it is just that, of the aesthetic distance taken by writers concerned primarily with the formal, objective view. It is not equivalent to the mask of Greek tragedy but allows for dramatic effects of equal intensity, assuming the difference in the audience. The Torchbearers, for example, could assume a knowledge of the myth at every degree of perception in the audience, out of a cultural unity expressed through an active religious belief. Neither Miss Gordon nor any other writer of fiction can count on this kind of reception. She must assume contemplation and some measure of critical apprehension on the part of the reader; these are her limits and her freedom. The reader, in turn, cannot ask of her absolute historic truth (if such there be) but can ask that her myth of which the image is the concrete surface will be coherent within its own terms. With the exception of *Green Centuries* she narrows her scene to the nineteenth and twentieth centuries, as that fragment of time more nearly comprising the clearest opposition of forces which is her general reference and dramatic impetus, the moment of equilibrium before the shattering of a social pattern, when the very air is charged.

Penhally, her first novel, covers the entire period. It is the progress, in a closely related set of miniatures, of the disintegration of a family, coincident with the disruption of a culture whose virtues are stable and traditional. The forces which triumph show in their triumph their monstrosity. The family is not entirely at the mercy of these forces from the outside: the complication moves from within as well as in the persons of two brothers, one the protagonist, the other the antagonist, and this process repeats itself over the generations.

The matter of the division of family property in *Penhally* becomes the internal sign of disorder, and the action seems to imply that the younger brother, who wants his share of land and a house of his own, in part sets in motion the nemesis of destruction from the outside through the revolution of the Civil War. In her other books she deals in larger canvases and in more detail. Although she uses the same family and its connections over and over, the same situations often, and the same characters, yet in her repetition there is always variation. Although her vision shifts and enlarges its perspective, the shift is never withdrawal from her circle of incantation, but around it. In *Penhally* the older brother, Nicholas, representing the traditional stability of family based upon landed property kept intact for succeed-ing generations through entailment, becomes the symbol of the restraints of the mores upon behavior. The identity of the family with the land is more than physical identity. It is first of all the proper fulfillment of pioneering as against the perpetual, aimless motion of the early frontier. It reaches back in an effort to regenerate the older Christian sense of order. Its use of nature is also the care of nature in terms of one locality, one farm, which has a name, as Penhally or Mayfield. The name of the farm and the name of the family become indistinguishable. They have a character which is a metaphysical crossing of certain bloodlines with the influence of natural environment. In terms of the plot the conflict sharply develops between the characters as personality and the characters in their blood relationships. This presents itself as the outward level, the texture almost of the historic center. Alice Blair and her male counterpart who courts Lucy belong to branches of the connection who marry the property. This would seem to the uninitiate the true expression of the pattern; but actually it violates it in two ways: it views property for personal use instead of as a trusteeship, and it violates the integrity of the person as person. Lucy's bitter complaint was that she wanted to be loved for herself (when she is no longer an heiress, her fiancé does not pursue his courtship), whereas Alice Blair chose Charles as the most likely match, though her instincts drew her toward John. The cata-clysm of war turned the tables on her calculations: Charles was killed, and when John renewed his offer of marriage, old Nicholas opposed the marriage of his heir with Alice, not on personal grounds but on the knowledge of her blood. She withdrew without a defense, admitting her position and making it plain to all. The irony is that if she had been true to her instincts of love, she could have also gratified, with honor, the traits of her branch of the family. The irony within the irony is that Nicholas could force the issue at a time when the defeat of the traditional pattern made his position, for future generations, meaningless.

But the irony is not simple. The central meaning of the book is its complexity, striking like an alternating current back and forth among the characters, the situation, the historic changes. Lucy in the end married John, which in happier times would have given their union meaning as the medium of the family's self-perpetuation; but since the defeat of the South, the marriage leaves them not even a personal fulfillment. When her son is caught sleeping with a young cousin in the house itself, the blow to Lucy is twofold. She is affronted by a girl who has been loved for herself alone, under great risk, which circumstance was denied to her, and also suffers the shame of her son's behavior—a violation of the house's integrity, if not its prostitution, which makes him an outcast and later sustains the wisdom of tradition in terms of its disappearance: the boy's wife cuckolds him and he shoots himself. The last act of the drama concerns his two sons who return to Penhally, but a Penhally that no longer has meaning in terms of the society as a whole. The younger son inherits the love of the land but cannot make it pay, since the land is now merely an area of industrial exploitation. To "love" the land is itself evidence of the change, a self-consciousness which is a sign of loss, and certainly an oversimplified view which never would have occurred to old Nicholas. As a further emphasis of what has happened, the position of the brothers is reversed. At the end it is the elder who commits the final act of prostitution, first of himself and then of Penhally. Nemesis no longer pursues; it overtakes both when the younger, driven to exasperation, shoots his brother. This act, both desperate and futile (for it can only be an act of protest), in its highly personal nature, the antithesis to the traditional concept and function of order, is the last comment, the final twist of the irony.

None Shall Look Back fills out by a more discursive method the fortunes of the family in the midst of a war which destroys the social basis of its way of life. The Garden of Adonis has for scene the country community about the time of the Great Depression, when the full effects of defeat have had time to show their marks. Aleck Maury, Sportsman is not outside her subject but treats it in a very special way; and The Women on the Porch shifts the location to the city, the full-blown symbol of the western progression or, more specifically in American mythology, of the end of pioneering. The heroine, the first to marry outside the connection (and this is significant), in her flight from the city with no intention of returning to the family seat, instinctively finds her way back, but this time to a place of ghosts and sibyls. But the startling disclosure of the book is the crystallization of what has been gradually emerging, the theme of prevailing interest. To isolate such a theme, as I shall now try to do, is an act of violence and distortion to the work as a whole. Briefly, this theme is what Life, the sly deceiver, does to womankind, particularly to the woman of great passion and sensibility. It is not that men do not come in for their share of sorrows and disappointments; it is, rather, that Life, represented in the only possible hierarchy of institutional and organized society, has a masculine determination. Very subtly the White Goddess reasserts herself as Miss Gordon's muse. The young girl in "The Brilliant Leaves," the various heroines of *Penhally* (such as Alice Blair, the dark sister), Lucy of *None Shall Look Back*, and, most eloquently, the wife of Aleck Maury, are all the same woman. Very few of the male characters—Forrest, Nicholas, Mister Ben are the possible exceptions—are able to measure up to the requirements of what the heroine thinks a man should be.

In *None Shall Look Back*, the only one of her books where tragedy appears over her prevailing tone of irony, this theme finds its closest identity with the structure and subject, which is death. Death as a part of the experience of living is to be found here, certainly, but is of no more value than any of the phenomena used to create the illusion of a world. Death is also used in the formal way of the great tragedies, as the fulfillment, which is also the release, the judgment, and the meaning of the tensions of drama. And since the setting of the book is war, death becomes the Adversary. But death as a feminine force appears with the surprise of all the freshness of invention, and the moment of greatest passion, the very passion of despair and bitterness, is the moment when Lucy recognizes her loss of Rives in the pre-knowledge of his death. The quality of this recognition lies not in just the loss of him but in the loss of him to a rival of greater charm, whom she has long come to know by the gradual supplanting of her image in Rives's thoughts by that of the Dark Lady so constantly with him. The heroine has a rival at last equal to the demands of her pride. With this in mind Rives's taking of his wife upon the battlefield becomes an affront. The transposal of the relationship defines their tragic situation. On his part it is the act of despair of the man who, rebuffed by his true love, takes another as substitute. Her despair is the knowledge of this, and it gives her the highest intensity of any of Miss Gordon's women. Lucy is her creator's most successful rendition within the dramatic context and her only woman of tragic proportions. At first reading she seems a cold woman, but it is the coldness of an Electra, of an excess of passion and pride before her stupendous rival.

As the envelope for this, with reference to the historical image, she marries Rives, a cousin who stems from an eccentric branch of the family.

The eccentric is the subversive element in a tradition, because his freedom is self-willed. Freedom in an ordered state is the freedom of the will and depends upon responsibility defined by place and degree. Self-identity is always realized out of the fiction among the complex relationships of a well-determined whole. The self-will of the eccentric destroys this identity. Ideologically the abolitionist is such a person. The eccentric ancestor of Rives gave up raising tobacco to go off to the gullied country of North Georgia (a proper Allard says, "I would hate to live in a country where my grave was already dug for me") to raise mulberries for silkworms. The family may seem to recover from such an internal betrayal, which in effect it turns out to be through Lucy's plight; but the defection persists and spreads. Lucy's mother-in-law, always concerned with other people's business to the neglect of her own, is the symbol of this, as socially she is the counterpart to the abolitionist.

The historical and personal destinies of the characters, in the context of subject and structure, at their different levels, are one and the same. The climactic moment is reached when Forrest looks down upon the dead Rives, at the moment when troops break around him for the first time, and realizes that death has been by his side all along, a knowledge the lesser men have known in their calculated risks. Like a charmer ignored, she has lavished upon him her favors; and one has only to consider her true nature to understand his heroic dimensions, his ignorance of death being not only fearlessness but the self-immolation of those few who by utter devotion to anything—the Church, war, love, an art—have already undergone the denial which makes them fit company for so awful a companion.

Those few of Miss Gordon's male figures who achieve the stature of greatness do so in terms of a near equality to the feminine principle as personified by the heroine; but it is such an equality as Adonis suffered before the triumph of the masculine principle in heaven. The social pattern and the constraint of its form is a derivative of a man's world; therefore at the moment of its dissolution, the woman is set adrift, as in *The Garden of Adonis*. The girl's father cannot, because of his situation, be properly responsible for her welfare (the same holds true of Ote toward his girl). Mister Ben's effort of salvation can only be a personal effort and for this reason miscarries. His delight in his farm is a withdrawal from the chaos around him, as well as a refusal to face his actual plight. His daughter's adultery shatters his position and releases the tensions of a complicated involvement which brings his death, a judgment upon the inadequacy of personal salvation at the same time that it comments upon the rapid advance since the Civil War of the disintegration of the social order.

In many ways *The Garden of Adonis* promised to be her best book. There is a loosening in the treatment of character and situation, a heightening of her people as persons, a sensuous clarity heretofore more restrained. Certainly Ote Mortimer and Mister Ben, as well as many of her minor figures, remain in the imagination, well-rounded and complete and as men superior to their circumstances. They will remain after the details of the action which defined them grow vague. But the girl has no personality; she is a shadow from the beginning, and so is her lover. Structurally the book is a failure. It is almost as if the freedom which the author allowed herself in the texture extended itself carelessly when she came to the structure. After getting one set of complications under way and the interest aroused in a set of characters, she stops and introduces an entirely different set in the center of the book, and this in great circumstantiality, so that you get the sense of two novels progressing side by side, some of the characters of each accidentally crossing over to make for disaster. For her central development all she needed, perhaps, was the impression of the industrial society, or its symbol personified in some way, to precipitate the catastrophe; or else she needed to make a much longer book. She has created such a symbol in *The Women on the Porch*—Mrs. Manigault; she has done it almost in the description of her hair. Mrs. Manigault is a woman of indeterminate age. At first glance one cannot tell whether the hair is actually gray or by the skills which money can command is cleverly platinumed. And if platinumed, is it merely some exclusive fashion of beauty or does it subtly deny the passage of time, as the green blanket of mortician's grass thrown over the red mound beside the grave disguises for the moment the gaping hole?

This ambiguity represents the death-in-life, the triumph which is defeat, of that pride of man's assumption of the godhead. Miss Gordon's strategy was right in choosing the woman, and not the man, as the descriptive image, for always it is the woman who represents the life-force and man only its direction. Mrs. Manigault's energy is the sterile energy of a restlessness comparable with the restlessness of Orion Outlaw. In her case it would be an aimless motion but for the tell-tale heart. She represents the woman, the latest ideal of the masculine image gone to seed. She returns to the country, to a place where things are still things and people people, where communion is personal; there she learns of her plight, but it is too late to do more than set about the destruction of her son. There is a true hatred between them: it is the only thing that gives her life. The older masculine dominance had more humanity and humility. In its defeat its womankind could still commit adultery and have that adultery carry meaning; but there is nothing that Mrs. Manigault can do that has any real meaning.

But to return to *The Garden of Adonis*: perhaps the actual technical flaw at the center is the use of Jim Carter. The dramatic plausibility of so discursive a rendition of modern society would be its corruption of Carter, but it is never clear that there ever was anything to corrupt, that he ever had more than a high degree of sexual charm and a callous insensitivity. Certainly there could have been a more economical way of showing this, a subordinate and occasional extension of the girl's complication. The relations between them intended more.

Although it was probably not the author's intention, *Aleck Maury* undertook in an indirect way, at least in the representation of the personal solution, what *The Garden of Adonis* treated more explicitly. For the personal solution growing out of a social disintegration of values, Aleck Maury is a rounding out of Mister Ben. The conflict here is not between a man who would develop his faculties to the full against the demands of society; it is rather of a man against time. Outside his special delight, he moves through the world with as few commitments as a titled foreigner would allow himself in visiting a friendly country. Behind his pursuit of the arts of the field and stream lies the ruin of the hierarchical values which he might have expected to sustain him. In this society hunting and fishing would have taken their proper place; but because of the ruin, and in his terms this meant a loss of identity since he had lost location, he instinctively turned to the one knowledge and love more nearly a substitute. But the pursuit of his pleasure becomes obsessive, so that in the end it becomes not pursuit but flight, and the hot breath of the Furies can almost be felt lapping the air he has just vacated. He is a more humane Rion Outlaw, the masculine image now desperate in its effort toward personal salvation. Like Outlaw he cannot isolate himself entirely within the hunter's arts. He cannot deny the need for woman nor escape entirely the consequences of union. One of the most eloquent pieces of understatement in literature is the death of his wife. The very manner of her dying is a judgment upon him, an eloquent and secret triumph over his feckless manhood. As fine a book as it is, one feels the limitations of the memoirs form.

The historical image that is so integral to Miss Gordon's work is not static. Behind it is a myth, and the process of rendition I hope by now will be seen as dynamic in the sense that the image enlarges as the development of the complication grows. And what comes through from novel to novel is this sense of growth which distinguishes what is permanent and what there is of change, but always in terms of the human predicament. In *The Women on the Porch* the world city is the latest and final symbol, the apparent triumph of the masculine impulse toward the godhead. But the reality, as the story implies, illuminates the ambiguity of this triumph, which has put into man's hands an instrument only a god can control, while it has kept him a man. The knowledge of his predicament renders him impotent, the woman sterile, which indeed to a god must seem a very trifling disability at the most, something to delegate out of respect to the understanding of lesser intelligences. But to the natural man, pretender to all knowledge, this comes to be a bitter miscarriage of his hopes, the final mark of defeat. Chapman's apostrophe to the City is the recognition, the bowing of the head, before the darkened husk which has led the way into the long, narrow corridor of no return.

> And the queen? O City, preparing for what strange, nuptial flight! Having stung her sisters to death, she rises on rapid wings, but when the dead bridegroom has dropped from between her feathery legs she will hurtle down, past the heaped bodies of dead and dying drones. Will not the odor of decay penetrate the royal chamber, interrupting even the processes of fecundation, so that, seeking a cleaner air, she may lead her hive forth in a last flight, in which, travelling high above orchards and the gardens, they will not stop to cull honey from the apple blossom or the rose, but will continue on, an insensate mass, until, dying, falling in a great cloud, they darken with their wings the whole west?

Besides having the quality and tension of the best poetry, this apostrophe is the essence of compression of the image in terms of the subject and the subject in terms of the image, and the final release of her meaning, where

the style and dramatic quality make perfect complements. The very dis-
creteness of the city's materialism gives it an insubstantial quality, the lack
of location of a state of mind. Appetites and even being, disembodied,
move about in a purgatorial air. The figures generate a kind of effluvium,
which is at once their sin and its punishment. The illusion of this, emanating out of the tone and tension of the style, follows the girl in her flight from
the city. The women on the porch who receive her are also ghosts, but there
is more substance, more privacy; they are haunting the world of matter. One
has the feeling that Mrs. Manigault, in spite of her restlessness, has never
had enough substance to haunt anything. She is that queen bee spreading
her feathery legs for the bridal flight, and soon she will take her incestuous
way, with her son drawn after her in a grim caricature of the young god
Adonis, because for him there will be no resurrection.

The heroine's sense of this, in her adultery, makes her realize that her
affair with the boy can come to nothing, as she understands that the women
on the porch can never restore her to any true location. This knowledge,
after a dramatic revelation of it through the electrocution of the stallion,
reconciles her with her husband, and they decide to remove. I am not quite
clear about their relationship. Is it that they come together out of the
knowledge that they are both victims of forces too great to encompass? If
this is the shock of realization which makes plain the vitality of their love,
and Chapman's effort to strangle her when she tells him of her infidelity
would seem to establish his love, then Miss Gordon has failed to do what she
did in "The Brilliant Leaves": make us believe in it. We may assume that her
flight was out of the injury of his betrayal; but it could as easily have been out
of injured vanity, for Miss Gordon's heroines have great pride and a knowledge of man's incapacity. At any rate the vision here is a little clouded; one
feels for the first time a dichotomy between the historical image and the
subject. But this flaw seems a crack in her structure which the perfection of
the prose will not allow to widen.

This examination into her work must be understood in its partial nature.
To expose, as I have done, a certain part of it for analysis is the violence of
all inquiry and merely an introduction for a more comprehensive study. I
know of no writer of fiction that other writers can study with greater profit.
Her tension at times seems too severe, as if her image as mask penetrates the
passion and, instead of objectifying, freezes it. It causes her characters at

times to appear immobile or cold; and the constant friction between mask and passion, or between form and subject, loses then its balance, and a kind of stasis results. But certainly she is one of the few distinguished writers of fiction, in the shorter pieces as well as the novels—and I do not limit this judgment to the immediate past—and it is a comfort to realize that her art gives evidence of its vitality and growth.

Caroline Gordon's The Forest of the South

I HAVE JUST READ AGAIN CAR-oline Gordon's *The Forest of the South.* I have known these stories almost as long as I have the author, but I put them down with that won-dering sense of surprise at how much better they are than I had remem-bered. Time in the way of the top-ical has left no mark. They are like old houses which have weathered all seasons and fashions, rising upon a landscape unobtrusively but with such authority they seem not to have been made by the hand of man but to have grown along with the flora and the fauna. This is a mark of objectivity. It is more. It is the mark of an artist who will last. To return to a book or story and find always more is the surest way to distinguish between the complex art of fiction and the simpler art of narrative.

Several years ago in the *Sewanee Review* I had something to say, par-ticularly about Miss Gordon's nov-els. I examined them in terms of the tools of the craft. The use of these tools is always twofold, conscious and intuitive. This process is the fundamental mystery of the art of fiction and, I suppose, of any art. In trying to re-create, the critic always takes a risk, but he takes less of a risk in watching the way the technique works, for the only way meaning takes form is the way the words are put together. I seem to be stating a platitude, but this simple truth is often obscured, and not only by the historical scholars.

It had seemed to me that up to *The Strange Children* the action proper of Miss Gordon's novels had always been cast against an explicit understanding of a sense of history. But there is a difference of approach between the novelist's use of past time and the historian's. The historian, as scientist, is interested in cause and effect, the discovery of principles of action. The fiction writer takes a different post of observation. Whatever the point of view, the action seen by the novelist creates the illusion of action taking place in the present tense. To the historian the past is dead. To the novelist the past is contemporaneous, or almost. There can be no absolute sense of contemporaneity in the re-creation of any age, or segment of an age, anterior to the time in which the author writes. Indeed, if this were so, the principal value of using the past would be lost: the value being just this illusion of the contemporary within a context of historical perspective, so that while an action is taking place it is rendered in terms larger than those of its immediate appearance. This is, I believe, the furthest extension, and it is just that, of the aesthetic distance taken by writers concerned primarily with the formal, objective view. The very illusion of life defines the difference between history as fiction and history as science. For this reason the well-done novel is the only way of recovering the illusion of past time, since people acting make history. I say illusion because we must leave the final truths to God. The question is not: Is the story historically sound? The question is Does the action represent the behavior of men and women in this given situation? Does it show what really happened, not the report of what seemed to happen? And secondly, does the form make the most of the subject, the subject the most of the form? The critical reader asks literary questions, which are the only questions he can ask about a literary form. His answers will show whether the history is sound.

Action takes place through, the natural man restrained by, the complex of institutions in any given society. The novelist and historian up to a point are together in recovering the look of these institutions. They must both do the same kind of research, but the novelist goes further. He must bring the people alive in their manners and customs, their habits of behavior. To the novelist the cultural pattern becomes in its broadest sense the enveloping action against which, and out of which, the action proper complicates itself. This action involves the conflicts, tensions, defeats and triumphs which are the constantly recurring deeds of the human situation. The enveloping action is the mould. Miss Gordon's structure depends upon a cultural loss, caught in a succession of historical images, a loss that impairs the possibilities of human nature. This impairment, made concrete in the action proper, makes explicit the meaning of history. The controlling image, therefore, is a double clue to meaning, through the action to the enveloping action, and vice versa. For example, in *Green Centuries* the image of the wilderness usurps Rion Outlaw's mind. The wilderness becomes the antagonist. Man has set himself to triumph over the natural world. This is a revolutionary change in the Christian attitude toward the world. Rion's very name of Outlaw is a symbol of this change. As Miss Gordon's novels show, the true antagonist is woman. Manhood best defines itself in the stress between the sexes, which is the source of physical and spiritual human intercourse. Rion's obsession shows itself for what it is in the disaster which overtakes him and his wife and children, indirectly commenting on the historic progression in Western society. The Indians are there to show the mystery, the supernatural suffusing the natural. That Rion should see them as feminine shows his blindness as it shows the cost of the distortion of his anima. In all her novels the progress of this changing attitude discloses itself in its effects upon her heroes and heroines, the true protagonists and antagonists. When Merlin withdrew with Niniane into the forest, he drew the magic circle of love about them, from which arose the shady hedges, flowers, and fragrant herbs to encompass the songs of knights and ladies. Niniane could not get enough of the music, but she understood only one verse: "Bitter suffering ends the sweet joys of newborn love." This is the oldest song. It is Miss Gordon's song, accompanied by the discords of history.

In one way or another this is the subject, as well, of her stories. In the title piece, "The Forest of the South," the conquest of the South is the destruction of a society formal enough and Christian enough to allow for the right relationships between the sexes. The Civil War was total war, not the restricted war of a Christian state. It returns people not to Merlin's forest but to the forest as wasteland. The madness of the girl makes its comment. Total destruction is madness. It shows itself explicitly and concretely in the basic relationship between man and woman. It is the conqueror's defeat, because he is fated to love what he has destroyed. The blowing up of Clifton is the controlling image. The roles are reversed between conquered and conqueror. The Confederate captain will die with this knowledge, so that his death is a kind of triumph. The victor has the flaw of being a gentleman who is in love. Blind, too, he has confused the response of madness for love. He is condemned to a living death, not the marriage bed but the madwoman's bed of straws.

In "Hear the Nightingale Sing" the theme is the same, except that the enveloping action becomes the home, that constant symbol of family, whose large connections, based upon a Christian sacrament, make up the structure of the state. When Barbara, leading the mule off the Yankee's dead body, says let's go home, the irony is obvious. The home is already gone. Both she and the soldier will be forever deprived of it. The soldier represents the violator, and his death enlarges the meaning of his act. It is his streaming and bloody eyes which give the manner of his dying, and the loss of eyes is an old symbol of castration, the absolute spiritual loss resulting in this instance in letting war go beyond its restricted concept. This Yankee is one of Miss Gordon's best characters. He is a sympathetic figure. His song, with its nostalgia, releases through the sense of hearing what it once meant for Barbara or what it might have been in love for Ladd, if only the music had played longer. What is common to both, releasing common memories, only sets them further apart, although twice the Yankee almost recovers his humanity: when he rises from the food and in the parlor. But he gives way to appetite, and the mule's thud brings him back to his part as enemy; yet he alternates between the brutal habits of war and feeling. He smiles, he sings, he is thoughtful of the mule's leg. He bridges his split by irony, but he cannot save himself. Irony is not enough. He dies by the feet of the brute instinctual forces released by war, symbolized in the sterile mule. The gift of the mule by Ladd to Barbara (her name foreshows her doom) stands for the hopelessness of their relationship. It does destroy the enemy, but it can stand only negatively in Ladd's stead. It cannot restore what the enemy himself has destroyed.

The most extreme statement of this reversal of roles results from the complications in "The Ice House." The Yankee contractor is a symbol of the revolutionary change in American society, the acceptance of materialism as the final value in the state. It is this which has triumphed in the Civil War. The defeat of the Confederacy destroyed in the Union the restraints of the checks and balances which took into account the depravity of man, at the same time as, socially, it smashed the values of a traditional hierarchy of relationships. Death, of course, is the final comment on matter. It reduces it to dust and the bare bone. By implication life conceived only in terms of the material aims makes of it a living death, by denying the spirit. The contractor is the embodiment of this denial in his own person and as representative of the Yankee attitude. In her use of symbol Miss Gordon never, as Hawthorne too often does, makes it carry the burden of meaning alone. Whenever she uses symbol, it is always matched by its natural counterpart, which is to say that she has discerned the inadequacy of allegory and propaganda for fiction. "The Ice House" stands for death, but it is also a place to store ice. The Yankee bones and decaying flesh are the symbols of death, but they are also the physical objects of death. The object and the symbol are further concentrated, dumped into the ice house. As well, the contractor's indifference to any meaning in the burial other than how much he can make out of it is a cultural debasement equal to social death. This makes his avarice sinister, particularly because of his unawareness. Further, the contractor's appearance resembles death. His belly, almost breaking through his breeches, brings to mind the image of the swelling, bloating stage of decay. The irony finds its point in his gray hairs, which anticipate his own end and coming up to judgment. This is all seen through the innocent eyes of the boys of the defeated people. Where he is insensitive, they are sensitive only to the physical nausea of death. They have naturally no affective reaction, for the dead is not their dead. Their feeling and reflections are all for life, which is struggling here with its opposite, and at the end it is life which triumphs. The triumph is more telling because the contractor is a man who ought to know better and they are boys. Their contemptuous laughter makes of him a low comedy figure, but a grim one, too. When Doug says, "There ain't a whole man in ary one of them boxes," he is saying more than he knows. Man who views himself only in physical terms is only half a man. He has ignored the crucial drama of the soul.

This is one of the few stories in which the complication lacks a woman. Miss Gordon rarely departs either in her novels or stories from the stress between the sexes, which allows for the most complete rendition of the soul's drama. At least there is the universal complication. Her attack is often indirect and always subtle, for example in the Tom Rivers and Aleck Maury pieces. These stories of field and stream and livery stable seem to belong only to a masculine world. But this seeming is only Miss Gordon's unique use of her historical image. Tom Rivers, Aleck Maury, and Ladd perhaps would be special cases in any society, but their singular aptitudes would merely bring to a sharper focus the look of their communities. They seem to flee their women, but what they are actually doing is seeking means of preserving their integrity. They are dispossessed men. The state in which they would function best has been destroyed. They would have been its ornaments and leaders. Men of integrity, aristocratic, they cannot become servile as the poor-blooded man who is afraid to pick his own cotton. Tom Rivers, by picking it, shows how the state has declined. Any aristocracy functions by instinctive action and within a code of manners, but its decisions need not be irrational because they are not always reasoned out. They don't have to stop to reason, because they know what they are and so can act instantly out of this knowledge. Tom Rivers' girl makes an impossible demand on him. She makes the literal error of asking him to promise never to drink again. She is asking him to surrender his sovereignty, which the Wife of Bath says is what woman wants of man. But her demand shows Tom she is unworthy of this surrender. She is presenting him with two impossibilities: first, that he deny the underlying conflict between the sexes; second, that he conform to a kind of mores which would be not only alien but destructive to him. She is unworthy because she represents these mores. All she had to say was, "Do you love me?" If she had, she would have destroyed him, because he then would have involved himself in a world he could not function in. His instinct for self-preservation, and by this much is the dispossessed aristocrat reduced, takes him away from her into a masculine world of horses and whores. His intercourse is diminished, and he will be a wanderer, but his integrity will remain. The action proper, the picking of the cotton, the treachery of the servile "new" men, unfolds his predicament and the meaning of the story. The boy's nostalgia for the old community of families, done largely through his memory of nature, the way the sun passes the garden fence at the homeplace, when land and family mutually identify each other, refers to the loss in the historical terms this image makes. The exile from this location is responsible for the situation the Tom Riverses find themselves in.

Aleck Maury is the Tom Rivers who married. He is a valiant warrior in love and wears his wife out, but almost too late. He tries to fill up his remaining years with the sports of field and stream. In this way he saves what he can by living as fully as he can. He, too, is an exile; but he has instinctively chosen the one ritual left which can more nearly use all of his resources. Of course it never quite does it. Hunting and fishing had their places in the society that was destroyed. They were not meant to fill out a man's total occupation. In "The Burning Eyes" he was given the image which would save him, but "To Thy Chamber Window Sweet" and "Old Red" show him never free of danger. If never free, his instincts always save him.

With one or two exceptions the other stories in the book deal more directly with how "bitter suffering ends the sweet joys of newborn love." The image of a changing or changed society withdraws further into the background here, as the pure drama of love comes to the fore. I cannot here go into these stories. I have hoped to show that Miss Gordon's use of history is the right use. It recovers history as a living set of deeds whose actions, as they represent the universal predicament, also interpret the changing flow of history.

Concupiscence and Power: Warren's All the King's Men

ROBERT PENN WARREN IS THE most distinguished man of letters in the country. He is a poet. He writes novels and stories. He is a critic. Even as an undergraduate his criticism, or a better way to put it, his reading in literature, was sensitive, apperceptive, and, above all, of sound judgment and taste. And he is a scholar and a teacher. Any one of these disciplines, performed as he performs them, would define a superior artist. Since they all come out of the whole man, it would be hard to say which he is best at. It is merely a matter of where he turns his attention. I thought he was set on being a poet, but then the poet is not limited to verse. Surely Plato meant that the man of imagination was the source of all forms. Warren's imagination boils with images. In speech his sentences explode in a chain reaction. Sometimes they would be gone before the ear could catch them; yet they are not volatile. This energy in the written work is concentrated by the particular form he is engaged by.

We were classmates at Vanderbilt. Frequently we would take walks together. A park was nearby, with flower beds and a stream and a replica of the Parthenon as its centerpiece. As the only exact replica in the world, it gave Nashville the sobriquet Athens of the South. Today it is called Music City, that is, the vaudeville town rather than the town of classical learning. O tempora, O mores! At the very gates of the park stood a giant oak tree. It was here that the Tennessee end of the Natchez Trace began. So we walked in the presence of an ancient inheritance and more recent history. But neither was on our minds as we walked and he talked, his head turned away from his stride as he sought your attention. I was a good listener but did not always understand all that I heard. At the time I was a dancing man, and Nashville was a social town. I kept two sets of tails, one at the cleaners and one on my back. I've wondered if what my ears took in on these walks, though, did not have a profound effect upon what has become my occupation.

There were other influences, including our companions. Some of them would become writers and one a sculptor. The professors encouraged writing, and not only the English teachers. Allen Tate, who was a senior, discovered Warren at Professor Curry's typewriter putting down a poem. They became roommates. Both were student members of the Fugitive group of poets. Unlike the Blue Pencil and Calumet clubs, both writing clubs for undergraduates whose works were judged by teachers, the Fugitives were only informally connected with the university. Men in the city—merchants and bankers and one mystic who thought of himself as a messiah—joined the professors and students in this common pursuit of discussion and the writing of verse. Often with fervor, high talk would come out of criticism of the poem just read.

That was a long time ago, and in a way All the King's Men came upon the literary scene a long time ago. It is a little shocking for a story I've always felt as present to become a "classic" and need an introduction. An introduction breaks the ice, almost reluctantly sometimes, between the reader and what he is about to encounter. In the theater it is called a curtain raiser. But it is also for the reader who wants to know what the author means.

In one edition of All the King's Men, Warren recounts the history and some of the influences that caused him to choose fiction rather than verse as his subject's final form. Whatever else he is doing, however, he is admonishing the reader to read for himself what lies between the covers of the book. It is there that the reader will find what the author means. Flaubert is saying the same thing to the Goncourt brothers when he tells them it was the color gray he had in mind as meaning for *Madame Bovary.* However, Warren does give a clue. He says, "And the story, in a sense, became the story of Jack Burden, the teller of the tale."

The teller of the tale, he who holds the point of view, is always the protagonist, unless he is the arbitrary voice of the author, in which case how did the author's surrogate get so close to the action without being involved? Jack Burden is totally involved, and not just in Willie Stark's life. It is his story. All the actors, in the world he explores, belong to his quest for a knowledge he needs, for Jack has a grief. The quest does center about Willie Stark and his drama. In serving him as investigator and confidant, Jack Burden is following trails that will bring him, at last, not only to a resolution of Willie's action, but also to his own. So, reporter that he is, Jack Burden is not just reporting Stark's disaster; he is affected and changed by what Willie Stark is and does. Both men involve themselves in larger matters than their own. Each has a wound that will not scar. In sending Jack to probe into Judge Irwin's past, which Jack feels is impeccable, Willie says, "There is always something." This something leads to Jack's mother's possible regeneration and makes of Jack his father's executioner.

All the King's Men is the third of three novels which concern the constant impulses of concupiscence and the drive for power. In Warren's first novel, *Night Rider,* the title is both literal and a pun. An internecine fight of normally responsible people engages them against a common oppressor. The fixed idea to break the monopoly of tobacco buyers involves the community and certain leaders in a more serious violence of human and civil actions leading to crime and death. In *At Heaven's Gate* the conflict centers about the industrial and abstract power of banking, but all the tales show differing aspects of greed and vanity and the insolent use of power. The licentious and succulent devices of sexual appetite complicate the greed for power, as power denies the sweetest expectation of lust, missing love's mark.

Particularly in *All the King's Men*, both concupiscence and power direct the means which bring the resolution. In themselves and as they affect each other, however, both are equal parts of the action. Together they reveal in a Protestant society at a deeper level a form of Manichaean heresy, that men are all bad, that there is nothing but the dark powers, and that the best to hope for (Willie Stark's formula) is to make good out of bad. The failure here is more than a failure of definition.

Warren experimented in these books with the technical invention of putting a short story within the novel as essence of the action. With such a device there is always a problem of where to put it without blocking the main action. In *At Heaven's Gate*, it is more like an Elizabethan subplot than a short story. But in *Night Rider*, Willie Proudfit tells a lyrical story of a boy who wanders west into his manhood and, after a vision induced by a desperate illness and Indian medicine, returns to his home. Here, in a pastoral setting, he finds the girl just as he had seen her in his fevered vision. It is a beautiful story, but it is misplaced. Lyrical though it is, containing as it does the essence of the larger action—among other things how greed destroys life—it comes too close to the end of the book for the reader to return with full attention to the main action, which has only one chapter left.

In *All the King's Men* the separate action, "Cass Mastern's Wedding Ring," has the essential meaning of the larger action; but it is also a part of that action. It is the clue to Jack Burden's quest. When it is given to him as a subject for his history dissertation, he is unable to decipher it. As he tries, his surroundings contain roommates living in the inertia of sensuality and sloth. This he flees, spiritually tainted by what he leaves behind. More profoundly he flees Cass Mastern's diary, but it follows him, unwrapped, the clue insistent but ignored.

The clue itself is false: Jack is no kin to Cass Mastern. The meaning will not be unraveled until the end, if then, in all its ramifications. The irony of this denies him an easy answer. His quest will be long, a part of the general irony which is the first property of the story's meaning, if not the meaning itself. Jack's search for the "something," on his own and at Willie Stark's behest, is an appealing part of the action, with the excitement of a detective story.

"Cass Mastern's Wedding Ring" is one of the oldest betrayals, that of a friend by a young protégé, Cass Mastern, who allows himself to be seduced by the friend's wife, Annabelle. She is a woman of thirty, to the youth of eighteen the irresistible *belle dame sans merci*. They meet at the ages when lust is the consuming urge of the youth's nature and she is at the moment of worldly and sexual knowledge intensified by the boredom of habit and Time's threat.

The husband, Duncan Trice, discovers the adultery, but he does not call his young friend out. He kills himself as if by accident. Publicly, this saves Annabelle's reputation and his honor, but by putting his wedding ring beneath her pillow, he means to let her know that he knew. That is his intention, but it is not she who finds it. Her personal maid presents it to her mistress, along with the knowledge that she shares the truth.

And this the mistress cannot abide, the unspoken, constant accusation of guilt. Annabelle sells the maid down the river, hoping to forestall exposure, but chiefly to remove the reminder of her betrayal. Later, when the adulterers meet in the summer house, she slips the ring upon Cass's finger, binding him in their guilt and announcing the nature of her husband's death. The ring, the symbol of union and conjugal fidelity, is now the symbol of a double betrayal.

Like Abu Kassim's slippers, the ring is part of the commonplace, the usual, the harmless furniture of life until, as such, it assumes another role, in this instance the baleful, self-induced punishment of a compound betrayal. The ring will not encircle Cass Mastern's finger. It can only hang, like the albatross, about his neck, for he, for neither, will confront what they have done. Neither will seek penance, contrition, or the hope of absolution by confession (which would have to be to each other or each alone).

Cass Mastern tries what all the king's horses and men cannot do: to mend what has been broken beyond repair. He will find the maid and free her. In this he fails, but the rebuke to Annabelle Trice separates them forever. Selfish in their lust, both lack the compassion of love, which possibly could have solaced if not saved them. Annabelle flees the scene forever. Cass, like the Puritan he becomes, puts evil in the object and good in his own will and so avoids the knowledge of his nature, that he is subject to what all men suffer and can do. He commits himself to the delusion of trying to turn bad into good, that is, to change the nature of behavior. He frees his slaves, but they will not work the land in a slave society. He then sends them up the river to an unknown future, which is in effect like Mrs. Trice selling her maid down the river.

He commits all the follies his society will not tolerate. When war comes, he joins the army but refuses to kill, even here failing to participate in what is common to all and by this obsession endangering the lives of his companions. A slight wound infects and kills him, alone and in spiritual distress from his evasions. Knowing he will die, he writes in his diary that he has done no man good and has seen others suffer for his sin. He doesn't question the justice of God, since the suffering of the innocent affirms that men are brothers. It is a comfort to him that he suffers for only his own sin. In this fashion he remains alone, his last evasion having shifted to God the responsibility he should have assumed. Perhaps this is the unknown sin, an assumption of divine knowledge through an immaculate ego which cannot err, cannot cry *mea culpa* even when it is beating its breast.

What Cass Mastern shows in private life, Willie Stark shows in the public world of politics. In these parts of the story, power, unrestrained by charity or moral considerations, dominates the action. The wedding band stands as a symbol of the meaning, for adultery disrupts public affairs, as it does the harmony and order of family life.

The two distinctions, public and private, with their manners and mores, are basic properties of order. Codes of behavior for both define the rules which sustain order in the state and in the family. Politicians must use their offices not for private gain but for the public good. Fathers must support and protect the privacy and the *lares* and *penates* of the household. Out of belief in the sanctity of these laws and codes, Duncan Trice, the cuckolded husband, kills himself. In the public drama of Willie Stark's power play, Judge Irwin, the adulterer this time, not the husband, kills himself in the same way, for the same reason, presumably by cleaning a gun. This convention was accepted, whether it was believed or not, for their community lived by traditional ways. Moral laws still worked, although morality becomes private prejudice when the light from Heaven fails, and it was growing dimmer all the time.

So it is, then, that Duncan Trice and Judge Irwin confront the act of darkness in a final way, out of a common belief. Belonging to a traditional society, they believe in something outside of themselves. Not so the Scholarly Attorney. Not so Willie Stark. After his public humiliation, Willie abandons his sense of the public office as serving others. His afflicted ego relies upon the power of that office to punish or control not only his enemies but his servants as well. How much he has forgotten that a man of principle can also assert power shows in his response to Judge Irwin's suicide: "God damn it, so the bastard crawled out on me?" What Judge Irwin has done is to set in motion forces which bring down Willie Stark and all of his followers.

These forces expose the inadequacy of the autonomous mind, which in crisis impairs instead of affirms men's humanity, that is, the humanity of Cass Mastern, the Scholarly Attorney, Willie Stark, and especially Dr.

Stanton. But not Jack Burden. He presents the facts as he discovers them. He never judges; he does not even judge himself after the shock which sends him fleeing to California, not to hide but to review his own past and understand it. He is his father's son even if his quest is for the truth, a vaguer matter than codes, honor, and the integrity of a family. At his return the truth seems the Great Twitch, but that truth does not heal his wound.

In the action of *All the King's Men*, this autonomy of the mind works in various ways but always out of the Puritan's singular heresy that he cannot err and that he can interpret God's will. The Scholarly Attorney writes religious tracts after abandoning his family. In practice he offers the palliatives of candy for the indigenous sorrows of life. At the last he tells Jack Burden to believe that the creation of evil is God's power and glory, which leaves the creation of good as the index of man's glory and power, since man is separate from God and to be separate from God is to be sinful. Obviously he ignores the lesson of Job, to whom God spoke out of the whirlwind in rebuke, saying, Who are you to interpret God's mind? He ignores as well that man was made, not begotten.

Willie Stark feels and is an example of this glory and power. He does not doubt that he will make good out of bad, although he fails to tell Adam Stanton just how that can be. The hospitals and good highways are monuments to his pride. At the same time, he offers them as aids if not solutions to man's deprivations. But good roads empty the communities they are supposed to serve, and the rapid traffic going to and fro isolates those who remain in the fields or the villages. And no matter how big the hospitals and how good the doctors—they alleviate and at times cure—disease and death remain. Willie Stark, then, becomes the example of the Scholarly Attorney's theory. But if Willie's glory is questionable, his power is not, insofar as it can ruin and break. Yet in efforts to make good out of bad, it fails. It does more. It is ruinous to Willie himself and to those who follow him.

Like Cass Mastern, Willie possesses a delusion about his power which blinds him to the true cause of his behavior—his injured vanity. Stark believes to the very end in the invincibility of his power. In his dying breath he says to Jack Burden: "It might have been all different. You got to believe that." Of course it might, but not as the governor meant.

Willie's blindness at the lip of the grave makes him a pathetic figure but a better man than his enemies—the functionaries of the political machines and their dishonest business associates. One of the minor ironies of the novel is that his enemies become his inheritors. They resume office after his death. Willie's boasts, his power to break reputations and reduce men to servility, had changed nothing. The seductions of concupiscence and the usurpation of office had made of Willie the archetype of Machiavellian politics.

And privately it is the same. He sees in his son the power of his loins. For lack of love the boy dies. Willie, seeking in his son only his genetic invincibility, induces a willful behavior in the boy that becomes the occasion for his father's undoing. And this comes at the moment when power and self-illuminated glory merge the end with the means. Concupiscence acts as a display of power. At that moment Willie's doom is foretold. Lust discards its object when it is through with it. When Willie leaves Sadie Burke for Anne Stanton, the action rapidly moves toward general disaster. When Sadie had become his mistress, Willie's wife, who loved him and remembered his early political integrity, merely withdrew until he could return to her and his senses. At least this is a possible interpretation, for she understood what power had done to him. At the height of his forensic triumph he came home to his wife's withdrawal. This is a crucial scene. It is also the moment when Willie makes his choice absolute. Jack Burden points out to Sadie that it is not she but Willie's wife who has been abandoned, but Sadie will not listen.

She sets out to knock Humpty Dumpty off the wall, in the same way Willie had used the state to destroy the politicians who had humiliated him in public. If Sadie had confronted her damage to Willie's marriage or even if Willie at the moment of his election had remembered the proper exercise of his office and not just his wounded vanity, there would have been another outcome to the action. Or even if Adam Stanton had served as *locus parentis* to his sister, which his unconfessed or unexamined incestual predilections prevented, there would have been another story. I see no better reason for Dr. Stanton's withdrawal from women, his murder of his sister's lover, his excessive professional commitment and practice, and his occasional violent release in music than what the athletics of the bed would have made unnecessary. He and Willie Stark display the same excessive, obsessive vanities, Stanton in privacy, Stark in public office. Rather than the governor's appetite, Dr. Stanton's puritanism shows the purest lust for power, in that the lives of others are in his hands, but especially in that he denies his sister her humanity, all of which serves as the blind screen between the oldest familial temptation and the self-knowledge which could have been his salvation.

It is his sister Anne who saves what is left to be saved. By sleeping with Stark, she frees herself from the threefold union of brother, sister, and friend, the impossible triangle, Jack Burden always the foil to the brother, helping his own courtship to miscarry. There is no end to the complexity of this action when you consider that it is Anne's need, not Sadie's malice, which scars the two wounds, one by death, the other by finding the truth he has sought.

Up to the moment Jack Burden learns of the liaison between Anne and Stark, his role has been that of observer, in the service of another, not responsible for the information he has passed on with a degree of cynicism which, however, did not compromise what he saw as the truth. This had kept his grief immaculate. As injured party to the domestic failure of his parents, he put this sorrow between his need for a fuller knowledge of his plight and what that would have done to relieve it.

But the shock of what he learns from Anne sends him to California, to his recovery of much of that truth about what he had done, and had had done to him, and about his mother and how he had lost Anne. From this self-probing, one crucial matter emerges: what a young male finds hardest to accept or believe, his mother's vain attraction which lures men. He had tended to blame her for the Scholarly Attorney's flight and the loss of what to the child is the basic security, the family integrity which is forever constant. But Jack could not accept with respect the Scholarly Attorney as a father, since he avoided his parental responsibility by giving the child candy before supper and making of the gift a matter for guilt. Jack's probing brought him to his marriage with a woman whose physical attractions were dominant, as if he were testing by proxy his mother's nature. The marriage had ended in divorce, returning him to his uncertainty.

After his return from California, not with the truth but the grounds for it, which he does not understand, he believes that the twitch extends even to God as the Great Twitch, and is the final impulse to action. At this point the fatal threads begin their twining. Willie's son Tom is accused by his father's chief opponent of getting a bastard on a girl, notwithstanding that she had been notably amiable. To counter this, Jack is asked for the "something" on Judge Irwin, to whom the opponent owes much. Jack refuses until he has the chance to allow the Judge to deny what he had found. Willie says he had never asked him to frame anybody, that the truth is always enough. When he calls on Judge Irwin, Jack finds this to be so. The judge warns him that there is something he could say that would cause Jack to withdraw his threat of blackmail. After the Judge shoots himself through the heart, Jack learns what it is. His mother's scream of loss and grief tells him, "You have killed your father." And as her son later learns, Irwin is the only man that she has ever loved, and furthermore to make her loss more bitter, neither she nor her lover had tried to avoid the circumstances which kept them apart. This crushing enlightenment makes her former and present life impossible, now that she sees it for what it was. She leaves the Landing with a feeling of pity for another. She goes to Reno, there to reflect in sorrow best defined by the controlling image from "Cass Mastern's Wedding Ring," that life is a spider web from which, once touched, there's no escape. But in her departure she has to know that her lover was what he appeared to be, that it was ill health and not a "jam" which brought his death. Out of compassion Jack swears to God that a lie is the truth.

This parting between mother and son is towards the end, after all the deaths, of which Judge Irwin's is the first. There is as much violence and death as in an Elizabethan tragedy, but the end does not leave the reader with the purgation of pity and fear. The general feeling is irony. Jack Burden and Anne Stanton are left to resume a life together, but their wedding attendants are ghosts. They live together in his father's house with the Scholarly Attorney, Judge Irwin having left Jack his property. With these survivors he at last begins to write the life of Cass Mastern, as his hurt begins to heal. But if the open sore heals, the scar remains.

It will remain, for the unblemished flesh can never grow back, as no truth is affirmed by a lie, even out of charity. The name of Jack Burden's charity is compassion, for his mother, for Sadie, and for Willie's successor, the imme-diate agent of his assassination, since Jack refrained from telling Sugar Boy, who would have killed him. Compassion, then, becomes the ultimate irony as the flaw to truth. Jack is a connection, if not kin, to Cass Mastern: Cass never probes for truth and so is blinded; Jack finds it but does not accept it. Perhaps he leaves it to God. At least if this feeling of compassion restores him to living, the edge is dulled. There is an autumnal tone to his reflections, even when he thinks he might join Stark's honest attorney general at some future time. He is like Pierre in *War and Peace* after his marriage to Natasha and their domestic life together. Pierre goes to his clubs, takes part in the philosophical discussions, but the fire is out. It is little more than habit.

It is no longer skepticism, but there is a part of Jack's understanding that is not convinced. It approaches, without defining or accepting, a religious belief. The feeling is there, but the leading actors upon the various stages live with a sense of history as the final judgment of man's actions and of his worth. But man can never be the ultimate judge of man's actions, so long as he continues to die. This may be accepted as the enveloping action of the drama.

It may even stand as a compassionate judgment upon "Cass Mastern's Wedding Ring" when Jack finishes Mastern's life and discovers just how that life and his are connected. But this will be after he and Anne go out of his father's house "into the convulsion of the world, out of history into history and the awful responsibility of Time." Afterwards they will come back to the Row, to the places of their beginnings, and they will walk to the pine grove, "where the needles thick on the ground will deaden the footfall so that we shall move among the trees as soundlessly as smoke." Almost as ghostly as their bridal attendants.

The Displaced Family

PETER TAYLOR IS THE ONLY American writer, and indeed to my knowledge the only writer in English, whose subject is the dislocation and slow destruction of the family as an institution.* He has fixed upon the one fact central to the social revolution going on in this country; how far it involves the rest of the Western world is not immediately relevant. It is relevant that Taylor is a southern writer or, better still, from the border state of Tennessee, which gives him a distinct perspective upon the historical situation and defines the aesthetic distance of his point of view. Nowhere else in this country is the family as a social unit so clearly defined as in the South. Its large "connections" amplifying the individual family life, the geographic accident which allowed the family in this greater sense (it was the community) to extend itself in a mild climate and alluvial soils where the physical barriers were not too severe, and slavery too, gave the family a clearer definition of its function as not only an institution but *the* institution of southern life. So it was else-

*The three works discussed in this essay are *Tennessee Day in St. Louis* by Peter Taylor; *The Homecoming Game* by Howard Nemerov; and *Sojourn of a Stranger* by Walter Sullivan.

where in the country, but never quite to such an extent. In the successive Wests the constant movement impaired its stability. In New England, at least in the coastal areas, there was always the sea to intervene, keeping its mind colonial and spiritually dependent upon England, holding up a distant image and not the immediate one of a constant scene such as land allows. Both the sea and land are feminine images, but the sea takes only men; and so the communion between husband and wife is disrupted. When you think of woman in New England's past, witch-hunting comes to mind; when you think of woman in the South, the matriarch shows herself. Land keeps the family intact. Husband, wife, children, the old, middle, and young generations all serve it and are kept by it, according to their various needs and capacities. The parts of the family make a whole by their diversity. The military defeat of the South, which was total in the sense of its structural overthrow and the acceptance of this overthrow, gives the writer a ground of comparison for the changes this defeat brought about. Most southern writers of necessity must be aware of this. None has so clearly made fine stories out of it as has Taylor. However, he merely implies the more stable situation of the family on the land in dealing with its predicament in town and city. "Exiled at home" might best describe Taylor's earlier stories. In *Tennessee Day in St. Louis* the exile is actual, as it is in most of the stories in *The Widows of Thornton*.

Families from other parts of the country, when they move, identify themselves most readily with their new surroundings. The southern family, like Lot's wife, turns back its head. The Tolliver household is the archetype of such a family. There are no heroes. The actors are all decent human beings caught in the situation of trying to maintain in absentia manners and mores which do not express their economic habits. The house has for its self-invited guest a former senator who will be the speaker at the annual Tennessee Day in St. Louis. It is also the birthday of Lanny, the youngest son of the house, as well as the anniversary of the parents, James and Helen. The family, as the curtain rises, discovers itself at a moment when both its public and private ceremonies happen upon the same day. Formerly, at "home," this would have seemed a happy occasion to combine the rituals of hospitality, birth, and the public thing. But the play opens in a different way. The *ficelles* describe a conflict between the public and the private ritual. The Senator has taken over the whole lower floor of the house, "evicting" the family while he memorizes his speech. But he has not been able to have it alone. Auntie Bet and Flo Dear, a rich old maid and her companion, defy the Senator by remaining downstairs working at a puzzle. They all have one thing in common: they are all self-invited. The ladies, however, have made themselves a part of the household; yet they feel insecure. The Senator, a temporary guest, as they once were, threatens their place. The "connec- tions," instead of working at and adding to the common occasion, jealously and selfishly find themselves at odds, if in the most civil fashion.

This competition between the public and private thing descends to a conflict within the privacy itself upon the entrance of James, the head of the house. He comes in as if he were intruding in his own home and hides his gift for Lanny, even locks it up. The reason given is that the Senator must not be made to feel his intrusion at such a time, and so the birthday is concealed. This is certainly a strain of manners, but it is more than that. If the Senator's kinship were true in the old sense, there would be no need for a guilty suppression of a private celebration. The guilt lies in the fact that there is nothing to be private about. The family is a husk, committed to keeping up the appearance of what a family is. The meaning of this shows in the father's gift, golf clubs, which he loves and his son hates, as he does all games, preferring history and literature. The gift should represent love for the child in the occasion: it represents instead self-love and appearance. With ruthless insistence the family holds to this.

The family in a Christian society has only one function, to operate as a family and perpetuate itself through its children. Each member is called upon to deny much of his individual nature in the service of the whole, and this service sustains the common love and life. But the service must rest upon domestic laws, the principal one of disciplining children and servants, if there be servants. This discipline is entirely lacking in the Tolliver house. Love becomes selfish, self-indulgent, and destructive; that is, irresponsible. William, Helen's brother, invites himself to the house, lives in it without paying his part; but the essential truth about William is that he rebelled against the family and its discipline back in Tennessee because that disci- pline seemed harsh. It seemed harsh because the family had lost its meaning for itself and the South. Lanny quotes the old Senator to Lucy: "There is no new South; there is only the old South resurrected with the print of the nails in her hands." Lucy supports her parents but flees their poverty. The Senator, who is more nearly the protagonist, came to manhood during Reconstruction and has a historic perspective upon the situation. He suffered more immediately the family's dislocation, because he had been brought up in the real thing. He comes to St. Louis to sponge on the exiles, "to enjoy all the familiar patterns . . . without any of the responsibility," where the kin are not too close for comfort. His self-indulgence is food and drink and comfort. All the actors recognize in moments of insight what is wrong, but they usually see the failure in others. To their own shortcomings they are blind or fatally committed. It is their need for family life which makes them see; it is the self-indulgence and self-interest which makes this insight blurred.

The Senator, as he gulps his host's whiskey (Jack Daniels, Tennessee whiskey), compares St. Louis families of Tennessee extraction with the colony of Virginians who, caught in Paris by the Civil War, became the favorites of the French court. But James Tolliver is more realistic: he replies that the men came to St. Louis of their own free will to make money in shoes, banking, and insurance. But James refuses to understand the full meaning of this in terms of the ex-Tennesseans' plight in that border city with the southern face. What he fails to understand is that these businessmen have substituted the means for the end, that is, money, not as a part of the family's economy, but as the end itself. Money, not the *res publica* nor the American Union, is now the common American dream, as earlier the Union, an abstraction, had supplanted the concrete image of the king with its long history and religious implications. These successive changes in the nature of the state up to the Civil War had merely altered the meaning of the family. In the play the family itself has disintegrated or is far along in ruin.

Money is got through competition. The Tolliver family has exchanged love for this competition. The controlling symbols for this are the games which fill the vacuum left by love. Helen, the wife and mother, is the priestess who orders all the play. She will allow no disobedience in this, lest the husk show its emptiness. William, with unconscious irony describing in part himself, says that gamblers are nervous, senseless sort of men who know they have nothing and ought to want something. He is about to take all his money and flee west, which he considers something new, fleeing west or making more money, just as he is deluded into thinking he can be "outside history." The Senator treats gambling with religious veneration, for it is not only skill, all that it is to William, but also luck: a small abstraction of life itself. "Luck is the most marvellous thing in the world, and no man knows whether or not he is lucky til he's seen his last day." With his historical perspective the Senator compares the present moment, where the family is the microcosm of the material society, with only competition and skill left, to the past, where the family was an organism out of which man came with a richer sense of the mystery and possibilities of life, not consciously seeking security but seeking, out of the only security possible, a stable society, the larger meaning of life.

The irony in the action, which Francis Fergusson describes as lying below the plot, is just this: that the family must keep up the appearance of amity and love and service, for that is all that is left to disguise their plight, which is selfishness and self-indulgence. All of the threats to the surface calm of the weekend take place: William flees with his money, abandoning his mistress, who breaks off her association with the family; the Senator affronts his audience by talking about old times, reminding them, we presume, of the parts they would like to forget; Lanny attempts suicide; Jim is going away to meet Nancy's people in Tennessee and ask for her hand (jumping from the frying pan into the fire). Any one of these incidents should mar the appearance of things; and yet they happen without in any crucial way disturbing the necessary fixation on appearance. The Tennessee society is entertained in the front part of the house, while the birthday and anniversary take place in the back room; the meaningless gifts are exchanged; Lanny's birthday cake is brought in all aflame. His father admonishes him to blow the candles out lest he set the house afire: that is, keep up the appearance or we are lost. Appearance is now the only salvation in a society which the Senator in the speech he never delivers defines as "the most frightful of all spectacles, the strength of civilization without its mercy. . . . It was artfully contrived by Augustus, that, in the enjoyment of plenty, the Romans should lose the memory of freedom."

But with all the changes and reversals which take place and resolve the plot, it is clear that even the appearance of the old family will go. The Senator, in his speech to Lanny, makes this plain. Lanny has hoped, by seeing the Senator and talking with him, to discover direct and authoritative connection with the past, "as if it were day before yesterday." But there will be by any sensible reckoning of history a thousand years between the

Senator's generation and the world Lanny will grow up in. This is the Senator's final warning to the boy, whose eagerness to know himself in terms of his past has forced the Senator to confront in himself his plight, which stands for the plight of all. As the curtain falls, we see that the appearance of family is doomed. Lanny sees it, and his insight is the beginning of manhood. "Give me time. Give me time," he says in the closing lines, not the time which his mother has killed with her games, but time to find himself in the reality of the situation which will be his in the brave new servile world.

Taylor's play is a fine performance. The well-done intricacies of the plot I have left for the reader to find for himself in the pleasure of reading the play or that better experience of seeing it done on the stage; for no matter how good the dialogue, a play must be seen. And this is a cause for wonder in Taylor's change from fiction to the drama. The drama is only the scene and depends upon the accidents of extraneous and numerous aids, such as actors, whom God made and not the author. Fiction as an art is more responsible to control in its entirety, and the best of actors can never supplant the pictorial or panoramic effects which summarize and prepare for the scene. John Crowe Ransom, in replying to someone who asked him why he had given up the writing of poetry, said, "It's a free country." After reading this play, one wonders again how free it is; or certainly how free the fiction writer as artist is to employ his time in a more restricted art form. One sees the Muse frown slightly, not turn away, for surely she understands Taylor's true devotion.

There is a cultural connection, at least, between Howard Nemerov's *The Homecoming Game* and Peter Taylor's play. In the play games fill the vacuum left by the loss of family communion. The hearthstone is no more. Nemerov shifts the scene to the institution of learning, the public occasion. The subject of Taylor's play depended upon what was still common between the public and private thing, as the Tennessee society implied the outward appearance of the inward nostalgia for the same general past and the traditional relationships between kin and connection and place. Nemerov only by indirection is concerned with the failure of the family as institution. With brutal directness and rapid pace the action of his book exposes a crisis in the community of a college.

Upon the eve of the homecoming game Charles Osman, professor of history, "a tentative, kindly, and ironic person," has failed the star football player. At once the pressures upon the professor begin, with the president of the student council asking him to "flannel" things over and give the boy a makeup test. The complication proceeds from this point up through the echelons of power and influence, with varying degrees of appeal to deny scholastic principles for the sake of expediency. The head of his department, the boy's girl, the president of the college (a former theologian), the coach, and finally two important alumni, a rich man and a senator (big business and politics)—everybody but the football player exercises himself over the matter, so that what might have been settled privately between a teacher and his student has become throughout public, institutional, and political.

Faced with the anomaly of the administration asking him, in effect, to deny its rules at the expense of professional honesty, the professor makes no promises but leaves the impression he will probably go along with the general wish. However, he insists that the boy make his own plea, as if it were merely a personal matter between them. The two meet, and Dr. Osman learns that it has been a public matter all along. Blent, the player, has been bribed by professional gamblers to throw the game. The young hero has faltered as hero, but has acted to recover himself by flunking the tests to make himself ineligible. As in fairy tales, as indeed in life, what at first seems a commonplace, inconsequential matter quickly precipitates the actors upon a quest of far-reaching and profound implication. Osman decides that the boy must play the game, to restore to the public and private thing not seeming but actual honesty. He himself undertakes to return the tainted money and also to convince Solomon, the philosophy professor, whose course the boy has also failed, to go along with his conception of the situation: to connive at a smaller dishonesty to prevent one more gross.

This decision, with the economy of a tight structure, carries the surface action through scene and episode, through Professor Osman's reflections and feelings and historical analogies, presented through panoramic summaries, to what can only be called anticlimax, to Ovaltine for the professor and to the general assumption "that it was only a game after all." For the game was lost, although presumably Blent played his best. But this is irony. The very anticlimax of the "plot" exposes the underlying meaning of the action proper, which has to do with the corruption in a power state euphemistically called a liberal democracy. Nemerov set his conflict in a college community rather than in Washington, for example, because the action concerns not the game itself but the failure of the institution of learning in its essential function of instruction, of making leaders (that is our boast) who will reduce the brutal forces of power, in themselves always irresponsible, towards order in the state and felicity in private life. Football is the perfect grounds for this. It is a power game; hence the occasion for the corruption of power or its restraint. Young Blent has all the makings of a hero. He has classic beauty, even innocence, if somewhat impaired, and integrity, if rather instinctive. He has survived the sordid training of his carnal parents. By rejecting them, he has set himself apart, although this cost him an abortive attempt at suicide and a bout with a psychiatrist. He admires Osman and with all the surrender of youth is prepared to be guided by him, for he senses the instructor's good intentions, his will to honesty and civilized behavior.

The courses he fails put the issue squarely: "English History" and "Modern Ethical Theory"; that is, knowledge of his past and a guide to conduct. In a traditional and Christian society there is a whole order of disciplines by which the youth may be trained for his mission, and an absolute concept, the City of God, which at an instant may reflect the degree of imperfection of an act in the carnal world. But in a society which is only technically Christian, that is, liberal, as is the society of this book, all that is left the prospective hero for guidance, once clear belief and faith is lost, is a knowledge of the past, by means of which the elect may have at least some chance of the right choice of rules of conduct. But Osman, while proposing to teach history for the end of discovering the "enduring realities," follows the one method which prevents this. He is a relativist. And Solomon, the philosopher, is a materialist. Young Blent complains to Osman of Solomon's instruction "that people in the modern world are divided into fools and knaves. That philosophies are merely procedures for dominating people. That in a hard world the smart man prepares himself to believe nothing, keep up appearances, and make money." When Osman defends his colleague by saying his precepts and example are far apart, Blent replies: "Do you expect us to hear what you teachers say just for kicks? I want some practical value out of my education." The boy is asking for moral tools, the necessary disciplines by means of which he can operate with integrity.

Confronted by this, Osman refuses to hear, as the priest refuses to perform his proper office for Emma Bovary by pretending not to understand her spiritual distress. He begs the question by referring to the bribe, but the boy has rejected this and is asking for counsel. Feeling his own share in the common guilt but not recognizing that it derives from his relativism, Osman takes the problem out of the boy's hands. By undertaking to return the tainted money, he usurps the role of hero. He is not only unfitted by training for it; but by pursuing it, he refuses to assume the responsibility proper to his own role and so, to use a legal expression, compounds the felony.

Nemerov has brilliantly seen this confusion of roles as the crux of the action and the source of our disorder. Osman's role, like that of his colleague Solomon, should have been that of the wise man who remains apart, that of the Indian guru or the Merlin who selects, protects, and trains the prospective hero, so that at the proper moment he can perform his act of salvation by rescuing the countryside, which has been laid waste by the dragon. In mythology we have come to recognize this aridity, this deadness in nature, as a metaphor for spiritual disaster. The dragon is the concrete image for those dark powers which rise from the abyss and overwhelm the body politic. Appearance instead of reality, expediency instead of principles, describes the peril, the giant brute force (another aspect of the dragon) which recognizes no restraints except that of a greater force and whose whims are ruthless and, like the small incident which sets the hero upon his quest, threatens either to save mankind or plunge it into the abyss. These dark powers become incarnate in the president of the college, the politician, the business magnate, the students, the criminal world of gambling, the two professors, and the magnate's daughter, the prospective heroine. As enveloping action, all these characters comprise a kind of allegory of liberal democracy, which, by giving lip service to its Christian inheritance, betrays it into accepting the worldly values as the end in itself.

As human beings, all these people need to be rescued, that is, restored to their proper callings by assuming a responsibility for the powers and functions they are invested with, in terms of money, politics, parenthood, instruction, etc.; and the agglomerate mass of the community needs to be restored to the constraint of ritual rather than mob violence. But the hero never sets out to save a countryside. He always has a specific object for his quest, the rescue of the maiden, whose release automatically and mysteriously restores order to the body politic and the orderly turn of the seasons to nature. This brings us to the actors as they perform in the action proper. By confessing to Osman, young Blent is asking for salvation. His own efforts to recover his integrity have brought him to only a neutral position: the refusal to play. But all the forces brought to bear against him will not allow him to maintain this position, which indeed is not that of the hero, who must act. Osman's failure as wise man lies in his refusal to give the word to Blent, which should have been the total risk of himself, his ruin as student and football star, that is, an open confession of the scandal. This would have brought it all out into the open and forced the college in its entirety to face up to the issues involved. Then Blent would have achieved manhood by assuming responsibility for his acts and, in suffering as victim, might have brought about the general purification of the community, including the heroine.

The wise man is always set apart. In this novel both Osman and Solomon are Jews. They are outside the Christian inheritance. Instead of being what they are, they want to belong. This desire to belong leads to their refusal to accept responsibility for themselves in their historic and human situations. Existing in two bodies instead of one merely emphasizes their incapacity before the reality of the situation. Solomon, as it turns out, is his own knave, for his precepts and example are in accord. His seeming principles are injured vanity at not being accepted. When he is given tenure and a raise in pay, he exactly takes his own advice of keeping up appearances (a Jew can never as Jew accept the Christian state) and making money. He surrenders to the dragon. Osman is a fool twice over, in refusing to be either a Jew or a Christian, and as wise man undertaking the role of hero. He considers himself a civilized man, but there is no such thing as civilization in general. At one moment he sums up civilization as a parody of its myths. By not being what he is, by misfitting the outside and inside, appearance and reality, he parodies the hero and becomes the fool. He is made a fool of by the restaurant keeper; but his folly reaches its climax when he takes the drunken heroine home, after the travesty of returning the tainted money, and she offers herself to him. His confusion of his identity makes itself clear in his refusal to take her. He thinks he wants to marry her, and his sense of decency won't let him take her in lust; and yet afterwards he is not sure how drunk she was and feels unmanned. Previously he has forced the girl to say she loves him when she has already told him he merely gives her pleasure. The reader knows no marriage will take place, as the reader knows she is a heroine in distress. She is described as an aristocrat who looks like a slave girl: the heroine in the clutches of the dark powers. Her invitation to Osman is, "Hurt me. Hurt Me," which plainly describes the nature of her enslavement. Young Blent treated her with all the innocence and circumspection of youth looking for its mate; but because Osman fails as wise man, Blent fails as hero. After the game, Lily the flower maiden gives herself to Blent and is discovered by Osman. All that Osman can feel is injured vanity and failure without understanding it. Young Blent, thinking of the proprieties, announces that they are going to be married, which we know will not take place, because both are lost now. Only Blent's risk of the abyss would have made him a man capable of assuming responsibility in the Christian sacrament of marriage. But he is no man, only a confused and corrupted youth, for he says, "it was only a game after all," in other words meaningless play, in which the real issues can be ignored.

This travesty of love represents the travesty of the entire action. In the end they all are a little deeper in the realm of the dragon. Osman tells the president: "Everybody seems to've won something out of the deal. Blent got his girl [but not the girl as he wanted her], I've got money [which he can't spend] . . . the people back of it have got enormous sums, probably [but with the insecurity which inheres in the criminal world], and you have your college [but an instrument of power, not learning]. Even Blent's parents are going to live together again" (until they separate again). This, I take it, is the final meaning of Nemerov's book, the failure of the liberals to control the criminal powers in the individual and hence in the state, so that the body politic hovers upon the edge of the abyss, with only the mask of appearance to give the semblance of order to the institutions, both public and private. Like Osman, the liberal as wise man, as teacher and guide, never takes responsibility for his instruction, for the place he occupies. He wants a better world—for somebody else. He sits in the high seat but refuses the obligations which go with it. He wants to save the situation but refuses the risk of loss which always attends salvation. In the name of the thing he betrays the thing. Conscience, decency, civilized behavior, noble intentions, abstract ideals in his hands become sentimental because of this final refusal to take responsibility. Nemerov has shrewdly shown the muddled incapacity for action by allowing Osman to try to act. Osman is a man of conscience but a relativist. Principles are never relative. A principle does not say on the one hand, and then on the other. It takes its stand and falls or persists at that post. It is why Osman is made a fool of by the restaurant keeper, who is the realist in the dragon's world, who accepts the power state as the condition of things and, with sympathy, patronizes such fools as Osman. The final turn of this screw is the refusal of the restaurant keeper's chauffeur to take a tip from the professor: he contemptuously says he makes more money.

The essence of criminality is the exercise of power without a responsible attitude towards it, which reduces human beings to their material qualities. The professional gamblers have truly interpreted Solomon's dicta. All the others—the politician, the business magnate, the president of the college—keep up the illusion of appearances, but they are just as criminal. The necessity for salvation, and its miscarriage, which the book's action so well shows, is apparent in their fright before the mob, which is disbanded by the president's surrender (allowing Blent to play) under the guise of the exercise of his authority. And the victim, who should have been Blent, with all the ritual of sacrifice, turns out to be an anonymous student who accidentally falls in the bonfire, to die meaninglessly; and his death is meaninglessly announced by the chaplain just before the kickoff to the community assembled for the game, who cannot listen, already caught up in the anticipatory frenzy of the show of power ("it is only a game after all"). For the voice of the priest is abstract and empty, its spiritual impotence echoing the physical impotence which the game now represents, which the knave Solomon and the fool Osman personify.

Tennessee Day in St. Louis has the tone and indirection of fiction. *The Homecoming Game*, in its pace and rapid succession of scenes, is far closer to the theater. It seems to go too fast towards the end; and yet on reflection it is all done. The protagonist, Professor Osman, is a pathetic figure, for all he has gone through and suffered leaves him, like the community, as he was before the action started. He has learned nothing about himself in his place. And yet he is not quite the same. He will teach history, as the school will continue, with less belief in himself and without quite understanding this. His irony, in all probability, will become cynicism now. I have the feeling that there is a partial failure of the post of observation on Nemerov's part.

The post of observation is that of the central intelligence, with the author hovering very close to the protagonist; yet at times he seems to withdraw arbitrarily. For example, there is the suicide of the professor's wife, which has caused him until the present action to withdraw from life. We are deep in the reflections of Osman's mind on this matter, but he reflects only upon the surface. He must have gone deeper in confronting himself over this matter, for his withdrawal represents a decision. This is not quite playing fair with the reader, and it leaves a flaw at the end of an otherwise excellent rendition. In history at another time comparable with ours God manifested himself through a Jew to save mankind. In this fiction a Jew assumes, not as God but as a confused man, the role of mitigating a worldly corruption in an institution. He is unequal to the role, and he does not understand why he has failed. One wonders why the author, who has made him an intelligent man and a historian, does not allow him to understand his plight better, and thus make him a purged man at least, if not a hero. By implication, in the enveloping action, we can understand that his relationship to a Christian society which no longer believes in itself denies him a fuller comprehension, but in some way this should have been clear in the action proper. Lacking this clarity, the novel seems to go too fast towards the end, and the reader is left with a turgid feeling, instead of release.

With Walter Sullivan's novel *Sojourn of a Stranger*, the basis of the complication comes from the act of Major Hendrick, whose disgust before the world's injustices turns him into a kind of liberal. In pre–Civil War Tennessee he marries an octoroon and has a son who in appearance shows none of his darker blood. Sullivan with bold strategy has avoided the more obvious kind of miscegenation. Here is a boy who, by various accidents, becomes the heir to a distinguished and rich Tennessee family. In appearance and feeling he is white, and yet the full reality of his situation cannot hide the small taint of the blood. Thus Sullivan states in his complication the extreme possibility of racial and social injustice; and yet miscegenation is not the full intention of the author's subject.

There is a quality of doom and pagan fate which hangs over the Hendrick family. The old general, the boy's grandfather, was unlucky in all things except the goods of this world. He was defeated in his campaign against the British in the War of 1812. His oldest son cut himself off from his place in the family and society by his marriage. His other son died of yellow fever, leaving only the grandson to inherit name and property, who because of his condition could not represent fully either name or property. Such is the situation as the book opens.

Behind any society lies the inequality of material possessions and social station. This was taken for granted by General Hendrick and his associates in the Old West, who in their development of this region assisted their own fortunes. Coming from the eastern seaboard, accepting the distinctions of a hierarchically ordered society, there was no doubt in their minds that the men of substance should rule, as there was as surely the acceptance that they should hold themselves responsible for their position of power. They did not deny the equality of opportunity, but they scorned as folly any belief in such equality in nature or man. By recognizing and accepting what their eyes showed, they maintained, upon the natural imperfections of the world, order in the state. Along with this, at the inception of the American union, was fomented what could only seem a social and political heresy to the rational minds of the men of property. We have come to call this the liberal attitude, the hope that Paradise in some way can be maintained in this brave new world of the wilderness.

Major Hendrick, the elder son of the general, with the fine instincts for justice and compassion for the human predicament and disgust at the procedures of property and power (this is often the genesis for liberal action), turns upon his father's world. He withdraws from a law partnership because of the abuse of justice: a master who should have hanged for murdering a slave was freed on a technicality. So far he acted as a member of his caste. Theoretically this kind of action was condoned by the society his father represented. It was a miscarriage of legal justice, which is as old as any society. But this leads him, later on, to withdraw from business rather than take advantage of a widow in money matters. Business by its nature gains only at the disadvantage of some party to the action, and Sullivan has not convinced me about the withdrawal, because technically he has not shown the human causes for it. He merely lets it strike Major Hendrick as if out of the blue, where there is the widow who could have, as a being, affected him. He does convince by involving Major Hendrick in trying to rectify a racial and institutional injustice in his marriage to a New Orleans octoroon who has been abandoned by her patron. He is successful in this episode because of a fuller circumstance which brings the octoroon alive in her various relationships, and particularly that with Major Hendrick.

Major Hendrick is one of the most convincing characters in the book. I know of no liberal in fiction who is so well done. He is made to suffer for his action, which derives from generous feeling and a soft head. He sets out to disarrange an established order. His act is an irresponsible act for two reasons: he ignores the inequalities in the social order, and he is unable to find any concrete means to better the situation. And so he isolates himself and his wife from the society which surrounds him. At least in New Orleans the condition of the kept octoroon gave her a place and a society of a kind, but in violating the mores, he cut not only her off from this but himself as well, establishing them both in a social vacuum. Gradually he takes to drink and trading in money; that is, he reduces himself as a person and as a citizen to the carnal minimum of his possibilities as a man; and yet he is a man and able to understand his predicament and to suffer for it.

It is upon the inadequacies of the carnal and temporal world, as well as the Jacksonian tradition of military success, that the octoroon mother places her hopes for her son, Allen. She is responsible for their removal back to Gallatin on the gamble, which succeeds, of having the grandfather accept his grandson as heir. The conflict of the book has to do with whether or not he can come into the fullness of his inheritance, not merely its economic base. The promise of the mother gave the boy hope. She recited to him how his uncle, a gentleman of color, fought side by side with the Tennesseans under Jackson at New Orleans in that great victory. Surely a society is yours if you can fight for it with no mention of a taint. But she oversimplifies, and her wishes are founded on false hope. To begin with, the military tradition she returns her son to is not victory, but, ominously, defeat; and in a traditional society there are many distinctions.

One of these distinctions is represented by the free Negro Ben Hill. The author uses him well. His freedom goes little further than a certain economic possibility. In spite of his emancipation he acts like any Negro who has not been treated right. This shows in his sullen dependency upon Major Hendrick, especially in his belief in the major's absolute knowledge and power over money, which is a part of Ben Hill's grudging acceptance of the white race's supremacy in all matters, grudging because he does not understand it. He regards the major's gifts as a magical formula, and he feels its ritual is being deliberately withheld from him. Not understanding that the major's gifts and intelligence are relative and that he takes risks, the free Negro blinds himself to the white man's sympathy and genuine desire to help him and others of his race. And so Ben Hill, believing in magic, betrays himself but blames his benefactor and later revenges himself upon Allen, the son.

Very subtly the author, in the larger pattern of the action, uses Ben Hill as a kind of symbol for an equal blindness in General Hendrick and what amounts on the part of this family to a belief in the magical power of money. It was the mother's belief in it which brought the son back, but it was the grandfather's possession of it which held out hope to his grandson that it might solve for him the ambiguity of his plight. So when Allen is rebuffed in a friendly manner as he tries to call on a girl of the family's acquaintance, the boy is made to confront the limitation of his inheritance. But he only partially confronts it. He remains blind: that is, he still has hope. When in Nashville on business, lonely and somewhat rebellious, he calls on the daughter of his grandfather's old companion in arms. She receives him; they fall in love, and she promises to marry him—but later. The situation is radically and socially reversed. The girl is white, and the boy has the taint, which is to say that both are brought squarely against the manners and mores of their society, which forbids more absolutely their union than in his father and mother's case.

The structure of this society serves for the enveloping action, and I would like to define it as it shows in this book, for we now have reached the action on its way to resolution. It is a society which, in the long decline of the European tradition, has lost the fullest sense of the Christian vision. Allen's father and grandfather, the liberal and the man of tradition and property, both accept the world as the end in itself, which is contrary to the original Christian conception, which made it the occasion for the drama of the soul. This is to say that the devil, the antagonist, has in his subtle way persuaded formal and public opinion to accept the means for the end. The liberal denies the fallen state of man and nature. He believes he can act upon others (rarely upon himself) and restore the former condition of wholeness and perfect justice; that is, he believes he can interpret at any given moment God's mysterious intentions. This is the sin of pride, and it destroyed Major Hendrick. General Hendrick, in his situation, is more responsible than his son. He accepts the multiplicity of variety in the state and nature, which is our fallen condition; and he supports the inherited Christian hierarchy that brings order to an imperfect world. He is a good man, a responsible man, and no doubt believes he is a Christian man. Nevertheless his sin is pride, too; and it lies paradoxically in his assumption of responsibility for owning God's land outright and the slaves, made in God's image, absolutely. But he is subject to the Puritan heresy, which is the direct approach to God, without any warning intercessor. The danger in this lies in identifying his private will with God's, so that his sin is not only in believing that he, as a man, is equal to his authority but also that his private interests and selfish purposes may seem to derive from God. He tells his grandson that tobacco is money, which is certainly an oversimplification. This promise, however, for so the boy takes it almost literally, is a promise that he will come into his full inheritance by marriage to his girl. If the Christian vision had been stronger in Tennessee at that time, Allen's problem would have been how to save his soul. His grounds for action would have been the limitation of his blood and place. The end of the action would not have been, as in this book, how to force a society to deny its structure to gratify his will. At the end he does achieve a kind of Christian humility. When he loses everything, including the girl, he sees that he has been selfish, thinking only of himself; and for this he seems willing to take the consequences.

But I feel that in the development of the resolution the author has failed to prepare the grounds for this. He has not made the love between them convincing. It is always hard to find the technical failure, but I believe it shows in his misuse of decorum. It works well enough in the seminary, where the two meet under the surveillance of a chaperone and in the stilted requirements of intercourse of that institution; but it does not entirely work even there, for a mutual attraction should appear more sensibly even under the conditions of their meeting. We are too much aware of decorum only. Manners and mores are the formal restraints upon action, and conflicts in life and fiction often begin with the natural man violating these very conditions; and when there is no violation, the very constraint heightens the response. I feel the author has in this instance been too much drawn into his hero's reliance on decorum.

On the whole, and very effectively, too, the pace of the book is measured and the tone is formal. The dialogue exemplifies this point. In one instance it becomes mannerism instead of manner, by the repetition of a name: " 'Allen,' he said. 'Allen, I am glad to see you.' " This has the restraint of measure, but it is repeated too many times. When Allen and his girl meet back in the country, secretly under the sky and at night, the formalities still prevail. This was the time, if ever, when the author should have convinced us of an attraction strong enough to deliver the final meaning of the resolution. But their responses are the same as in the drawing room. Here certainly he should have used the senses, got into the hero's mind more thoroughly. Instead of using decorum to heighten the pathos of their situation, Sullivan has allowed it to muffle feeling. The point of view remains too close to the outward appearance of the scene and not at the post, where the restraints and inward feeling could be shown working against each other. This same criticism holds for the Civil War section. I feel here that he could have recovered himself if he had used the mind of his hero to reflect more sharply the changes the war makes in Allen's feelings about his reason for entering it, instead of paraphrasing battles, good in themselves but the wrong kind of middle for his conflict. The girl's father has promised him that, if the war is won, he will get the girl. His action becomes related almost entirely to this *idée fixe*. The larger violence of experience which the war must have wrought upon a person of his sensitivity is too briefly shown, and it is hard to believe that such would not have made progressive alteration upon his growth. It does so in the case of the girl. She refuses him at the end on the grounds that too much has happened.

This is a first book, and Sullivan's talents are many. The subject which engages him is a complicated one, perhaps such a subject as one should attempt at the end of a career, not at the beginning.

Helen's Last Stand: Faulkner's The Town

FAULKNER'S POST OF OBSERVA-
tion usually lies with some individual who, out of his need for self-
knowledge, even salvation from
those complications of the human
scene which "outrage," tells the
story and, in telling it, resolves it.
But in the resolution there is usually
a fuller knowledge which rescues
the protagonist from the accidents
of his own situation or allows him to
see it in a larger context of meaning,
by means of which he can "endure";
or his plight in the end illumines by
its shock some disaster of epical proportions implicit in the enveloping
action. Or else the point of view
roves from individual to individual,
each of whom discloses differing in-
sights and revelations of the complication. But whatever the point of
view adopted, it is essentially bardic, with the difference that the
bard himself is crucially involved.
He is not merely telling the story to
entertain or out of curiosity. His tale
is told out of a compulsive need for
understanding of self or community.
The tale is usually part of the county's saga, but the versions are partial
or differ. His function is to fit the
true story together, to find out what
actually happened from the contra-

dictions of legend and gossip and special pleading. Technically some part of Yoknapatawpha is the enveloping action: its manners and morals, conventions and mores, which locate and restrain the natural man, sustain or corrupt him. The action proper concerns those individuals who represent the opposing forces which will determine the county's changing destiny.

In "A Rose For Emily" the town speaks with an anonymous but communal voice. Chick Mallison's intrusion into the dust is an intrusion into the complexities of his cultural inheritance, out of his need to find his place. The risk he takes is his initiation into manhood with the attendant assumption of responsibility for his public and private personalities. By piecing together the fragments of the fatal story of families not his own in *Absalom Absalom!*, Quentin—almost hectically—hopes for greater knowledge about the son's part in the family life, either to save himself or give grounds for his suicide. At any rate this understanding does not save him from his peculiar situation in *The Sound and the Fury.* V. K. Ratliff in *The Hamlet* seems merely the interested observer of folly as he travels about the county gathering and spreading its news; but there is a quality to the tone of his protest and "outrage" which is not that of the disinterested observer. What he sees informs him of his own vulnerability, a threat which any moment may involve him, too; and it does, for he succumbs to the same moon madness which the painted horses release in others, and he is taken in by the salted mine Flem Snopes prepares for him and Armstid.

It is unnecessary to repeat for Faulkner readers the rise of Snopesism out of the ruins of the structure of southern society, but it may be well to recall that, as Faulkner sees it, its hierarchical degrees and rituals were always temporal. Nowhere does he take the church house as image or symbol. Always his symbols for order are civic: courthouse, jail, the square, the farm dwelling. Of course there is the greater symbol of the grandmother, the matrix, but she extends beyond an image. In *The Town*, Faulkner has Gavin Stevens say the various Protestant denominations define themselves not so much by puritanism as by nonconformism. This was the crucial flaw, and a serious one in a society predominantly agricultural, for the experience of the farmer before the mystery of the seasons and nature was always more complex than his theology could explain.

It may be that Faulkner feels that the church as institution is no longer effective in guiding and ordering behavior. The two preachers in his fiction who appear as true men of God are both from the country, the one who buries Granny in *The Unvanquished* and the one who is brought into town to bury Eula Varner Snopes. They never appear in church houses, but only in the open air. They are simple men of simple belief, plain men who are close to nature and suffer the hardships of the plain man's conditions. There is little distinction between them and the one-bale farmers (although Faulkner oversimplifies here in using one bale as the norm of the hill country) except that they have had "the call." They are learned neither in theology nor dogma, but they know that evil is in the heart and not in the object, where their more learned brothers would put it. Like saints, their connection with God is direct, and their hardships would compare favorably with those of saints. Their compassion for the human predicament lies in their power to suffer and withstand it. So Faulkner is conscious of the part religion plays; he merely does not elevate it to the dignity of his more temporal institutional images.

These institutional images, which are the cultural symbols of not only southern but American society, operate in Faulkner's fiction as the controlling images for the larger and implied action, the true action which underlies the surface tensions and conflicts. Faulkner's neglect of the Christian church as comm-union must be deliberate in an artist who has consistently relied upon the symbolism of archetypical behavior as the source of his enveloping action. The multiplication of our Protestant denominations impairs that unity in belief and faith which maintains the equilibrium in a healthy society; it tends to make the divisions, both geographical and cultural, partial and sectional instead of parts which represent and contain the whole, contain it by means of the very diversity and uniqueness of their functional and organic differences. The American union has been merely political and so eccentric. The true communion of sovereignty under God, which medieval society at least in principle recognized in the powers delegated to king and bishop, God's temporal and spiritual surrogates, with castle and cathedral as concrete symbols of this sovereignty (not to mention the persons of king and bishop), has been supplanted by an abstraction which is self-contradictory: the sovereignty of the people. The very nature of sovereignty is its supremacy, which only God possesses, and so only He can delegate its powers. It is why, perhaps, the aristocracy which dominated the South before the Civil War disappeared after its defeat, for, although historically an aristocracy is an extension of temporal rule, it degenerates without the formal restraint of spiritual rule.

The moment sovereignty passed from God to, not even man, but to man in the abstract, the state lost a clear image of itself. Ritualistic representation of spiritual rule being lost, the aristocracy had only its civic and private codes to discipline itself in the performance of its service to the body politic. But even in its proper civic function it could have no formal image of itself. Where the people is sovereign, an aristocracy must pretend to be what it is not to be able to rule. Its caste is too private, as the spiritual comm-union is replaced by a too private and therefore personal approach to God, which only the saint can risk. But a code has teeth in it, such as the code of honor, demanding of the holder a civic and private principle of action, but with sufficient belief to back it up by sacrifice, both of goods and life.

Its integrity in private life, reflecting a public attitude, centered about its conception of the role of woman. Faulkner has seen and dramatized this, and woman is pretty close to the center of his epical treatment. The aristocracy's intention was to preserve not so much her purity as the image of this purity, which, of course, when the threat becomes overt always fixes upon an individual woman. Superficially woman was put into the role of a creature above the brute nature of man, which delimited both man and woman; romantically she was raised to the "divine" and set upon a pedestal, which actually derives from our pagan inheritance. What the aristocracy really depended upon but rarely made articulate was its protection of the woman as guardian of the family blood and mores. This heightened sense of the family was one of the things which made the aristocracy function for everybody, for in a farming community the family is the basic unit, and by family must be understood the ramifications of its "connections." It was a real comm-union, if a social and not a religious one. Further strengthened by common economic interests and the sense of being threatened from outside (the quickest way to bring people together), the aristocracy became truly representative in its rule in the antebellum South.

Then how were the Snopeses able so easily, or rather so persistently, to usurp its place? The clue is not in Flem so much as in his forebear Ab Snopes. Ab was an outcast, which meant he had no place in the hierarchical system in the society upon the fringe of which he lived. He could only prey upon it. He was one living in the condition of the frontier after it had passed, the frontier conditions being only bearable so long as they were temporary, the beginning from which the more successful rose to an ordered life. In the chaos of war Ab found his occasion; he found it because he brought to it the unmoral pragmatism of the frontier, which was able to corrupt the grandmother, since war had shattered the social order and so rendered it, like the frontier, with no recognizable standards of behavior: only cunning and strength or whatever was fittest for survival.

With moral righteousness the grandmother went into the enemy camp demanding the return of her property; she went in the name of civil and domestic order, which internecine war had already overturned. Colonel Dick recognized equally her courage and folly in the irony with which he gave her more mules and slaves and trunks than she actually owned, which should have informed her but which she failed to recognize was now an agglomerate loot and not property. Ringo understood the possibilities of this as a weapon. It was he who was the first instrument of the grandmother's corruption; he prepared the way for Ab. When she began to use the paper beyond its specific meaning, she was guilty of falsification: that is, she lied, and a lie is nothing, no thing, and so the devil's instrument. Even though her reasons were noble at first—the service of others—she was doomed; for one lie begets another, and the declension of lying is moral chaos. It proceeded from the general interest to a selfish interest, her family, and the judgment upon her was death. Her fate is tragic, having both the moral flaw and the force of circumstance. It might be said that her fall was due to insufficient theology. She prayed, but we doubt the sincerity and efficacy of her prayers, for she never confronted her acts, only gave lip service to them and that literally, making the boys wash out their mouths with soap, and this usually for the violation of a propriety, which allowed her to ignore the true nature of her sin. This has to do with the grandmother as action. As enveloping action she represents the matrix, the core of the doomed South. It was her part as symbol and person to be protected by the Colonel Sartorises. That she herself must enter the conflict describes the failure of manhood in general and the aristocracy in particular. Drusilla's unsexing of herself and fighting as a man makes this clearer, showing the precarious balance of society based too specifically upon a temporal order. So Ab Snopes not only betrayed the grandmother as person; he was the agent of a larger fall.

When Flem enters the scene in *The Hamlet*, Snopesism has already preceded him in Will Varner. *The Hamlet* is the first in a trilogy of which *The Town* and *The Mansion* are the second and third parts. The mansion, of course, is a symbol of the aristocracy, which in the possession of the Snopeses can only be the final degradation. *The Hamlet* represents the farming countryside. The place is merely the focus of country life, having no identity apart from this. There is no longer any personal code to make decent or order the brutal uses of power, for by this time the aristocracy is suborned, dead, and its forms empty. It has no effective social influence. Money now rules; not money as the counter for the exchange of man's labor, but money itself, the sterile and bare sign of material force. Or rather *The Hamlet* shows the beginning of this advance toward the state where this is so, where materialism usurps the sovereignty first of God and then of the civil state. Its sign is the usury of Will Varner, that is, the preemption of the labor of others without responsibility toward those others.

But there is still manhood left in the hamlet, and this is defined in terms of the trade. The very fact that no quarter is asked or given in a trade defines the nature of this manhood. Any advantage taken is merely seeming, for the ethics of trading presumes that each man knows what he is doing—knows his own advantage and how to outwit his opponent. The most courageous and admirable trader is Flem Snopes, because he has only himself and his wits to oppose the most powerful man in the community, Will Varner. The very paucity of his material possessions, the unbearable nature of the hardships out of which he has come, defines his heroism. The difference between him and the other Snopeses is there to show it. Brutal, lacking in human sympathy even for himself as a human being (since his devotion to his aims makes him impotent), and with nothing but his persistence to rise and his wits, Flem is able to defeat Will Varner. With only the ethics of trading as a measure of man's intercourse with man (the state has been reduced to this), Will's defeat is the defeat of his manhood. It is why his hatred for Flem is so long and lasting. The loss has a double edge. It is not only the old French-man's Bend place. Flem uses the daughter of Will's flesh to bring about his triumph and the older man's defeat. Already we are shown how inadequate is the ethics of trading to deal with the human predicament. It takes no account of man's relations to woman. And the woman, in Will Varner's wife, steps forward to put him at a disadvantage with Flem. She forces her husband to find a husband for his daughter and a father for his grandchild, a bastard, as yet unborn. Give it a name and a home, although a home degraded and without love, for the father at least will be spurious. Will's selfish devotion to his manhood undoes him, but degraded though it is, the family as an institution is preserved. Officially the child is not a bastard, as officially Eula's fornication is made respectable.

In *The Town* we discover how frail is this respectability before the complexities of love and order in society, the two being closely connected, for this very order depends upon love. Carnal love is no longer defined or restrained by the love of God. It is sex and instinct. To such a wilderness have we traveled, and the town is its sign. Unlike the hamlet, which is a part of the country, the town is set apart. It represents the county less and preys upon it more. Its symbol is the bank, a necessary but abstract usury; and unlike the personal usury of Will Varner and Flem Snopes in *The Hamlet,* moral blame is less easy to see, and the punishment less easy to understand. There are still decent people and people of responsibility and good will and kindness, but they are less effective because the forms and rituals which should sustain them are gone. The civil functions, severed from their spiritual counterparts, keep some kind of order, but the order has no larger meaning, and therefore it is implicit by 1927 that even this order (the police) will decline.

The decline is on its way when we enter upon the action of *The Town's* story, for the town as enveloping action is Snopesism. It is his understanding of this which emasculates, not actually but psychically, Gavin Stevens, for he is immersed in the very thing he would like to overcome. The action has to do with man's attitude towards and responsibility for woman, which of necessity involves love. Eula Varner, the heroine, is a Helen, a Semiramis: that is, she is the archetype of all man can hope for in woman, and not only hope for but be willing to fight for; and to possess her he should willingly surrender his sovereignty. In *The Hamlet* she is waiting for her rape, inert in the fragrancy of her flesh, in a kind of primordial aura of woman. The image is the rocking chair, forward and back, the motion of love and the only motion she is capable of, for she is presented in a suspension of all other motion. Her destiny is McCarran, a man of courage and fighting capacity but lacking in moral responsibility for her as wife and mother. He fornicated with her and abandoned her and her child to the—as it turns out—respectability of the town. In *The Hamlet* she is the abducted virgin. In *The Town* she is wife and mother.

In the enveloping action womankind appears in triad, Linda as virgin, Eula as wife, and Maggie, Gavin Stevens' twin sister, as mother; but they appear in all the isolation of the qualities of these archetypes, none of them, unless it is Maggie, uniting the three possibilities in her own person. Manhood also appears in triad: Flem, Gavin, and de Spain. None of these possesses total sovereignty. Each in his relation to Eula represents one quality rather than the wholeness of man which woman demands of her partner. Flem, the legal husband, is impotent physically; de Spain, the lover or physical husband, has none of the legal or moral rights to her. Gavin Stevens assumes the moral rights (but limited to keeping her respectable), but he turns out to be ineffective because he has neither the legal right nor the physical capacity to maintain his feeling of moral responsibility. The three rights, separate, not the three in one, describe the fearful impairment of man's competency towards womankind. Legality becomes meaningless; love is lust; and morality a kind of sentimentality, for it is merely a moral sense and not morality, which always operates in terms of the formal rites and sacraments of social order, based on a total and responsible possession.

The forms in the town as society have degenerated into respectability. Respectability does not represent reality, only appearance. It is maintained by keeping the proprieties, but since moral action has been rendered unclear and personal because of the impaired sovereignty, they are negative and variable. It is Maggie, the female twin, who risks her respectability by introducing Eula to Jefferson society; not Gavin, who wants it. It is not the same risk as the grandmother took, for she lost her life, while all Maggie can lose is her position. (Gavin and de Spain act like boys before the ball, which is to say they are not fully responsible men.) This is a parody, perhaps, on the Dioscuri, fighting men both; the masculine aggression and risk are given over to the feminine side, and the male fighting by indirection, without much risk to himself, such as giving the poetry of Donne to a teenager, giving it not to save Linda but merely to make her dissatisfied with her condition. This leads Gavin in the end to deny whatever moral stand he has, for he lies to her, to keep the appearance of truth, swearing Flem is her father.

But in the end it is Flem who is the most masculine of the lot. He takes the measure of respectability. He never confuses it with the reality, which is money. He knows it for appearance, a means to be guarded but manipulated for the protection of the reality. So Faulkner with the surprise of true poetic insight makes Flem the protagonist of *The Town*. Flem can scarcely be called a hero, but he represents one in the terms in which society now governs itself. An impotent man shows himself to be the most masculine. This is real irony. He is almost a sympathetic figure because of the high price he has had to pay for his kind of manhood. If this is identified with money, he does not disguise it or try to palliate its sterility, as respectability does. He manipulates respectability for his greater freedom. So long as it is maintained, he can practice usury or anything else. The one sin which must never be committed is to be found out. He can be president of a bank and a cuckold, so long as de Spain and Eula are not caught. He can be the father of another's bastard, so long as the moral Gavin will lie to Linda about it. He can destroy the members of his family, so long as it is done in the name of virtue and probity.

The family is disappearing. Ratliff has difficulty in keeping the degree of kin in his mind, and the real reason shows itself at the end, not only for the family's plight but for the state's as well. The men of God fear not God but respectability. When Eula commits suicide out of boredom, boredom we presume from the failure of men to fulfill her demands, the four preachers of the town come in a body and offer to bury her, not in life to instruct her in the ways of virtue, but to bury her. They condone her action by refusing to recognize the adultery, so long as she keeps the appearance of virtue, so long as she and de Spain are not caught; the irony is that the preachers are willing to consign to hallowed ground a person who is both an adulteress and a suicide, facts known to them and the community, because her death begs for them the real question of mortal sin. To such a condition has the spiritual and temporal state been brought. Even Gavin sees this won't do, and proposes to preach the funeral himself until his sister says, "Do you want Linda to have to say afterward that another bachelor had to bury her?"

The three men appear at the funeral not in their true relationships but in the appearance of respectability: de Spain's armband might be merely the official mourning of the bank; Gavin appears as the official friend of the family; Flem was the grieving husband, who was no husband and had no love. But the final image to concentrate the meaning is the monument raised presumably in Eula's memory but actually to entrench Flem in his new position of respectability. Upon the shaft, embedded in marble, is the face of a woman carved by the Italian artist. In spite of the photographs and the care of Gavin, it is not a likeness of Eula but, in marble and not in flesh, the image of the woman all men desire. This is the final irony, the costly appearance of love reduced to the uses of respectability. The very words underneath the face are a lie.

A Virtuous Wife is a Crown to Her Husband
Her Children Rise and Call Her Blessed

The lie, the no-thing, Satan's instrument, is death, and it stands for all the town to see. To this has the archetype of Helen, the central issue of the great war between Europe and Asia, been reduced. Troy is indeed fallen.

This is the argument, the logical decline of the previous losses. The rendition is not entirely successful. The point of view roves between Gavin, Chick, and Ratliff, but the technical advantage is slight because little is gained by the roving. Each voice has the same tone, and with the exception of Gavin, the tone is reportorial. The passion of involvement, the passionate need for knowledge and salvation which suffused the rhetoric of the earlier books, is absent. The old words such as *outrage* appear occasionally, but they are as ineffective as Gavin's moralism. It seems to me that there is an error of strategy here, of attempting to make comedy out of an epical subject. The narrators seem particularly flat, for we remember them in their earlier roles. They stand behind our reading like Banquo's ghost. Faulkner should have learned from Balzac that you can't do this. Even the sheriff, Hampton, seems remote and uninterested. The only one who can view it all as comedy is the old Negress, Het. She has come upon such hard times that she is out of the action and can view it as she does with delight. "Gentlemen, hush," she said. "Aint we had a day." And she is involved in the one episode which is comic, the burning of Mrs. Hait's house by a mule. This episode comments on the action but not with the same authority that the painted horses do in *The Hamlet*. The tone of that book is dominated by Ratliff, and the outrage he feels is of a quality to allow for a kind of sardonic comedy. Not so in this book. The episode of Byron Snopes's children is a little out of tone. It introduces the exaggeration of myth with which we are familiar, but respectability can have little to do with myth. The problem was a hard one, how to take an epical subject at the moment when the actors can only play pathetic parts, can only show their action as a travesty of what they should be and feel. But it is a book that shows the master's hand, even though the bard is no longer crucially involved; he is telling a tale to entertain.

The Son of Man—
He Will Prevail:
Faulkner's A Fable

BUT HE THAT SHALL ENDURE UNTO
THE END, THE SAME SHALL BE
SAVED.

MATTHEW 13:24

IN THE STRICTEST SENSE
Faulkner's *A Fable* is not a fable. Nor
is it fiction, strictly speaking. It is
not even an allegory proper. It is
perhaps a morality sometimes using
the form of fiction. It is certainly
homiletic. The text is the Son of
Man in search of identity with the
Father. The enveloping action—
that animated condition against
which the action takes place or out
of which it comes—is man's dual
nature as it involves "the problems
of the human heart in conflict with
itself . . . beginning when his first
paired children lost well the world
and from which paired prototypes
they still challenged paradise, still
paired and still immortal against the
chronicle's grimed and blood-
stained pages." The book's legend
derives from the Hebraic root of
Western culture—from the first part
of the synoptic Gospels, especially
where the Son bears witness of the
Father. It certainly does not derive
from the Book of John; Christ
speaks there as the Son of God. In-

deed Faulkner departs even from the religious interpretation of the final acts of the synoptic Gospels. He limits himself to the body of the world, not that that body doesn't contain the spirit. It is only that he leaves what is beyond life strictly alone. Whatever is supernatural in this book lies in the mystic balance of the life-force itself.

Every man has that within him which saves or damns, but Faulkner seems to be saying that he is never saved or damned absolutely. The scales are forever dipping their alternate weights. Man endures his situation not because he is immortal: he is immortal because he endures. What he endures is every degree and gradation of his dual nature. The old Negro preacher, Mister Tooleyman (all the world), says to the Runner: "Evil is a part of man, evil and sin and cowardice, the same as repentance and being brave. You got to believe in all of them, or believe in none of them. Believe that man is capable of all of them, or he aint capable of none."

The action proper concerns a mysterious Corporal and twelve followers who try to resolve this dualism. The scene is the western front at the time of the false spring armistice. It is false because it is no true armistice, and further, the hopes aroused prove to be false hopes. A regiment mutinies in the trenches. The Corporal is responsible for it. His mission is to convice individual men that, by acting together, by refusing to go over the top, they can put an end to strife and bloodshed: that is, men acting with purpose can establish the Kingdom of Heaven on earth. The conflict arises between the Corporal's party and those in authority, who, presumably out of fear and hatred, have kept the bloodshed going.

Since conflict is the basis of life (Faulkner states it in one place as the initial primordial flaw), a world war is the extreme occasion for and definition of man's situation; and this particular war, which has locked men in trenches deep in the earth, is the clearest statement of it. The four-year stalemate not only returns man to the mud and slime; it imposes the condition of the earthworm, one of the lowest and blindest forms of life. Man, so reduced, is denied his humanity. The long trench is an orifice from which he, confined there in the sweat and ordure of his body, is evacuated to his death, to the condition of total physical excrement. The General, for whose benefit the attack was ordered (it was intended to fail), is a commander of a group of armies whose mastery derives from his passionate concern with his own orifice. This is to be interpreted not merely that he went Napoleon one better, changing belly to anus, but that man, since he has been cast out by the Father, is at the mercy of his physical processes. It is in this army group that the Corporal does his work, in a corps whose commander believes that the whole moiling mass of man is the officer's enemy. The division commander, Gragnon, interprets this belief into a principle of action: men must and can be ruled by fear of and hatred for their officers. To this attitude the Corporal proposes mass disobedience. He offers hope and courage and compassion. The success of the mutiny raises this hope, for the mutiny spreads over the entire front. War stops on both sides. But there is a catch. It stops, but the men are still in the trenches. All they have to do is make the simple physical movement of walking across No Man's Land, with hands out, weaponless, in the hope that the enemy will do the same, to bring peace and render the generals impotent before hope fulfilled. But their leader, the Corporal, and his followers have been put under arrest and sent to the rear, as have the mutineers. The catch is betrayal. One of the Corporal's own has gone to the authorities.

But there is still hope. The Runner, whose occupation has put him in a position to know what is going on, thinks there is time still to beat the generals. But his mission is a little different. He must deal not with hope but with man's cynicism. He will have to force man to save himself. He has previously committed an act symbolic of the action of all the characters of rank. He had once been an officer himself. But because he came to hate man for submitting to the degradation of his condition, he forced the authorities to break him. He became an outcast both to authority and to the men in the trenches. All hold him in suspicion; yet his act has set him on the way of salvation. Faulkner mentions in his foreword the hanged man and the bird. He gives credit to James Street's *Look Away*. I couldn't find the book, but in the tarot deck of playing cards, Le Pendu, social death, is card number 12. It comes just before number 13, the death card. These two cards represent the two kinds of quests which the chief characters undertake. There are many interpretations of the tarot pack. Heinrich Zimmer in *The King and the Corpse* thinks that the meaning might derive from an "esoteric order of initiation of gradually amplifying enlightenment whereby the initiate, beset by as many characteristic temptations, at last arrives at the stage of mystical union with the Holy Trinity." In *A Fable* all Faulkner's heroes, and everybody is a hero there, suffer the deliberate loss either of rank or of life. Each protagonist and antagonist, and each is protagonist-antagonist, is a criminal. Each violates in varying degree the civil or military code. Each kills that of himself which he values most; or upon his quest he kills his fellow man. But if he is a murderer, he is a sacred criminal, somewhat like the priest-murderer at Nemi. Lose life to save it; "Suffer little children to come unto me, for of such is the Kingdom of Heaven": paradoxes interpreted in terms of the quest mean that man must plunge himself into degradation to be reborn out of the perfect knowledge of and triumph over himself. And sometimes he can only find life through physical death, and always at the risk of the loss of himself.

In Chrétien's "The Knight of the Cart" the cart stands for social and legal disgrace, as the animal is carried in it on the way to the gallows. When Launcelot and Gawain undertook the quest to the land of no return to rescue Guinevere, both were invited by the driver to mount. Gawain, Arthur's nephew and the perfect hero, refused to sully his knighthood and lose his rank. Even Launcelot hesitated two steps, but he did get in, symbolically sacrificing his rank, as he would later his life. These symbolic acts were necessary to restore the soul to life from the realm of the dead, and because Gawain refused the cart, he was denied the highest degree of the adventure. This is an interpretation of the older mythological meaning behind Chrétien's romance of medieval chivalry. Guinevere is the flower maiden, as are Persephone and Blodeuwedd and others in the pre-Christian myths. She is the life source and, like all goddesses who demand complete and unthinking devotion, is cold to her savior for his moments of hesitation. But saviors generally hesitate once before their agony: Christ says, "May this cup be taken from me"; the Buddha hesitated to preach.

Faulkner has modified the myth. There is little hesitation and there is no flower maiden in A Fable. Rank must be sacrificed and even life, but the conflict is in other terms. The hope of salvation is largely masculine. It becomes the quest for self-knowledge, for man's relief from his own nature. And this nature's lot is so deprived, the trials so severe, as scarcely to allow for that communion of a true marriage between man and woman. This brings the protagonist-antagonist to self-victimization, acting both in the confinement of an internal conflict and outwardly in the conflict of man with man. Neither aspect is neglected. The search becomes, therefore, the quest for the Father, not the rescue of the "Mothers," the Father of absolute authority, the all-knower, the chastiser who also loves. The question the Son of Man asks himself is, Why am I outcast? "Eloi, Eloi, lama sabachthani?" Why am I forsaken? Why have I had to undergo the dolorous quest of pain and sorrow and death? Since the Father is all-perfect, the sin, the imperfection, must lie with the Son. An unconscious guilt of innocence is the source of the mystery. A reunion with the Father presumably will expiate the guilt. To emphasize this, Faulkner has made all the heroes orphans. He allows to some a mother, but she is of necessity a widow. Orphanage is the common plight; bastardy is the absolute statement of it, since the bastard is abandoned even in the womb. Deprived from birth of the right to give up his social rank, he must undergo the harder role. The number of his card is 13.

The Sentry-Jockey is wonderfully deprived even for a bastard, whereas the Corporal, like Jesus, is of high birth. The Jockey and the racehorse represent the centauric nature of man, but the roles seem to be reversed. It is the horse, winning races on three legs, which at first seems to carry the higher virtues, the Jockey now become groom, the lower. The Jockey has nothing but this purely instinctive and intuitive aspect of the human creature; he seems even to have been foaled in the stable and cannot be imagined apart from it. The accident which breaks the horse's leg sends the Jockey upon the quest for the more human side of himself. He, too, becomes a criminal along with the old Negro and his grandson as accessories. He "steals" the horse (and this theft entails others) to let him, impaired as he is, win races, do what he can do best rather than what any horse can do, breed others. This becomes a heroic adventure. All the power of the law and society becomes his opponent. In the pure, impassioned pursuit of his animal nature, made surrogate in the horse, the very heroism which it entails brings the Jockey to accept the supernatural fatherhood of God and the brotherhood of man: he is baptized by the old Negro and taken into the Masons. But this belief is as yet unsure, for the moment comes when the opposing powers overtake him. He has to shoot the horse to save him. It is a moment of spiritual peril for the Jockey, as it is a moment of symbolic death and rebirth. He is reborn to despair and stoicism. He renounces his faith in God, but he has advanced over his previous state. He comes into the fellowship of man: that is, he accepts the condition as bad, but he faces this knowledge and prepares to endure it. The Jockey's incomplete initiation in the swamps and upon the roads carries him to the Tennessee mountains, to a remote cove that is well out of the world. It parallels the Supreme General's initiation, but at a different level, in the desert and other remote mountain fastness. As foster child to a poor mountain couple the Jockey recovers the image of parenthood, but the very image makes apparent his lack of the real thing. From animal intuition he has reached the human state. This is an advance, but a greater trial awaits him. His card has not yet turned.

It is the old Negro's role to affirm the heroic and immortal nature of the quest by giving himself up to the civil authority. He is the father in search of the lost son, but his action causes man in the mass and the chief agent of authority, who has already understood and surrendered his office, to witness the heroic quality latent in all men and the capacity of man in mass to act. The court house is taken over by a quiet but resolute mob, and in it justice is given. Civil authority and power is vanquished. The house of justice prevails over the jail house: the spirit of the law over the letter. But the action is incomplete. The father does not find the son. The quest continues and finds itself in a larger field of action.

The court house and the jail house are the dominant symbols for man in times of civil peace, as the palace and citadel serve for war in the older, hierarchically ordered Europe. The jail is here, too, and the trench, as the Place is the counterpart of the Square. Just as the quest in America is performed in terms of the animal nature of man, so that quest in Europe involves at its height the intellectual and spiritual, the deliberate surrender of self in search of salvation. The Jockey–old Negro–Negro youth, a trinity of instinct-faith-innocence, has its counterpart in the Corporal–old General–young airman, spirit-wisdom-innocence, at the top of the hierarchy. The structure also opposes the plain lowborn against the highborn with power and great estate. There is also the forerunner, the John the Baptist, who announces the coming of the savior: the Runner for the lower level, the old Quartermaster General for the upper. But with these, Faulkner, as elsewhere, distorts to his own interpretation the tradition.

The controlling image for the action is rank; for the enveloping action it is the wasteland of the desert and the wilderness. The great quests of mythology eventually lead the heroes into either one or both, the arid desert or the Celtic forest, aridity or the superabundance of nature. The

forest, mythologically considered, is the realm of the soul entangled in
nature's maze; the desert more nearly fits in this book—not the seasonal
death of the sun god, which must freshen with the rise of the tanist, but the
opposing death in hell of Christian theology. All the generals who compose
the council of power receive their initiation in the desert. They are either
sent there or they go willingly: Mama Bidet, Gragnon, Lallemont, the
Quartermaster, the old Supreme General. But they go as young men. They
go to Africa, the Dark Continent, but they do not go all to the same place.
How far they penetrate the desert determines the degree of initiation. Only
for the Generalissimo and the Quartermaster are reserved the furthest
reaches and the highest measure of sacrifice. The paired prototypes who
have well lost the world are not man and woman. They are father and son.

Mama Bidet's preoccupation with his orifice, which gives him his nick-
name, dramatizes the loss of the feminine source of the quest, much older
than the father-son interpretation as it is considered in A Fable. Yeats's view
of the dualism, that love and excrement have one organic location, found
the mystery of the continuum of life in what would produce it. Mama Bidet's
preoccupation makes a radical reduction. Leaving out love, the creative
love between man and woman, there is left only excrement. The conflict is
purely masculine, and the responsibility for it is man's. War springs from
"the loins of man's furious ineradicable greed. We [the captains and the
colonels] are his responsibility; he shall not shirk it." In the tarot pack
Mama Bidet's card would be number 23, the next to last, the Dancing
Hermaphrodite, that embodiment in a single form of all the pairs of opposites, but inverted, since the female part can find itself only in the vague
resemblance in the male organism, in a mockery which affirms the insol-
ubility of the predicament so long as the search is restricted to masculine
terms. A hopeless hope is the only relief. Mama Bidet tells Gragnon: "Let
them believe that tomorrow they will end it [war]; then they won't begin to
ponder if perhaps today they can. . . . That's the hope you will invest in
them." Until the word Fatherland is obliterated (and he knows it won't be),
war, the supreme definition of the dualism, will continue. He knows this
because he is a widow's son. His yearning for a father has brought from his
quest this understanding.

Gragnon, a man entirely alone, brought up in a convent, refused the
solace of impersonal parentage and with no help from anyone raised his rank

from sergeant to major-general. His response is obedience. Disobedience means death. He is willing to shoot the last man in support of this principle. But he is only a major-general. There is greater authority over him. This is his damnation and will be his martyrdom. He sacrifices his rank out of belief in a principle, but that is not the end of his quest. A foundling bastard, his card, too, is number 13. He has to die physically to be resurrected in glory. A professional killer without fatherland, he will be glorified by the official lie that he was shot in the chest, though actually the bullet had gone into his back, where, struggling, he forced it to lodge as the literal mark of the regiment's betrayal of him, and the principle which to him was his integrity.

The culmination of the extreme possibilities of social and physical sacrifice falls to the lot of the old Supreme General and his bastard son, the Corporal. At this level the refinement of meaning reaches its crisis. The Corporal, from the ranks but the son of his father, is able to gather about his mission all the degrees of the quest. The highest degree is earned by his father. Instead of a trial presenting the choice of the surrender of rank, the acceptance of the outcast state as the means of resurrection, he by will and choice makes the sacrifice. As a youth, he is endowed with grace and beauty, gifts of the mind and the flesh and the spirit. He is an orphan (the image of his parents hangs in a locket about his neck), but he is the heir to supreme world power, the two kinds of power which complement each other and are the source of all world power: economic and political. His uncle is a cabinet member who dominates the government; his godfather (the irony is very broad here) owns munition works so vast that they pass national boundaries and suffuse the body politic like cancer. And then there is Paris, the city of the world supreme in her gifts, ready and anxious to offer herself to a youth so well endowed. All of this he renounces, and "all" means the ultimate which the world can offer. He begins by denying sloth. He makes himself first in his class at the military school. With his backing this is unnecessary. He doesn't even have to go to school. He needs only to ask and it will be given. And this is what his fellows expect. As world opinion they are at first baffled, then outraged by his refusal.

His adventure is similar to that of John Golden-Mouth, who at sixteen, by divine and natural means, was raised to the priesthood. John felt that he was too innocent and ignorant for his high office and so fled into the wilderness of life, where he was initiated into the experience with and final overcoming of his elemental nature, even taking on the posture of the beast. He fornicated, and to save himself from this sin committed a greater, murder. Officially the sacrament is valid when given by any ordained priest, but he felt the priest should be a Knower. He refused to be merely a dignitary of the Church, just as the Supreme General in his youth refused without earning them the highest offices of officialdom. The Quartermaster, who was second to his first in class, recognized this quality of renunciation and thought him chosen to save mankind. Like Jesus, he who is to become the Generalissimo disappears from the world to prepare for his high mission.

He goes into the wilderness of the desert, to the command of an outpost so remote from Europe and even from the settled parts of Africa as to seem out of the world. It is a place representing the extreme opposite of what his inheritance could have given him. He commands a segment of the foreign legion, outcasts of society, whose crimes will not permit their return. The knowledge this quest brings him is this: freed of temptations, self-abnegant, he cannot free himself of man's dual nature. He is at the fringe of the world, but the world still retains that fringe; there he causes the death of a man. His motive is good, officially and privately. This one death is deserved. The criminal repeats an old crime: in the love act he kills a girl. The surrender of this man will not only free society from an incorrigible criminal but, in so freeing it, will spare society a small war. And yet this criminal is a man, and the taint of his blood is on his commander. The Quartermaster by choice relieves the Generalissimo, believing the crime is no crime or that at least he will expiate it, still believing him the chosen savior.

The Generalissimo now flees to the mountains, that other retreat, so remote and so above the world that one in its fastnesses scarcely knows of the world beyond and below. Here he enters a monastery (comparable with the Essenes?) surrendering any semblance of rank, denying any need of the body. And yet he is in his body, and it will not be denied. He commits adultery with a married woman, gets her with child, abandons her and the child in her womb, and returns to the inheritance he has tried to refuse. He repeats the very crime the soldier he sacrificed committed, for the woman he abandons dies.

The Generalissimo's initiation is now complete. He knows the limits of man's possibilities: that he cannot escape his nature. He has learned by the sacrifice of himself, within the limits possible to him or any man, what the old Negro preacher knows, that man by dying to himself, or even by dying, cannot save mankind or even one man from the mystery of his predicament. This is the wisdom with which he returns; and it is this which, when he is Supreme Commander, allows the absolute knowledge of what man is capable of, that is, to accept man in terms of the cooperating opposites of his nature and circumstance. When his John the Baptist, the old, sickly Quartermaster General, accuses him of fearing man and betraying him, he initiates his subordinate into the truth that man betrays man always. Like the Runner, the Quartermaster has thought that by action man can resolve the insoluble. The Generalissimo says that he does not fear man—he respects him. He will later tell the Corporal, his son, who says man will endure, that man will do more. He will prevail.

After a long pilgrimage the Sisters bring the Corporal back to Europe, giving him a home, location, and what serves for parents. But this parentage is a substitute. The Corporal, deprived of the Cart, must undertake the harsher role. His sacrifice must be complete. As the anonymous corporal going among the soldiers inciting them to mutiny, he has already recovered certain of the qualities of fatherhood, all but the actual physical bond. From him the privates receive hope of release from the evils of their plight; he comforts them; he redresses social ills. He promises marriage to a whore, gives status to her outcast state; he arranges the marriage between a soldier and a girl with child by him, thus assuring to the unborn child a father in the flesh. He does this with the knowledge of the risk he takes, the final test of fatherhood, sacrifice of self for the child. Thus far the Son of Man becomes the Father of Man.

His next to last test parallels the temptation on the Mount. The old Supreme General takes his son above the town and offers him the world. The old man understands the full measure of the sacrifice of his own youth, now that he is deprived by age and is near to death. This makes authoritative his plea that breath is worth the sacrifice, that life is its own boon, the sorrows as well as the good. This is the same revelation the song of the bird announces to the criminal about to be hanged in America. This revelation is the central kernel of meaning to A Fable. Yet the Corporal is offered not only life but life in abundance. The offer is accompanied by a price: betrayal. This the son refuses; but as the two part, the Corporal thinks father and son have perfected their reunion, that the guilt of innocence is expiated at last. He says, "Father," as they part forever. Sir Launcelot of the Lake has become Sir Galahad of the Baptismal Fount.

But not quite. The old General knows there is one more test. He warns his son of the blood with which he resists him. The Corporal dies the death, but in dying reaffirms the old primordial flaw. He repeats his father's adventure in the desert. He cannot die immaculate, only in the stain of Gragnon's assassination. This is the insoluble antinomy, the sacred paradox. Both father and son thus suffer the double role of priest and murderer. The Corporal, rather than betray man's hope in salvation, accepts the role but now with full knowledge. This junction of relationship between the Corporal and Gragnon is the union of worldly and spiritual rank, but only the rank will be resurrected as symbol of no body, only hope. The old General opposes the highest sacrifice to the lowest: the highest possibilities against mere breath. Out of this did the Corporal come to be, did the old drama repeat itself. The perfect reunion between father and son is denied, but hope of it is renewed. And in the end, in the terms of this dualism which makes all plights common and degree meaningless, man will not only endure, he will prevail; and this is mortal immortality. To such an extent is the divine understanding of the Passion Week reduced.

In the section called "Tomorrow" it seems for a moment that the wisdom which keeps order in the world and the hope for man's return to the innocence of Paradise will be reunited in death. The Corporal is the unknown soldier. The perpetual flame of hope burns above him in the triumphal arch. The old General, now dead, in all the pomp and circumstance of high degree and the pageantry of the death cart, but the death cart resurrected in glory, is brought before the son for the revelation of their final reunion in death. That hope of bringing to an end the evils of man's condition, and that knowledge that it persists in terms of the eternal quest, for which Fatherland is the symbol, join together in the eye of the mass man lining the way. In this common eye only the symbol of the Father is apotheosized.

But at this moment the Runner steps forth from the crowd. When the Corporal was arrested, when the higher purpose failed, he turned to the Jockey-Sentry, who was reborn into a cynical sense of brotherhood, instinct become superstition, believing in blind chance (who holds his outfit in the palm of his hand as banker through whom the men gamble their lives against the temporary spree of military leave: life against the body's basic needs). In a sense the Jockey-Sentry has exchanged attitudes with the Runner: he hates man in himself and in others. Like the German general, he uses men for his gamble with lives, practicing Mama Bidet's concept, his hatred almost as abstract as the German's attitude. He at first kicks in the teeth of the Runner when the Runner tries to tempt him to a noble risk. Having lost any belief in spiritual or any kind of salvation, he refuses to listen to the Runner, who tells him that if he will only take his men over the top, the enemy will come out, too, and man acting in the mass will thwart the generals of both sides (man's common enemy) and bring the conflict to an end. He has tried already to defeat authority and has failed. The old Negro has followed him to France, as the friendly comforter from all the world to all the world, but the Jockey-Sentry will have nothing more to do with him. This is his situation. Having used gambling as a means to an end in the horse-race episode, he now uses it as the symbol of the end itself. The Runner, who believes that the end justifies the means, understanding the common man's belief in signs (the dice and the Mason's sign), will force the Jockey-Sentry, who controls both, to save himself and mankind. The Runner uses violence to end violence (again the paradox), even fooling himself and the old Negro with the fire and the roar of the artillery as signs of the coming of the end. At the point of the gun he forces the Sentry over the top; men from both sides come forward in brotherhood. But it is too late. The generals have got together. A barrage from both sides, turned not upon an enemy but upon mankind, destroys them. The Sentry, dying, cries "we" instead of "I." This is his final test, the dying of selfhood which becomes a resurrection into the brotherhood of man.

It is with the knowledge of this failure which is also a triumph that the Runner, who has survived it, lunges out of the mass and casts the military medal at the old Marshal's death cart, defying and denying the symbolic reunion of Father-Son, reaffirming the hope of man that Paradise can be brought to earth. Except for the police, the emblem of authority, he would be torn to pieces by the man in mass, again forced by him to recognize the hope of man's relief from the dualism of his nature. The Runner appears to be not a man now but an upright scar, one arm, one leg, one eye, on crutches, in his being death-in-life and life-in-death, the walking representation of the dualism and man's hope that he can end it. The book closes with him in the arms of the old Quartermaster General. The two levels of action are thus joined not in terms of the saviors but of the John the Baptists, the one weeping for lost hope, the other with little more than breath defiantly affirming the immortality of hope. It is because of this hope, at some far distant time in the future, that man will prevail. How and under what conditions Faulkner does not tell us.

"This passion, this immolation, this apotheosis" has always been Faulkner's subject. It has never before been so explicitly stated. The insistence on endurance as the measure of immortality in mortal man is a stoical attitude that appears in late stages of civilization. Whatever virtues it lends to behavior, it remains a naturalistic interpretation of man's predicament. Jesus is either divine, or he stands for an archetypical performance, the essence of which remains in man's consciousness to be repeated again, say in the twentieth century at the time of a false spring armistice in a world war. A *Fable* takes all the circumstance of the Passion Week's progress and repeats it by reducing it to a natural explanation. There is a savior with twelve disciples, a Judas, a last supper, a barbed-wire substitute for the crown of thorns (this must have seemed a little forced even to the author); there is even a corpse shifted by gunfire for resurrection. Characters in life or fiction, knowing the Passion, might conceivably try to reproduce it under certain stimuli. But neither in life nor in fiction can they repeat the initial circumstances by means of which the Passion was acted out, for these are beyond control. And yet the author does this. The reader asks, Upon what authority? Certainly upon no historic authority, for history may repeat itself, but never under the same set of conditions. Does the author in the episode of the three witnesses who have seen the Corporal die in three different times and places imply a supernatural resurrection? It seems so, until we remember that the Corporal is the old General's bastard. Is it a supernatural manifestation, or is it accidental resemblance? We cannot know. From this failure to solve the basic technical problem of authority, the author impairs and renders ambiguous his meaning, and hence his form.

What is the form of *A Fable?* It sometimes seems to be a morality, sometimes an allegory, sometimes fiction. The characters are differentiated by the degree in which they represent this version of the Passion, not as men who differ in their personalities. As mouthpieces of Faulkner's rhetoric they are so far allegorical. The clearest instance of this is Marthe's impassioned denunciation of the old General. Her station and upbringing are not such as to lead us to accept what we hear her say. Is she speaking under some supernatural influence? This can't be, for the whole message of the book denies the supernatural. The long oration about Sambo in *Intruder in the Dust* seems to be the author's voice; and yet there it is put into the mouth of a lawyer who conceivably would have thought such thoughts and been able so to express them. But Marthe is a peasant woman and, furthermore, a mountain woman, and mountain women are notoriously silent and subservient before men. And where did she get her training in diction?

Nor is the Corporal ever seen as a person. Even the *ficelles* who talk about him do so in terms of the mystery which he is supposed to be. He is no Son of Man. He is begot of the sound of the author's voice upon an idea. This makes the great scene above the city between father and son miscarry, for there is no son but only an abstraction to be tempted. In spite of the variety of the General's plea it never quite has the human warmth of a parent trying to save his child. The accidental machinery of another drama intrudes to divert the reader, who perforce must think of the temptation on the Mount or find himself wondering if the old General stands for both God and the devil. Anything which diverts the attention from a scene, which destroys the illusion of action, is a fictive flaw, for it makes the reader aware that he is reading. God made incarnate in man cried out as man, in the prayer to have the cup removed and again on the Cross. And yet Faulkner is dealing with the natural man and that only. Surely he should have given him flesh and the body's needs. Action should never be resolved in symbolic terms only. Reality and symbol should fit as the glove the hand. He sacrificed too much to inducing mystery about the Corporal's movements, all of which are reported. He is in the death cart with his disciples, passing rapidly, making a heroic posture. And in the scene of the last supper there is felt the strain of effort to make him a human being with other human beings, but this comes late and even here the arbitrary "plot" again intrudes to divert the attention, and to inhibit the creative act.

It isn't as if Faulkner doesn't know how to do it. The shock of meaning in terms of mystery he handled superbly well in *The Bear*. The concrete footprint disappearing before the boy's eyes made present the invisible bear, evoking the awe of the immortal in the mortal beast. The print of the foot vanishing in the swamp's water, two objects acting together in one image, is one of the finest examples in fiction of Flaubert's law that an object exists because it stands in relationship to another object or objects. There is none of James's weak specification here, nor in that other instance when the bear, again invisible, looks at the boy out of the forest's screen. How does Faulkner do it here? By having the bird suddenly grow silent. The sudden cessation of sound produces the silence because it affects the boy. The very fact that it is a bird which in no way can be harmed by the bear makes the ominous quality of the danger immediate. In the first episode sight and touch are used; in the second sight and sound, sound against silence, sight complicated because it is blind. It is sight which doesn't see opposed to the seeing bear, itself unseen, that gives the shock of awe and terror. All of these specifications are made by the boy's mind out of the legend of the bear's immortality, fixed in a crooked paw, which the author has carefully established.

This comparison is relevant, because Ike McCaslin is cousin-german to the Corporal. He undergoes a self-immolation, refusing his inheritance to rectify the sins of the fathers. By his act of renunciation the taint is removed at least from his private conscience; its self-victimization shows the way to regeneration. But he is no abstract symbol. He is a believable individual, of a certain heritage, in a certain time and place, acting among individuals who perform out of the mores of a society and the particular ritual of the hunt. Furthermore the sincerity of his belief and his sacrifice is accepted, because we see—are not told about, but see—what it costs him in the scene in the boardinghouse at high noon when his wife offers her naked body, a renunciation of her modesty, the measure of her desperation, for the sake of a communion of real marriage. And marriage as an institution is certainly strengthened by the physical location in property, as the personal communion is fixed in the sensible joining of flesh. Young Ike is the exemplum of the Puritan hero, who holds in fee simple the body of the world and is incapable, as are all men, of this responsibility. To this is owed his unconscious guilt which makes him reject the inheritance. The old Christian order of a God's wealth which gave to the divinity the ownership of the world had in his day become a commonwealth. Action always comes down to the individual. The rejection of the social body required the sensible rejection of his own. His father and twin brother tried to correct the injustice by a social sacrifice, which was also symbolic, of moving into the cabin and putting the slaves in the Big House. But this was a compromise between social responsibility for property and the injustice it entails. The ritualized chase of their half brother—emphasized by the formality of the necktie—in which he was never caught, shows the perpetual recurrence of the dualism, which became the enveloping action for Ike's own specific act of renunciation. Man's plight and his effort to do something about it appear in *Go Down, Moses* as they appear in *A Fable*: as the enveloping action and the action proper. The pursuit of the mulatto brother causes the "fall" of Ike's father and the renewal of the conflict in Ike's birth, just as the "fall" of the old General begets the Corporal. But *The Bear* deals only with card number 12, the surrender of social position. The poker game is essentially the same as the dice game in the horse episode with the Jockey, a means to an end. It has not become the end in itself, as in the later stages of *A Fable*. The woman as the root of all evil, because pursuit of her involves the use of the senses, is the Puritan attitude; but she has only symbolic reality in this last book. Perhaps when she disappears entirely, then will the son complete his reunion with the father. But card number 13 turns for many of Faulkner's heroes: Christmas and Quentin and Bayard's grandson, for example. Bayard himself risks his physical life to put an end to violence and gains a moral triumph. For him there is the ram in the bushes; but as I shall try to show, his action is no resolution. The old dilemma remains.

In these previous novels there was generally, in technical terms, a fusion of the action proper and the rhetoric. The rhetoric at its best was an impassioned reverie, sometimes spoken, sometimes in the consciousness as on a stage. It was made authoritative by having it depend not upon the author's voice commenting out of some omniscience but by attaching it to the characters in their fictive parts. At times in *Sartoris* and in *Sanctuary* the author intrudes his omniscience, but it is restricted, as if the author were deliberately trying to avoid reporting the action instead of making the action reveal itself. Even in "A Rose for Emily," before he had more surely mastered the form, the Voice of the Town narrating is strictly a local boy. He might have been a particular individual, sensitive and apperceptive, who saw Miss Emily not as a symbol but as an individual whose private situation gave symbolic meaning to the more general predicament of the town. Nor did Faulkner depend upon the symbol alone to make the resolution. He made the image of the indented pillow and the gray hair beside the skeleton of lost love do it, just as earlier the odor of decay came from the desperate act of her private anguish. The dual nature of the central intelligence, while making the action show itself, also served for a choral effect, revealing, commenting upon, extending the violence into a larger context of meaning. He later perfected the techne of this point of view, but "A Rose for Emily" is instructive for showing it in a cruder form. Not that the story is unskillfully done.

The post he has come to take is a variant of James's, and his use of the senses is nearly always as skillful as Flaubert's. What is unique to him is a kind of bardic quality and tone, modified by the incantatory homiletics of Protestant rhetoric. The bard tells the well-known story but known incompletely until he brings all fragments into their true relationship, thus revealing the fuller truth in the mould created by his greater talent and knowledge. It is why Faulkner can begin anywhere, often in the middle, and work in any direction. His temper of suspense is dependent upon this. It implies on the part of those involved a passionate but obscure understanding, and it implies on the part of the central intelligence the focus by which the meaning of the action will be disclosed and made whole; or it implies the intention, also the compelling need, of the central intelligence to unravel it. He becomes the interpreter with special insight as the sewing-machine agent in *The Hamlet*. Or he is Quentin in *Absalom, Absalom!*, who must find out the secret of the dark violence in his community out of a compulsive sense of his close communion with it. He feels a responsibility where the action of a part involves the destiny of the whole, of which he is another part. He hopes, from the understanding he will get, to inform himself of his own dark nature, explain himself to himself in terms of the common social scene, and in so doing perhaps regenerate it. His quest is a full measure of participation. This quest explains why so many of Faulkner's protagonists, when they hold the point of view, become victims, at times selected, at times self-appointed. They have only gradually worked up to the role of the archetypical savior, as is to be found in *A Fable*. The irony and disaster of Quentin's search are that he failed upon the larger scene; or perhaps it was no failure but a revelation that all he could do to save his immediate family was die. The force of the irony lay in the impotence of his act. The spiritual impotence of suicide is only another, if more conscious, reflection of the family's spiritual decay.

Faulkner's roving point of view, placed now with one person, now with another, with the author above or looking over the shoulder, is not a shift of view but segmented cones depending from an intense point or core. So it is that the action proper in one part becomes the enveloping action for another. The opening section, for example, of *Absalom, Absalom!* has Rosa Coldfield for protagonist. The fury she feels from the treatment she has received makes for the intensity of her denunciation, a vocal reverie. This reverie contains an action complete as far as it affects her, but to Quentin it is the enveloping action against which he finally hammers out a truth; that is, her action contains in essence the enveloping action, which is Sutpen, but not until the other stories are unraveled will it show itself to Quentin as a part of the pattern which at the same time has all the ingredients of the whole. This is another way of saying how the gradual disclosure makes for suspense.

The extreme extension of the bardic tone, as it is the most instinctive, belongs to Faulkner's mobs. They seem to act out of a blind understanding but with the force of mass and the incorruptibility of a natural movement which is beyond good and evil. There is nobody except Tolstoy who handles crowds of people so well as he. Tolstoy does it by focusing mass action upon an individual, or the action is seen through and felt by one seeing eye. Faulkner at his best does this, too. He has a spokesman for the chorus, but the chorus, unlike Tolstoy's, has a life of its own, indeed almost a personality, at once physical and metaphysical. In the opening of *A Fable* he uses it well, inducing mystery and suspense. We don't know who the individuals who step out from the crowd are or what the Sergeant represents; but at this point we don't need to know. Unfortunately, later the suspense lags, and the mobs grow monotonous, and there is a reason for this.

This reason will best be seen by examining his best mob action, which appears in *The Unvanquished*, one of his most successful and least understood books. The uprooted slaves going along the roads and woods to Jordan are a technical triumph. They represent the hope of earthly paradise and the loosing of chaos, all those elemental forces which an ordered society keeps in place by ethics, a code of morals and manners. Society can solve none of the repetitive involvements which are man's plight and inheritance. It can only hold in abeyance the most destructive aspects of these forces by rules and orders, accepted habits and the convention of property. The animal nature of man is transformed by form into what is called civilized behavior. There is restricted war and total war, the first a convention of the Christian state, the other the freeing of violence which will destroy the state. Such violence allows for no sanctuary. The Civil War was the first Western war to do this. (Napoleon only partially did it.) It was instituted by Yankee generals. Historically the moment is clear: when Buell and McClellan were replaced by Grant and Sherman. Previously the convention, certainly the eighteenth-century convention, which Lee followed, was that armies fought armies, that the population would of necessity be injured. But when Sherman said war was hell, aside from admitting an incapacity to defeat the Confederate armies in the field, he meant specifically that there would be no sanctuary, that the entire society would be destroyed. At war's end the forms would be no longer the same. He began it in Mississippi; so the scene for *The Unvanquished* is not only right dramatically. It is right, too, historically.

Rosa Millard, the protagonist, in her person opposes all the moral and ethical mores of Protestant Christian life to the loosing of these forces of total war. She does not consciously see the war for what it is. To her it is the usual folly of man raised to its highest power. Her silver and mules and Negroes have been stolen, not levied upon formally, as the articles of war allowed as late as the Revolution. She sets out to the proper authority to get them back, on the assumption that it is a crime against property. And Colonel Dickey among the enemy shares her attitude, but with greater knowledge. Her failure to see the actual state of affairs is made clear by her actions. She sends for a more formal hat, since her call is to be formal; she "borrows" the team; she carries rose cuttings, as if everything was going on as usual; she makes the boys wash out their mouths with soap when they lie or use profanity. This is the usage of social order, small evidences of manners and ethics of the decent behavior she knows. It is comedy, but it becomes a grim irony as the action progresses. More and more the nature of the war shows itself. Her house is burned along with others. The success of her mission sows the seed for her destruction, which symbolically foreshows what total war will do to the civilized order. Gradually she is forced to violate her moral code out of the ambiguity of her situation and, except for her last act, for the better reason. This contradiction between means and ends finally brings her to her death. There could be no finer image to focus the meaning of her action than the appearance of her body in death. She looks like a few thin sticks with a piece of calico thrown over them. This image makes a shocking revelation, in the apposition of spirit and body, in terms of her fall.

The uprooted slaves moving in mass towards Jordan and freedom, towards that deep-laid hope of Paradise on earth but to the actual betrayal of death, also represent the destruction of the society of which they are a basic part. Putting Rosa Millard and the boys in the midst of this mob allows the chorus to make an implicit comment on her quest. Her personal fate and the fate of what she stands for is foreshadowed. But like all tragic figures, she is blind to it. To her it is another evidence of the folly she expects. She is outraged when it engulfs her and sweeps her into the river. Her impotence before it, the release of chaos in man joined to the natural chaos of nature, the river, is in the umbrella which she lays about her. But she is not allowed to drown like the characters of a lower order. The strength of her moral nature demands a longer struggle. All the five senses are used to give effect to the mob, to relate it to the protagonists in the wagon. They hear it moving in its mysterious power, but most of all they smell it. Smell of all the senses is most mortal. The dust the mob raises overlays them, a symbol of death, making a composite effect in sight, touch, taste, and smell. Sight is used to make present the human, individual delusion. As in the story of the Pied Piper of Hamelin, one falls behind. A mother and child cannot keep up. In her human frailty and blindness are foreshadowed the self-betrayal and the hope of the mass. Rosa asks her why she doesn't go home. But the Negro woman can't go home. The gleam she follows, like the children of Hamelin, has already destroyed it. Rosa, too, is blind. The two blindnesses complement each other as they expose the meaning.

In *The Unvanquished* you have practically the same impulses, the same motives for action, the same prototypes for the heroes, as you do in *A Fable.* The grandmother and the Generalissimo, out of differing knowledge, both stand for order in the state. The enveloping action is total war. Not only does the war destroy the rank and place of great and small, but it is against this background that the private actions of the succeeding protagonists, grandmother and grandson, of resisting and restoring the shattered forms by the risk of self, take place. The bushwhackers who kill the grandmother have for leader a man whose costume is a parody of that of a gentleman, representing the release of the forces of chaos, made sinister by the inversion of the form of leadership. In his terms Ab Snopes becomes a force of evil only after he has been able to tempt the grandmother. The boys in pursuit of the murderer give death for death, but the act of vengeance, in spite of its motive, is private and dangerously close to chaos itself.

Colonel Sartoris is the archetype of the leader whose rank has been subverted by the triumph of total war. He is closer now to the parody of the gentleman bushwhacker than he is to his former self. He is the traditional leader changed by war into the leader who makes his private will into the law. The race of the two engines, which seems to the boys a chivalric tilting, becomes in his hands the image of private, irresponsible power. The railroad is the instrument which will prevent the reestablishment of the family in some location, although it is the motor car and the airplane which will later more successfully set individuals adrift upon the earth and above it. The uprooting finds its clearest image in what is done to womankind. Drusilla realizes that her role as sweetheart, wife, and mother, the formal succession of woman's roles in the family order, will disappear. In dressing and fighting as a man, she symbolically unsexes herself. The grandmothers refuse to believe in the heroism of her act. In their choral role they carry on the resistance against the disruption of society's form, for which one grandmother dies by forcing upon Drusilla a loveless marriage to Colonel Sartoris. The futility of their act, their failure to recognize what has happened, is seen in the travesty of the marriage itself, delayed by an action of two private interests, each taking the law into its own hands, the carpetbaggers and the defeated, no longer acting as soldiers out of some formal obedience to the state but out of a private sense of injustice and betrayal. The irony is completed by the wedding gown which Drusilla, the unsexed soldier, wears even as she rides as one of her husband's men. The final betrayal of family takes a critical turn in the incestuous attraction between stepmother and stepson, which the father is not even aware of for his self-absorption in his private violence. Colonel Sartoris frees himself, out of weariness, by death. His son, Bayard, refuses the pistols offered in the odor of verbena, violence identified with love, and becomes a moral man in the double denial of love and physical life. The enemy misfires, and he wins life, but ironically, as is seen in *Sartoris*, there is no longer any clear convention which can contain and give it meaning.

Although *A Fable* and *The Unvanquished* are dealing essentially with the dualism of good and evil in terms of total war and man's effort to resolve it, there are crucial differences in the technical handling of the two books. It seems to me that action in a novel must rely upon the social conventions. No action takes place in a vacuum. It is always somewhere. Even if it is in the mind, the mind reflects the images of life. It is the convention, whether it be of manners or morals, which restrains the natural man and makes that which is common to all men (the elemental forces) take the varying shapes of a particular culture, the source of which is some religious belief. The loss of this belief is always in evidence through the fragmentation of the convention. The fragmentation of the convention has been Faulkner's enveloping action in books previous to *A Fable*. But in this book he treats too specifically of Everyman, no particular men. The trench is a symbol without a natural counterpart. We are told of the ordure and the sweat; we are not made to smell or suffer it. We are told we are in France. We see no Frenchmen. This is one reason the mass action grows monotonous. We are told men sacrifice their rank, what is dearer to them than even life itself, but only with the young airman in Europe is this rank made concrete. And this is done by use of the senses. We see the phosphorous bullet strike his uniform, the mark of his rank and his belief; we smell the slow burning of it, which becomes the sensible focus of betrayal, and its slow smell of disintegration is always there as the specific reference for his revery. In America the author is equally successful with the horse race. When the great scenes which center around the old Generalissimo become scenes, it is because of what the eunuched staff officer does with the door or what Faulkner does with the old batman. This servant stands for loyalty, but a human relationship is established between the two men. It is the batman's presence in the death cortege (he is a human being who is also a symbol) which helps make the pageantry visual. The young airman, the old General, the Negro, and the Jockey-Sentry more nearly take on the particularity of people. Therefore when they appear, we more nearly get fiction.

But I rather feel the total impact is that of a morality. An author can take what form he chooses, to say what he pleases; but certain literary forms are more successful in one period than another. Our sense of history, for example, would not have been understood in the twelfth century. I rather imagine that in the twelfth century genealogy expressed in dynastic terms whatever sense there was of history. But perhaps its most explicit form was that of a memoir such as Joinville's, which implied the soul's trials and self-discovery in terms of its religious belief. War had its natural side then as now, but war, foreign and domestic, existed as a specific kind of action reflecting the image of religious man. There was no disparity between economic man and religious man. When the king was counting losses after a certain battle in the Holy Land and asked about his brother, he was told, "Sire, he is in Paradise."

And so it seems that a morality or an allegory, whose materials are mortal sins and moral principles and not the uniqueness of individual men, could make a better effect in such an age of belief, because this belief suffused all degrees of rank and particularity. A man witnessing a morality would, in the action dealing with the drama of the soul, automatically specify whatever was unique and personal in himself. But today, when we have conventions empty of belief and institutions being reduced to organizations and forms which have lost the natural object, a morality lacks authority. It is why fiction as a literary form appears now and not in the fourteenth century. Everyman now must first become unique man. He is no longer composite of spiritual and natural parts, related and defined against an absolute set of values. The fiction writer can best recover him through the artful use of the sensibility of naturalism. This is what Flaubert learned after *The Temptation of St. Anthony*. (*A Fable* is Faulkner's *St. Anthony* or Tolstoyan *Resurrection*.) It is why the natural man discovers himself in opposition to the conventions. He is in search of that which will contain him, and what can contain him is fragmentary, the broken artifacts of a culture.

If I had to sum up in a sentence what I think is *A Fable*'s technical limitation, I would say that the author's omniscient viewpoint has used his rhetorical gifts to report the action instead of using the rhetoric, as previously, to extend the meaning of the action's violence, thus depriving himself of that extra dimension which his subject needs for its fullest rendition. An artist has only one subject. It does not come to him full-clothed and apparent; else there would be no travail, no delight, no creation. He spends his life in an enforced discovery, so that in the end the objects of his imagination will be set in the proper relationships to each other and his vision appear whole, to himself as well as to the reader. This, at least, is the ideal situation, that shock of recognition which joins the observer to the observed in a renewed understanding of the common predicament or some aspect of it. The stale becomes fresh; the old, new. This regeneration the artist performs for society. This is not to say that he alone knows such an experience. The great oak puts forth each spring a leaf as tender as that first leaf upon the switch whose roots still know the rotting seed. So do most men make according to their skills. The artist does not preempt the creative act. He confirms it by turning chaos into the labyrinth. And this only the great artificer can do. And he can do it because he has confronted his dual nature, accepted and assimilated the beast, and so out of this knowledge can make the lair to contain him. Without the knowledge of evil and its place in the divine scheme, there is no life. The innocent try to exclude from themselves the possibilities of evil. This is the universal meaning of the young airman's fate in A *Fable*. Instead of doing as Bridesman must earlier have done, come to terms with the complexities of the world, he cannot stand the violation of the illusion of his innocence, and so, since he is honest and courageous, there is nothing left for him to do but kill himself and choose the latrine, symbolic of what he has refused to confront, as the place of suicide.

This is the self-betrayal which denies maturity. Theseus, that other hero-innocent, made the second error of immaturity. He thought he could dispose of evil once for all. It was not by accident that he killed the Minotaur in its sleep. This condemned him to the wanderings of perpetual immaturity. The knowledge of himself forever denied him by his refusal to confront the beast lurked in his unconscious to become the ruin of friends and loves. How quickly Ariadne was betrayed! The black sails which plunged his father to his death foreshow the nature of his quest. Incapable of mature love (and this is best defined in man-woman involvement, rather than father and son) because of his refusal to know himself, he must go on to the end, to exile, to be murdered by his host once a friend, seeking what he has refused, with the bones of wife, father, and son to mark his way.

The labyrinth we inherit from that other source of our common culture. It is a myth particularly instructive for artists. Daedalus and Icarus inform us of another meaning to be got from the father-son myth. They make another pair of criminals, but the guilt this time is the father's. Because the labyrinth is his handiwork, he can offer the thread of understanding to all men. The intercessor is a woman. The state in the person of the king would have him subvert to an arbitrary political end his knowledge and his devotion. The king imprisons him within his artifice. But like all arbitrary power, it is stupid. Knowing the limitations of his craft, Daedalus finds the way out. The nature of an artist is composite of an Icarean recklessness—the pushing of matter beyond its limits—and restraint. The medium of a craft is always waxen; it is the limits of form which give it flight. It was Daedalus, who did not forget the limits of his craft, who kept his course.

Regeneration for the Man: Faulkner's Intruder in the Dust

IN *INTRUDER IN THE DUST* Faulkner has taken a subject, and almost it seems deliberately taken it, which the propagandists of the party line have preempted as theirs to have and to hold and fulminate about; for that matter, it might have been taken by any of the intruders upon the art of fiction who violate the Muse for pragmatic purposes, whether at the state's command or out of private need or through sociology's quasi-revelations. These last pretend to illuminate situation and performance, but in effect, by meddling with the craft, they obfuscate even their debased cult of good works. It is irrelevant, actually, whether Faulkner either out of irony or from some more private impulse chose what seemed a contemporary issue as subject for this novel. Such choice is beyond the artist's capacity. He does not choose his subject; his subject chooses him. And because his imagination functions in a certain way, craft against reverie, even if he were deliberately to set out to make a plea to action or to treat the accidental accidentally, he wouldn't be able to do it. The artist is simply one who cannot debase his work even when, pressed, he thinks

he gives in to circumstance; certainly he cannot do so after his apprenticeship is behind him. There always seem to be a few exceptions to prove
the rule; but on close scrutiny I doubt if these could show more than a
technical virtuosity such as magic shows.

Dickens' passionate interest in the social evils of his day and Bleak House,
that one of his books which stirred England to reform the courts in chancery, together give the best example I know of the artist's inviolability. The
excitement of the day and the social action Bleak House set afoot were
residual to the central experience, the literary truth, of the novel. It happened that the injustices of the courts in chancery served Dickens as the
complication which discovered his subject. The effect of the inertia, the
circumlocutions, the mazelike ritual of the court upon the characters gives
to its injustice the absolute quality of Fate, with which man struggles but
about which he can do little but realize the combinations of his character
against circumstance; so that the proportion of good and evil in the nature
of man is implied in all its variety through the central drive of the action. If
Dickens' concern had been with the evils of banking, say, instead of the
cases in chancery, the literary truth would have been the same. The book
would merely have lacked the residual effect of reforming the banking
system, which at that time the public interest had not identified with its
sorrows. The artist may use anything, since whatever he uses will be absorbed by his imagination and rendered by his technical skill, and this is the
artist's integrity. He will only use what his vision sees, and that according to
the degree of its intensity. The surface and density of the object, illuminated
in its totality, is form. Whatever failure there is is a failure of human
fallibility, not of intention.

Intruder in the Dust bears comparison with Bleak House, with the difference that Dickens' concern is with a single institution, whereas Faulkner
deals with the complex and fundamental involvement of a whole society.
The supposed murder of a white man by a Negro, a threat of lynching, and
even the Bill of Rights, which certainly brought the material up to the
moment of publication, appear to be the author's subject; but actually they
are only one aspect of it. In the first paragraph Faulkner reports sparely,
tersely even, an act of violence. At noon the high sheriff has reached the jail
with Lucas Beauchamp, although the entire county has known since the
night before that Lucas killed a white man. The act of violence has already

happened. But the pastness of it is not static. There is a continuum in the information about the spread of the news; and given the particular kind of news it is and the lapse of time between the murder and the jailing of Lucas, we are made to feel a mounting suspense which gives to the delay, as the story unfolds, a quality of mystery. This suspense and a feeling of the dark unknown is further tightened by the emphasis on time, not any hour but the hour of noon, a crucial division of time which we sense will be of importance, if for no more than that the narrow limits it suggests will contain the action. That it also will imply a symbolical reference we cannot know but later find ourselves prepared for. This introduces us to the structure. Instead of leading up to the murder as the final release to the tensions of involvement, Faulkner, by putting it into the past, uses the act as the compulsive force to catalyze the disparate fragments of appearance into reality, for the story is not about violence at all. It is about a sixteen-year-old boy's education in good and evil and his effort to preserve his spiritual integrity.

Charles Mallison, Jr. (he is called by name once), is not merely a sensitive boy in whom resides the consciousness of his race, although he is this, too. More particularly he has a grief. The cause for this grief comes out of the dichotomy between the races, brought about by the long assault from the outside which has isolated southern people and made him, along with them, overly sensitive to his racial distinction, to the extent that the integrity of his manhood has become identified with his distinction. This identification between race and manhood represents for the boy-man both Nemesis and Fate, since he is neither responsible for the imperfection of his view nor for the pattern of the action which the dead white man releases. He resists flight (washing his hands of it). His effort to escape his predicament lies in his decision to discover the truth by digging up the grave of the dead man to see what bullet killed him. He will face dangers both physical and metaphysical comprised in an undertaking beyond his capacity to perform, but in his decision he assumes the moral responsibility for his humanity. The impulse behind this decision, however, is mixed. On the one hand he hopes to wipe out the shame his manhood has suffered at the attitude of Lucas four years before the story opens (Lucas' denial of his racial preeminence, or so it seemed); on the other, it is to avoid the shame of lynching that attaches to any mob action, since this is another kind of emasculation for both the individual and society, as in either case the will is deprived of its function. Or to put it another way, the individual's violation of his code of conduct and society's subversion of its laws become a kind of suicide, especially in the instance of traditional man and a homogeneous society. It is his innocence as a boy but his pride and conscience as man which in the end clarify the confused impulses and bring him into a fuller knowledge of the truth. In one sense the historic isolation of the southern culture by a victorious and hostile force serves for the fateful drive of the story: it is at once the cause for action and the clue to its meaning. By focusing it in the moral destiny of a boy, the story becomes dramatic instead of didactic, that is, a novel and not propaganda.

There is for any southern writer of imagination an inescapable preoccupation with his native scene and especially with its historic predicament. He can no more escape it than a Renaissance painter could escape painting Her Ladyship the Virgin and the Court of Angels. He has been made to feel too sharply his uniqueness and the uniqueness of his society in the modern world. His self-consciousness does for him what blindness did for Homer. He has been forced to achieve aesthetic distance. It is this which gives to the boy protagonist (a culture hero almost) in this book the authority for his undertaking and allows him to absorb into the working out of his fate the entire complex set of relationships which represent the contradictions, the mixed virtues and vices, the agonies, even, of the southern sensibility, containing a vision at once objective and involved: the poet-prophet who defines a civilization bereft of historic destiny but which refuses the role.

It seems to me that criticism all too often attempts to isolate an author's truth by abstracting it from the context of his performance. It is the writer's nature to discover for himself his meaning by matching his knowledge of experience against his imagination. This never comes in a burst of light; it comes out of a gradual exploration into the dark places of the mind and heart of man. The process of writing forces the discovery, or rather it is the discovery. What saves the writer from losing himself (the points of darkness are infinite) is his point of view. To this he may return, and by this he may relate, reduce, and absorb the seemingly unrelated matters of experience until they become what to him is truth. Given the creative function, what follows is style, and style is that breath of life which makes of texture and structure, or body and bone, an organic whole. In this novel Faulkner has achieved a oneness of style and point of view which is of the first order of literary distinction. It is all effortless and so fused (which has not always been the case in his other books—he has not always removed his scaffolding) that to probe for purposes of analysis becomes a kind of bloody operation.

I shall let the point of view more or less envelop what I have to say. It lies in the close sympathy which exists between the boy and his uncle, a sympathy so intimate that at times the transference of thought does not need speech. There are many advantages to this. The novel is freed, but not entirely so, from the indistinct image the narrator-actor must present to the reader. By having two sensibilities instead of one—he would have done better had he made them more personally distinct—each is able to give to the other the grace of humanity. The boy's innocence and the uncle's maturity set up an interplay both at the center and on the periphery of the structure. Their relationship becomes strophe and antistrophe, enforcing the formal pause, defining the action as it is taking place. The center of the structure depends upon the treatment of time. For the physical action a very narrow limit is set; but the physical action, while performing at its own level, releases the flow of reverie and comment which becomes the embodiment of the intrinsic meaning. Since within this area lies the realm of truth, where all is timeless, the dual consciousness moves through past, present, and even into the future, according to the needs of the particular stage of the story's development. But for this flexibility the continuous beat of the prose would grow monotonous—with its inversions and parentheses, the dreamlike quality of its tone (again the sense of timelessness) often threatening to make the skill of its complex delivery too apparent, which would be fatal. But always at the right moment there comes the pause, the break of dialogue—and Faulkner's dialogue surpasses itself—the added information when it is needed, the image in a new light subtly changing the texture, or the posturing of a character as sudden as the shock of the tragic mask.

Gradually as we come to understand the achievement of the boy's education, and the achievement is manhood, we discover that the point of view has not shifted but was more inclusive than it first appeared. It is still posted firmly with the boy-uncle relationship, but it has expanded beyond the boy's discoveries, though it is still contingent upon them. It rests at last not upon the boy's coming into manhood, but upon manhood, or its essence: the Man. The boy sets out to restore a spurious manhood (appearance), but thanks to his innocence and the guidance of his uncle he reaches instead true manhood (reality). The Man is the representative of the homogeneous society. His symbol is the fire and the hearth. He maintains the right relationships between the sexes, preserving to each its natural function; guards the blood's purity; is ultimately responsible for order in his household and therefore in the state; attends to his business, does not intrude or allow intrusion. He punishes and rewards toward this end and is the trustee for the earth out of which life comes and by which it is maintained. He, not freedom, which history has shown no man can stand, is the realizable image for society.

But in the South of *Intruder in the Dust* there are half men or men hamstrung out of their instinct to preserve this manhood. The uncle who understands so much is blinded by "the facts and circumstances." The sheriff, the hunter who guards the jail for five dollars as he reads the funnies, the jail keeper who is outraged that he may lose his life for seventy-five dollars a month but will still risk it, and old Gowrie, the father of the murdered man, are all men in Faulkner's sense, but each is circumscribed by some phase of the South's darkened image. In Miss Habersham's action the functions of the sexes are transposed. She, an old woman, does what a man should have done, if it had to be done—dig up a grave at midnight for justice's sake. And yet she was the only one who could assist the boys. Her caste and feminine intuition both informed her beforehand of what she would find, intuition acting truly, her caste function misplaced: she was a lady peddling eggs and vegetables at the town's back doors, wearing Sears-Roebuck dresses, but her thirty-dollar handmade shoes and fourteen-dollar gloves were symbols of gentility, whereas the dress was not and therefore could represent her economic status. But slavery or any like subordination is the specific image of emasculation. The South's hope for regeneration lies in its struggle itself to restore, not from outside pressure, to that part of its population the rights of manhood of which it is deprived. Understanding of this is proof of the boy's initiation and his right to the toga virilis. But his possession is still precarious. He has not yet, as individual or symbol, established himself, because one man cannot maintain this state alone, against an environment where the spurious image is predominant and where the unrecognizable sin, the impossible sin, has been committed: fratricide. A Gowrie cannot kill a Gowrie, but one has. The fraternity of the state cannot be destroyed by internecine conflict, but it has been. Out of the South's resistance to this impossibility, which exists, has come an integrity mixed with turpitude, the misplaced functions of the sexes, a misdirected and fragmentary homogeneity.

When this is understood, Lucas' relationship to the novel grows clear. He is the basic symbol of the southern predicament. He never actually performs as a character; that is not to say he is not characterized. He is the hone upon which all is sharpened. He is the society, both black and white, his white grandfather having been the founder of the plantation. He has inherited the manness (the signs of this are the handmade beaver hat, which was the grandfather's; the gold toothpick; the pistol; and the old frock coat), while his white cousin, the present owner, has inherited through the distaff side. Each is misplaced; each is confined by the isolation of this displacement and will remain so, so long as Lucas says: "I aint got no friends. I pays my way."

But there is hope. The boy's uncle tells him, "Don't stop." Don't stop trying to rectify injustice or to restore the true order. It is still possible to regenerate southern homogeneity, because of and not in spite of the sheriff, the old one-armed Gowrie, the hunter, the jail keeper, Miss Habersham, and himself. The uncle says: "The white and the black in the South should confederate: swap him the rest of the economic and political and cultural privileges which are his right, for the reversion of his capacity to wait and endure and survive. Then we would prevail." For at this time the man will dominate again, justice will be restored, and all will be ordered according to place and function, even to the exact degree of place and function. Then will the blood be purified of its foreign bodies.

There is one other point to make: the boy's active identity with the basic symbol. At the opening of the book, on a hunting trip to the plantation he falls into a creek of icy water, in November, goes under three times and comes up to confront Lucas: the first encounter. The shock of the experience and the sight immediately afterwards of Lucas (he appears almost miraculously), who does not help him, who even orders the boy's colored playmate to remove the pole, the only assistance offered (the crutch of matter), so that the boy can get out by his own effort, is a kind of baptism as a result of which he will be forevermore changed. Even the time of year marks it, the dead season which always precedes regeneration. The boy's recognition of his involvement, in spite of his efforts to free himself, even to the temptation of flight, sends him to Lucas' cell and commits him to the central adventure of the book. Lucas' attitude toward him at the creek and in the cell emphasizes the underlying symbolism of his presence. He asks nothing of anybody, not even the boy. He is intractable, even indifferent to the inherent threat in his situation. He merely directs the boy to go dig up the grave. Even in this he is impersonal and without specific information of what is to be found, so that the burden of the action is shifted to the boy as his, not Lucas', responsibility, as baptism in the Church puts the burden of salvation upon the communicant.

This extends the point of view still further, saying in effect that in the action of the boy, or of such as him and Miss Habersham, will the South's crucifixion be prevented; since it is persons such as they who can or will restore the true image by removing from within the initial injustice which has obscured it, at which time the threat of crucifixion, which comes out of the North, will have lost its excuse for being. This is the final enlargement of the point of view. The use of time in the action, from high noon until midnight (actually it becomes longer), is suggestive, and even the image of the three before the grave is suggestive; but quite rightly Faulkner does not belabor this. Within the needs of the action of a story the symbol to work must perform at every level as it does in this book. To do more than suggest the specific Crucifixion would weaken his narrative by introducing comparisons extraneous to his own truth and so compromise him.

Literary Portraits

JOHN CROWE RANSOM

A GENTLEMAN TO WHOM SO many are beholden has now reached his sixtieth year; twice the years, if we can believe another poet, it takes to drain the cup of folly, the moment in time when a man may pause to consider his worth, to judge and be judged. And yet not a time to be done with time. As so often in the past, John Ransom makes the occasion for his friends to observe the amenities. This in itself bears upon his worth. In the midst of confusion, rude hurry, when the very shards of society are pounding together, his birthday allows us to be civilized. The custom of praising one who has distinguished his profession reminds us that birthdays have meaning beyond the accident of birth, for the occasion predicates values, and values suppose forms and institutions; else there is that vast dissonance, the chaos of the accidental.

Of the men I have come to value, whether as teacher or friend, he has seemed the easiest to communicate with, the most natural in his ways; and yet one could not go further afield than to approach him by way of the natural man. The ease of communication depends upon something to communicate; the naturalness upon a great reserve. The presence of any superior mind in any given time or place is perhaps more than accident. It is best to accept the fact of the mind, then move as quickly as possible toward the qualities which make it unique. It is very hard to pin down the extent of his influence, because so much of it lies in the personal interchanges between him and a continuous stream of students. But it seems to me that one fact is of great importance: his relationships depend upon a sensibility that functions always in the same way. Any difference is a difference of degree, not of kind. I should like to explore this a little by way of an inheritance and a training.

His family, from an early settlement, flourished in two Middle Tennessee counties, where he was born and brought up. I think that this circumstance at this particular time, 1888 and the two decades following, is a matter of importance. Tennessee was a part of the Old West. It had been laid waste by the Civil War; but because its tradition was old enough to have roots and because it was a general farming country—particularly stock farming, which requires greater humanity than specialized planting—and again because Tennessee was a border state and returned quickly to the Union, it missed the extreme waste of Reconstruction and was able to resume fairly quickly a pattern of life.

But it was a chastened society. The people had believed so absolutely in the support of a just God for a just cause that when this cause went down to defeat, it became plain to all that they had sinned. Out of this grew a great questioning of the heart and a genuine humility before the fact of defeat. Religious debates were held all over the countryside, and they were heavily attended. If the subjects were unimaginative points of doctrine, the dialectics was learned. Spellbinders were about, but not overwhelmingly so. At the same time, along with this turning to God, there was a sentimentality which, feeling pressure from the outside, perverted and weakened the formal patterns of conduct. Vaguely felt was the shadow of coming events.

I have a point and I will make it briefly. John Ransom reached manhood under the training of such a society. Because of his father's calling, he must have been especially aware of the strength and weakness of the Protestant discipline. His secular education was at this time in Tennessee in the best tradition of humane learning. Certainly his training derived from a coherent view of life. It was the last possible moment to get so completely this particular kind of education, for this was a historic moment everywhere in the Western world, the latter part of the nineteenth and the first part of the twentieth centuries. It was the last moment of equilibrium, of peace and the enjoyment of the peaceful arts. It was the last time a man could know who he was. Or where he was from. It was the last time a man, without having to think, could say what was right and what was wrong. For almost overnight, with the automobile for symbol of the change, the community disappeared.

Although the historical shift was sudden, the stages of the revolution would proceed more slowly in the case of the individual; and especially was this so in the case of John Ransom. Because of what he was, he would be slow to accept the validity of the change. His was particularly the kind of sensibility which absorbed all that was form and style, the permanently recurring truths which a tradition hands on and guards. In a time of contradictions, where the lasting and the accidental intermingle, he might have expressed in his person the confused vision afflicting so many of this time. The critical part of his mind allowed him to distinguish the impurities, the sentimentalities, and the narrowness of a doctrine unequal to the complex, insoluble matters of experience. The dualism so eminently descriptive of his point of view allowed him to compare the richer tradition of Western civilization with the more limited strain of the particular Protestant Tennessee variety. His medium was the freemasonry of literature; but he by no means limited himself to this, although it absorbed a large part of his imagination and interest. Instinctively his position asserted itself whenever the occasion demanded, because his mind and sensibility were so tempered. Perhaps his more intuitive performance demands greater consideration than his conscious assertions. Others have critically presented the case for traditional value. He has represented it.

It is worth noting that he was slow to recognize the great change in attitude, in habits and manners, already well under way at the end of the First World War. It was his association with younger poets and critics, many of them his students, whose training contained the contradictions of their time, which served as the shock to his imagination and set him in the way of his mature work. The younger men more nearly represented the private sensibility before the spectacle of a breakdown in the common sensibility. His dualism contained a less ambiguous center of reference. His poetry, both in subject and form, was less private in its appeal, for he assumed a more common sympathy and understanding for the ever-recurrent contradictions of life, the disparity between form and content, between the Word and its exegesis. This provides the source of his irony and creates, in part, the tension of his style.

During the twenties and the thirties one had to reckon with the fact of general disorder. One wonders if a situation so foreign to his instincts may not have been responsible for his neglect of the Muse in favor of criticism and philosophy. But there was no betrayal of his innate conservative view of order. And now it seems that he is coming more and more into his own, for there is everywhere a search for some kind of balance. Never do the forces of disorder reach an absolute and final triumph. Never are they contained from below, but always by those who are able to withdraw the Image from the desperate shiftings of the pragmatists, who among themselves offer the part for the whole. The need now is for the wholeness of his view, and perhaps this defines the essential qualities of his value. Although his medium may seem isolated from common affairs, the artist and thinker does not work in a common way.

ALLEN TATE

It was John Ransom who introduced me to Allen Tate. I was at Yale working with George Pierce Baker (where I learned what a scene was), and he wrote me there and gave me his address in New York. So I owe to John Ransom, among other things, a long and cherished friendship. It could be said that I owe him my wife, since it was Tate who some years later introduced me to her. But in this kind of sorites where does gratitude end? It neither begins nor ends, for friendship cannot afford to measure the occasions for its uses nor mark too narrowly the moments of communion. Certainly all this was in the future. Yet the future may be no more than the suspension of what is always present, awaiting the moment, the seeming accident in which it finds its substantial form. In the Old West of Tennessee and Kentucky people of like interests and station were bound to know each other or at least know the stories of common friends whose personalities were interesting enough for gossip or tales. I'm sure I must have played with Tate at Mont-eagle, and Nicholson Springs was only a few miles from Estill Springs. And who can say it was not the tone of Captain Beard's voice reciting poetry upon the veranda of the summer boardinghouse at Estill, pausing only long enough to call to his wife, "Maria, Maria, the hogs are in the yard," which marked the little boy with the enormous head?

At any rate the day I presented myself at the basement entrance of 27 Bank Street I was met with a severe and courteous formality—it was as if the eyes reflected but did not see what was before them. Later I came to recognize this as a mask to keep the world at a distance, because of the artist's necessity to be saved interruptions while at work, or merely to save himself boredom, which he cannot hide. I learned this necessity for withdrawal in his house, as I learned that the artist's discipline is almost its only reward. Once a caller asked for Katherine Anne Porter at this same address and was received with grave decorum and told, with a bow, "The ladies of this house are at the riot in Union Square." The bow, as well as the words, was a conscious emphasis upon the irony of his situation, the common situation of the artist living in New York who belongs to no cliques and demands that the profession of letters be accepted as a profession. He, more than any other writer, has upheld this professionalism of letters. This attitude is obviously more French than English and is, I feel, unique in the English-speaking world, at least to the extent he carried and carries it. Ford Madox Ford had this sense of himself as a writer, but he would have claimed not England but Europe for his habitation. Tate would see Europe for what it is historically, as it relates to our common inheritance. To hold this position has not been without its price. I have at times thought that he had advanced himself into tactically untenable positions or used too much force upon what seemed only an outpost engagement. But in a rearguard action, after the campaign and, indeed, the cause is lost, strategy and tactics become one and the same thing; that is, "no bulge," as General Forrest called it, can be allowed to the enemy as your force retreats, lest all be swept into oblivion.

Every serious writer has one subject, I believe, which he spends his life exploring and delivering as fully as he may. Tate's subject is simply what is left of Christendom, that Western knowledge of ourselves which is our identity. He may be classed as a religious writer, and that from the very beginning. The literary historian is likely to see his work as the best expression of the crucial drama of our time. "We've cracked the hemispheres with careless hand!" Does language more poetically describe the plight of Western civilization? He has many voices: verse, biography, criticism, essay, even fiction—but one language and one subject. In rereading him, I was surprised to find that, even as a young man, especially a young man in the twenties, he saw the religious doubt, the failure of belief, as crucial. In the same way he accepted the South's defeat not as a private or local affair but as the last great defense in a going society of those values, particularly human, we know as Christian. Even in the earlier verse such as "Causerie" and "Last Days of Alice" the ironic complaint derives from and hangs upon this ambiguity of belief. In *I'll Take My Stand* it was his essay which argued the religious position. The diversity and range, certainly in the verse, can be seen in the manner in which he divides his collected poems into sections. Early pieces are put by the latest, but the book opens with the larger treatments of his position, the historical and cultural past, not as background but as vision immediately related to the poet and all others now living. The first section opens with "The Mediterranean" and closes with the "Ode to the Confederate Dead." The final irony of the sound of nature's soughing of the leaves serves for a transition to the other parts of the book.

The sixtieth year is a wonderfully anonymous marking of time—not yet three score and ten; nor, alas, that station where time reverses his light heels; yet it is the last station where one may look both forward and back. Behind him lies a body of work anyone would be proud to call a life's work. And yet there is time for it to be only the great body which awaits its crown. As I myself skirmish the borders of this anniversary, I find that I am close enough to hear the secret so well kept. Ours is the immortal generation. And how do I know it? I know it with my sixtieth-looking eyes, which see now, at last, that it is not we who are getting older, but the young who are getting younger, smoother-cheeked, more innocent-eyed, so that it is a marvel to find that the sounds they are making are words, perhaps language even.

CAROLINE GORDON

Reading Miss Gordon's fiction, you are rarely conscious of the sex of the writer. This is the definitive measure of her craftmanship and of her devotion to its practice. Given an equal talent and luck, the major artist is distinguished from the minor by energy. And Miss Gordon was endowed with all of energy's properties. I only know of one other who sustains the same kind of extravagant display of vitality. I can hear the gallop of Miss Gordon's typewriter in correspondence. She rarely paused for typing errors. In action her mind could not delay. As in her fiction, the drive of her sentences delights the eye. The untidy page of the letter is a part of its form. She used to complain that it takes as much time to write a letter as it does a page of fiction. She further said that if you waited long enough, you didn't have to answer. Her letters all had the quality of her fiction. Wherever the word was concerned, she showed herself a devoted, committed writer. The master was Henry James, introduced probably by Ford Madox Ford, who worked with her on her first novel, *Penhally*. Ford himself was such an artist, but no one could have suffered the act as did she. Allen Tate, her husband, in the fierce concentration upon his craft, whether verse or criticism, or his one novel, sustained in her presence this ancient practice. But she was more vocal about it. Flaubert was usually her example, and her fervor was catching, despite her complaint that it was like being on the chain gang.

I have not mentioned her generosity to other writers, particularly beginners with a sure talent. To their work she brought the same attention that she would bring to her own. The great example of this patronage is Flannery O'Connor. Letter after letter of instruction and advice passed between them. Nothing was withheld on the one part; nor did false pride show on the other. Indeed, it could be said that fundamentally their subject was the same: what a society, materialistic and mechanical, does to the human psyche. They were both Roman Catholic, Miss O'Connor by cradle, Miss Gordon by choice. This distinction made the difference in their work. They were both southern to the marrow of their bones. Being set apart by her formal religion gave to Miss O'Connor a perspective on the Protestant world about her. Miss Gordon was born into that world but understood better the range of its hierarchy. She had a peculiar sense of it as it was before its defeat and degeneration. But her view was historic and tragic. The defeat of the Confederacy and the consequent destruction of southern, that is, the transplanted segment of European, society, and its effect upon the succeeding generations gave her the substance for her earlier fiction. Her later fiction concerns the damage into the third generation of what cracked and broken forms do to human beings. Her actors belong to a different category from Miss O'Connor's. Most of her work was done before she joined the Roman church, and it seems to me that the fiction whose complications derive from her immersion in the new faith is less satisfactory. A universal church that in her known society is not universal cannot find the concrete images or manners to deliver a satisfactory fiction. She must have felt this, as she turned to the Greek-Roman world of myth and fable for her last book, which was to be completed by another book laid among her family in Kentucky. This book was never completed. Presumably it would reveal in the disparity of time the same constant myths but with forms composed of differing mores. Now that she is elsewhere, in a place or condition where presumably all things are known and all hearts clarified, if I have misunderstood her intentions, I can feel reasonably exempt from a scarifying descent upon any imprudence of statement. I hope.

FLANNERY O'CONNOR

Years ago at Iowa City in a rather informal class meeting I read aloud a story by one of the students. I was told later that it was understood that I would know how to pronounce in good country idiom the word *chitling*, which appeared in the story. At once it was obvious that the author of the story was herself not only southern but exceptionally gifted. The idiom for her characters rang with all the truth of the real thing, but the real thing heightened. It resembled in tone and choice of words all country speech I had ever heard, but I couldn't quite place it. And then I realized that what she had done was what any first-rate artist always does—she had made something more essential than life but resembling it. She had done this by the use of crucial words and the proper rhythm raised to a higher power. She was making her own language for the subject already seen to be uniquely her own.

This, of course, was Flannery O'Connor.

There is never any mistaking the authentic voice. And she had this voice if anybody ever did. It should be noted that she was from Georgia, because people in life and in fiction do not exist in a vacuum. The bad kind of provincial writing anywhere emphasizes costume and ornament or the convention with no content. This is one definition of local color. But Miss O'Connor made formal by use of southern manners and mores the subject central to Christendom in its imperiled plight in our time. The world now, after a long decline of the order of Christendom, is predominantly secular. The general enveloping action of her stories is a state not predominantly but absolutely secular and material, in which her heroes and heroines miss salvation because of complete selfishness and self-love. Actually it is impossible to find any society so given over totally to the evil nature of man. This can be done only in an art form. Hence the monstrosity and grotesqueness of her characters. Her action comes closer to allegory, but since her actors do not represent abstract qualities but enjoy the roundness of humankind, I would say that her fiction resembles more nearly a morality play. By showing the terrifying nature of a society entirely material and secular, with little or no relieving charity, she intended, I think, to shock us into an awareness of the present disguise the enemy of man now assumes.

She was courageous in her work, having to resist a mortal disease with a medicine no less dangerous, to which she finally succumbed. She was a young woman, but perhaps her work was done. One can admire her long fight against herself so that her work might get done. The personal annihilation is the habit of all serious writers, to die in one way and be revived in another. So after all, with Miss O'Connor we may grieve but not regret the greater intensity in her life and death of the artist's common plight.

Part III

History and Vision in Tolstoy's War and Peace

I SHOULD LIKE TO TALK A LIT-
tle about the novel whose subject
lies in the past. I must say right off
that I am distinguishing fiction as an
art from the mere storytelling habit
and need, which is universal and
continuous and of itself may or may
not have form, except of course in
the most rudimentary way. But certainly to be an art, it must be formally conceived and delivered. To
comprehend the shape and qualities
of such a work, it is necessary to read
it for the totality of its meaning, an
undertaking more often promised
than done. Such reading at once
brings us up against the larger matter of terminology. Percy Lubbock
regrets the novel did not appear a
hundred years earlier, so that it
could have fallen into the hands of
the schoolmen of the seventeenth
century, who, he feels, would have
given it a proper nomenclature. At
any rate the lack of some commonly
accepted set of terms has got both
the writer and the critical reader
into talking at cross-purposes and,
even with the best of instruments,
into reading badly.

For example, very often we find a
novel discussed and indeed read in
terms of the social sciences. If we are

going to apply one area of knowledge as the means of rendering the meaning of another, we are bound to compound confusion. The very shape of tools is defined by the work they do. No cabinetmaker in his right mind would pick up a foot adze to shape the inlay of a tabletop; and yet how often and with what facility is it said that Dostoevsky is a psychological novelist. Naturally the writer confronts the psyche of his personalities, but so does the cabinetmaker his wood. And whose psychology, Freud's, Adler's, Jung's, or the Chicago School's? There is less confusion in this matter at least upon Jung's part. In *Psychology and Literature* he warns us that there is "a fundamental difference of approach between the psychologist's examination of a literary work and that of the literary critic." What is of decisive importance for one may be irrelevant to the other, and he adds, "Literary products of highly dubious merit are often of the greatest interest to the psychologist," for example, those of Rider Haggard and Benoit.

But I think the case is clearest in the so-called sociological novel. This area of study, at least in its public expression, commits in a secular way the Puritan heresy. It puts evil in the object. If we keep changing plan for plan, it seems to say, we will finally happen upon one which will solve all of man's maladjustments. What a curious inversion of Platonism, or anarchic Platonism, for the ideal image is never present, only a vague feeling for the ideal, which practically never lets the right hand know what the left is doing. I can't help thinking of King Lear. Just what plan would have made Goneril and Regan proper daughters? Certainly the king's didn't. Anyway, such a conception, put to the uses of fiction, directs the emphasis of meaning not upon the action but upon the residual implication of the action. It deprives the author of the very center of his concern, the humanity of his actors. If evil lies outside mankind, man can only be good or neutral. In either case no action is possible. At the best you get a poor kind of allegory; at its usual worst, propaganda.

This brings me to my particular enquiry, the novelist's use of a field where he has rights along with another social scientist, the historian—and not only that, but where he must use certain methods of investigation which the historian himself uses. (I would like to add that it seems to me highly arbitrary to place the historian among the social scientists.) The entanglement here seems harder to unravel, for criticism has come to accept a joint authority over the same area: that is, literary criticism has. Witness the term *historical novel*, everywhere accepted by writer, publisher, critic as a special kind of fiction. The term has bothered me for some time. It makes an ambiguous specification which more often than not obscures the proper reading of a book. It implies that if the book is not all it ought to be as fiction, the reader can fall back upon its history. But can he? Does history exist in a vacuum, apart from the actors who make it? And obversely, where the *history* is doubtful can you say the fiction is good? How can you separate it? And how often does criticism pass over blocks of history in a book, lumps of yeast which have not worked the dough; or how often does it pass briefly over public figures so obviously public, who move over the scene stiffly like papier-mâché figures or poorly disguised in some quasi-mythological dress. Andrew Jackson—must he speak with flamboyant illiteracy because he gave his name to a certain kind of democracy? Or Lincoln, the poor young lawyer who joined the Whigs, the rich man's party, the lover who left his affianced at the pulpit—how does this behavior modify that compassionate heart which died that Jay Gould and the freedmen might thrive with equal opportunity? Old Hickory and the Great Martyr may belong to the mythologizing instincts of a people but not to a work of art. They will not stand up there, for they lack what Andrew Jackson and Abraham Lincoln had in life, and that is humanity. And this is the first concern of the novelist. If his people lack this, no matter what he achieves, he fails in fiction.

This very illusion of life defines the difference between history as science and history as fiction. For this reason the well-wrought novel is the only way of recovering the illusion of past time. I say illusion because finally, I think, we must leave the truth to God. The question, then, to ask is not, Is the story historically sound? It is, Does the action represent the behavior of men in this given situation (which must include the author's imagination)? Does it show what really happened, not the report of what seemed to happen? And secondly, does the form make the most of the subject; is the subject all used up in the form (paraphrasing Lubbock)? The critical reader asks literary questions, which are the only questions he can ask about a literary form. His answer will automatically determine whether the history is sound.

Action can only take place by means of the institutional restraints of society. It is just here that the novelist and the historian are closest together. They both must do the research necessary to recover manners and customs, codes, public and private disciplines, all those habits and rituals which make up a pattern of culture. But the novelist must go further than the historian. He is not in search of principles and causes but of people. He must become the research; like Alice, he must walk through the looking glass of time and be there, where strange manners are no longer strange but familiar, at least acceptable. He metamorphoses the pastness of the past into the moving present. The reader becomes the witness. He is there; he sees; he tastes; he smells—if the author succeeds. This involves all the technical knowledge and vision which goes into the making of any good novel; but when the fiction assumes the past, it places an extra burden upon the artist. And this pressure makes another value which raises the sense of contemporaneity to a higher power: you have not only the illusion of the present, but the past permeates the immediacy of this illusion; the fictive personalities take on a certain clairvoyance, the action a double meaning, as if the actors, while performing, disclose the essential meaning of their time, even of all time. (This is possible.) This is literary irony at a high level, an irony that restores vitality to tradition—the past is not dead but alive; the contemporary scene then seems merely one division of an accumulation of the segments of time, wherein live people act out their private destinies in the context of a common destiny which is their history. This paradox of a past which is the present is the peculiar possibility of fiction whose subject lies in some definite period of history.

If the recovery of the total experience of a book is the critical reader's task, what I am saying, I suppose, is that the novel must be judged and accepted on its own terms and that any specification not literary distorts and falsifies it, extracts from it a half-truth or another kind of meaning. Now I come to the real difficulty: what are those terms? I have quoted Lubbock wishing for an anachronism: those schoolmen of the seventeenth century. I will have to confess that the situation, to use a military euphemism, is rather fluid. James and Flaubert made great sense in an effort to clarify this terminology, which certainly is the reasonable place to begin. And Lubbock, interpreting James, adds fresh terms and a retooling of terms taken over from the material arts. His essential position is this: the artist creates; the critic becomes an artist by re-creating as nearly as he may what the artist has done. The critic must proceed in a workmanlike way. The artist is a craftsman; the critic cannot be less. In pursuit of this method I began to ask myself what device there might be which was crucial to the development of the fable. In novels which are dramatic, which render the direct impression of life, this device seems to me to be a central image, which might also be a dominating symbol, placed at the post of observation and at the center of the author's seeing eye. It was right to begin here, because it is here the author began. This image will not take the final measure of a book, but once it is located, there will be less risk of misreading, for there will be a common referent. The risk remains, since finally the creative act cannot be described, even by the creator himself. To embody in words, formally, some intensity of vision affirms a mystery. It is a mystery anyhow, but more of one because a concrete method acts upon the intangible, invisible content of the mind to effect this embodiment.

You will not find a controlling image in the memoir type of novel, nor in the narrative which reports the complication. Such works always give it to you secondhand. The reader is never the witness. There is, to paraphrase Lubbock again, always someone standing between him and the action, talking about it. He may talk very well and hold you to the end, as does Thackeray; but it is a lesser art, because a report is never so dramatic as the action itself. Mark Twain's *Joan of Arc* is a specimen of the failure of this kind of novel. There is not a scene in it, not even the trial or the burning. Everything, even the battles, is secondhand. If any subject ever cried out for a controlling image, it is the story of the adolescent girl who saved France and undid the results of the Hundred Years' War. It is ready-made. Through a Virgin, God gave the world its Savior, and the world crucified Him. Through His angels another virgin saved France, and France let France's enemies burn her. Here is the oldest subject of Western civilization— betrayal, open to individual and universal complementary action. Twain muffed it. His narrator is a follower, in afteryears remembering the sequence of events, all with the blurred edge of hero worship and nostalgia. I do not believe it is the way old soldiers remember. They forget the sequence of events; they remember the sharp image. Even Twain's humor fails him. He either would not or could not confront his material. The image was there for him, but so was sentimentality and special pleading.

But I want to take a book that succeeds, not one which fails. It is a book with a great historic scene, one recognized to be brilliant, one continu- ously read, and one whose direction shows the hand of a master. This might be *Kristin Lavransdatter*, but it is *War and Peace*, because the feeling in certain quarters is that Tolstoy presents a mountain of material which he never actually reduced to its proper form. Lubbock feels that "*War and Peace* is like an Iliad, the story of certain men, and an Aeneid, the story of a nation, compressed into one book by a man who never so much as noticed that he was Homer and Virgil by turns." He contends that the subject is youth and age, the revolution of life marked by the rising and sinking of a certain generation. It was with this cycle that Tolstoy began, only to let himself be diverted by the drama of Napoleon and Kutuzov, Europe against the imperial destiny of Russia. Out of this confusion, he says, Tolstoy allows himself, before the turning point of the book is reached, to assume a change of attitude and method. Nicholas, the delightful boy of all time, and Natasha, the delightful girl, become simply the hero and heroine of a particular story. That rendering of the spirit of youth, with which the book began, is therefore diminished, this loss being reflected in the lack of the large humane irony so evident in the tone of the book at the start but which does not persist through all its phases.

In spite of Lubbock's brilliant critical intuition and clarity of judgment he falls short here of his own precept: that of being fully re-creative. A glimmer of doubt crosses his mind, for he asks whether Tolstoy has "intentionally coupled his two themes," that is, whether he "set the unchanging story of life against the momentary tumult, which makes such a stir in the history-books, but which passes, leaving the other story still unrolling forever. Perhaps he did; but I am looking only at his book, and I can see no hint of it in the length and breadth of the novel as it stands; I can discover no angle at which the two stories will appear to unite and merge in a single impression. [What about Prince Andrew wounded, under the blue sky?] Neither is subordinate to the other, and there is nothing above them [what more *could* there be?] to which they are both related."

There may be nothing above the action, but there is certainly something below it, at the post of observation, where it should be; and this something is the controlling image. The technical procedure of looking for some such image would have saved him a blurring of the eyes in his search for meaning and that old mischance of putting our partial impression as the author's whole—in this instance "the unchanging story of life against the momentary tumult." The Image denies that there are two stories, one of war and one of peace. War and peace are the extremes of action, the discord which is the source of life, the means by which the totality of man's experience may be rendered. Peace is no more the unchanging story of life than is war. Both, the memory of man going not to the contrary, roll along forever in timely alternations, and who is to say that peace does not have its momentary tumults, too?

No, it is one story, if a story of the scope of life itself. Only one other story, *Kristin Lavransdatter*, allows the reader to experience so fully the variety and complexities of private and public action, from the largest panorama to the small but sharply done scene; from an incident so clear, illuminating some moment of truth, to the military campaigns and battles involving hundreds of thousands of men and the destinies of races and peoples, focused upon the curve of the distant view or close up as the experience of one man. Whether it is a young girl at her first ball or a mother who will suffer any humiliation for the well-being of her son, it is all there. It is Russian, but it is life anywhere, anytime. No one person, then, could carry the burden of meaning. Only the recurring image can contain it.

At first this image to focus the double vision (sight into the world and insight into self) might seem to lie within Tolstoy's historical argument about the man of destiny and the forces he thinks he controls. But this won't hold up; it leaves out too much. And technically it is anterior to the writing of the book, a part of the scaffolding the author did not remove. It *is* part of the feeling out of which the book was written. It is the feeling insofar as it can express itself by argument, which is hostile to artistic procedure. It has marred his treatment of Napoleon and his marshals. At times they seem allegorical figures, at times caricatures. As representatives of his theory, too often their humanity is excluded, a humanity his Russian characters and certain individual French soldiers always have. When he thinks of the people as forces which desecrate Russia, he cannot objectify his feeling, place it outside himself. It is a failure of artistic discipline. Tolstoy the Russian, not Tolstoy the artist, is speaking in this instance. These essays in a book of fiction are, therefore, a flaw. The author has withdrawn from his post of observation to argue. But when he is at the post, this feeling, purified of all that is extraneous to art, becomes the Image, at once the essence of the subject and its form. This Image I take to be somewhere in the dramatic plight, the dichotomy, in which Russia found herself after the arbitrary Europeanization by Peter the Great.

Such is a hypothesis got from a conscious search for the Image, and it must be examined against the detail of the action which ought finally to reveal the author's vision. You can begin almost anywhere: for example, in the two distinct sets of characters which the author opposes in the conflict. There is the worldly set which revolves about the court, whose habits are predominantly European. Petersburg, that capital representing the artificial synthesis of culture, is this set's actual and symbolic habitation. On the other side you have those others, the Rostovs, the peasants, all who look to Moscow, the holy city, as their spiritual and physical center. This division extends to the armies: Napoleon and Kutuzov, of course; but in the army itself the split is distinct. There are the Russian generals like Bagration, who dies on the left at Borodino, and the foreign generals, particularly the Germans, whose interest is not Russia but their professional ambitions. These abstract theorists seem almost abstractions themselves beside the failing, battered, too-ready-to-weep but how human Kutuzov, who goes to sleep in staff meetings and at moments of crisis listens not to the messenger's words but studies his face, and there reads the true condition of affairs. It is to this old Russian, against the wishes of the czar and the court, that the people commit the defense of Russia when Napoleon actually invades the holy soil, when the war, in effect, ceases to be a matter of European politics and becomes a matter of Russian life or death. Kutuzov has the two qualities which the protagonists risk in the action: humanity, with its frailties and strength; but more important, that mystical communion with the soul and body of Holy Russia, which is every compatriot's inheritance. When Kutuzov takes command, he mentions no strategic theory. He says, "They'll eat horseflesh yet." And because he instinctively knows that the real issue is the Russian inheritance, which he never loses sight of, even when Moscow is abandoned, his policy symbolizes the trimph of the true over the spurious. When the last foreign soldier goes away, his function is served and he quickly dies.

The Czar Alexander personifies this division. In his handsome, youthful person reviewing the army he is the presence of Russia, the little father, whom the soldiers, and especially Nicholas Rostov, spontaneously recognize as such and instantly love. But he is also the monarch, imbued with the liberal ideas of the French Revolution, the defender of Europe against its common enemy. In this role it is implied that he wastes the blood and treasure of Russia to no purpose, at least to no Russian purpose. When he makes peace at Tilsit, the fraternizing between Russian and French officers seems to Nicholas, through whose eyes the scene is witnessed, not only a betrayal of the Russian dead but unnatural in the literal meaning of that word.

The subject, then, seems to lie in the conflict which these two kinds of people represent and personify. The thing at stake is the Russian inheritance. Externally it is threatened by foreign ideas and a foreign army; internally, by a cultural schism, still by foreign ideas which intrude upon the patriarchal and oriental relationship between rulers and the ruled, but more particularly, in the case of individuals, between the soul and worldly temptation. In body and spirit it is a question of salvation. In war and peace, in public and private affairs, in the rise and fall of families, the antagonists and protagonists meet always in the terms of this dramatic involvement. The burden of this action is specifically carried by two families, the Rostovs and the Bolkonskys; but if you should try to find one individual who more nearly represented the intention, the structure hidden in the "abyss of the nucleus," this person would be Pierre Bezuhov.

He enters the fashionable drawing room of Anna Pavlovna and the central complication is under way, in the very first pages of the book. Beneath the glittering and well-groomed surface of this Petersburg drawing room, Tolstoy lets you understand, is played a cynical and brutal game of self-interest. In Anna's salon fashion governs. Its maneuvers are always tactical. There are sudden advances and retreats, always brilliantly executed, which must follow the shifts of politics and worldly interest. Anna manages her entourage like a good general, never allowing any genuine belief or emotion to intrude, for such belief would disarrange the artificial conventions which are able to control reality, keep it at a distance, only so long as the surface becomes the limits of action. With the instincts of a good general she views the entrance of Pierre with alarm, "as something too big and out of place." It is just that Russia is too big and out of place for her house. Pierre has already been compared to a bear, but a bear lumbering and hampered. He is massively built, but he wears glasses. Since he has just returned from a long foreign residence and education, does this suggest a vision impaired? Certainly he embarrasses his hostess by naïvely speaking out his true beliefs.

Tolstoy, as if he were afraid you would miss his intention, soon after brings Pierre into the Rostov household. This is in Moscow and in every way is the direct antithesis of what has gone on in Petersburg. The entertainment is not for some celebrity of the moment; it is the traditional name day of the mother and daughter Rostov. Here Pierre is accepted as a person, lovable but eccentric, interesting for his prospects. He is accepted as a human being, in a given society, in terms of his position in that society. It even has the exact opposite of Anna Pavlovna in Marya Dmitrievna. She is old-fashioned, guarding the inherited mores with her free tongue, always speaking her mind, always genuine, with a good heart beneath the brusque exterior. It is not necessary to list the characteristics of her opposite in Petersburg, but time and again, with a too-obvious comparison, Tolstoy makes his point. Behind the formalities (not the formalism of Petersburg) of the name-day occasion one sees the true purpose of any society that has a history. Its people come and go, are together because they want to be together or because families must attend to family interest and pleasures. And here the entertainment is guided not by fashion but by manners, the institutional means of intercourse, maintained by the individual and family discipline and code, which may outlast the individual but not the family.

These two households are brought before the reader early in the book because, as well as serving his larger intention, Tolstoy specifically needs to prepare the right kind of mise-en-scène for the two wives which Pierre takes unto himself. The one from Petersburg is the false wife; the one from Moscow is the true wife. So it is that his sincerity sets him apart in Anna's salon; but his ideas, blurring his vision, set him apart at this date from Russia. But Tolstoy has set him apart even more radically. He has made him a bastard of a great house, that is, the blood denied its inheritance by no act of its own. To intensify this isolation he is given a foreign name: Monsieur Pierre. His story is the conflict which arises out of his search for this inheritance. It takes place at two levels, the worldly level and in his own soul. In his fortunes the subject central to the book is made literal and specific.

Each level has its internal complication, conflict, and resolution; but the action of each never discloses itself separately, as Lubbock suggests it does. The growth of the novel's structure is organic, in its two main aspects and in the aspects of all its parts. The different stages, to be specific, of Pierre's

search for the matter which will embody his spirit appear first as complications in his external fortunes; and as they appear there, they also affect the
private fortunes of individuals and families, and these the larger cultural
issues Petersburg and Moscow stand for.

Pierre recovers his temporal inheritance first, an inheritance so immense
it seems almost Russia itself; but as far as the action is concerned, he is
entirely neutral. He is in no way, except as a pawn moved about, involved.
He is not even aware that the conflict of one of the richest episodes concerns
him. The protagonist here is a minor character, a woman wellborn but
penniless, and certainly powerless in the counters used by the world. But
she has one thing, passionate and selfless devotion to her son. Hoping to
gain a moiety of the inheritance for him, she frustrates the worldly power of
Prince Vassily, who brings to bear all his talents and prestige to steal the
inheritance from Pierre. The woman's triumph is the triumph of the human
and the devoted; and the world, in spite of its power, its vast pretensions,
and its cunning, loses.

The episode in another way concentrates the meaning into symbol. The
dying prince, Catherine's favorite and grandee, stands for an older order,
just as Catherine stands for a Russia unimpaired by newfangledness. She
who used old Poniatowsky's throne for a toilet seat had little in common
with the liberalism of Alexander. The relationship of this prince to this
queen does more than suggest the personification of the masculine counterpart to Russia, for Holy Russia is Mother Russia; and that means essentially
the mystical union between man and woman, forests and plain—the my-
thologem of mother earth, out of which life comes, suckling all things but
above all the peasantry, its natural children, inarticulate, brutal, instinctive, irrational as the force of life is irrational. Even dying, the old
prince suggests the control of this power, with his almost metaphysical
beauty, his leonine head and a strength even in his helpless condition which
makes all those around him seem small and ineffectual.

But he is also a symbol of a greater symbol. Remote in his inner chamber,
there is a space around him and an air, and it is not of this world. The
scurrying, the confusion which is everywhere about, moves withdrawn from
the ominous quiet of his invisible presence (he is seen only at the end of the
scene)—for he is also death. And death is the reality which decisively
reveals the world's vanity in a larger action and in so doing intensifies the

more specific action of the novel. It is there to warn that there is a counterpart to life, which Lubbock feels Tolstoy meant the book to be about, in
spite of the title and all the evidence to the contrary. Technically, as scene,
it prepares for and works through all the other incidents which have to do
with the two great realities, particularly when Prince Andrew, wounded
almost to death, under the expanse of the sky, looks up at Napoleon, his
former idol, and understands the nothingness of power and worldly vanity.
And coming after the frivolous persiflage of the young princess' words about
her husband going off to get himself killed, it points towards the consequences of such frivolity.

Pierre's legal inheritance is only the outward form. Within he is still
bewildered. The spiritual bar sinister, disassociating the moral and natural
parts of his being, remains a barrier between himself and a true expression of
his being. His story now becomes the search for that which will express the
innocence and integrity of his being. Because he lacks this, he aimlessly
drifts, wasting his strength, his good nature, his amiability, his great gifts of
feeling, enchanted by carnal appetites, the very food Petersburg eats. Everybody loots his inheritance. He cannot say no; his good nature sees need
everywhere; but it is because he feels the shame of his position that he
cannot act. Prince Vassily, thwarted in his effort to steal the legal inheritance, is able to get it by marrying him to his daughter Hélène. She appeals
to Pierre's lust, to that which makes the bastard; and he knows it, knows he
is being tricked, but can do nothing. Marriage as a sacrament, subduing the
natural man to a spiritual end, and as an institution, bringing children into
being and so perpetuating the family, the true unit of society, is absent here.
This absence indicates that Pierre, in spite of his legal possession, is still lost
on the left. And by implication Petersburg, in its view of marriage, wears
the bar sinister.

His wife cuckolds him; half-heartedly he fights a duel, feeling that he is
the true offender. He separates from his wife and gives her the larger share of
his income. This is the period of enchantment by illusory images. Still in
search of himself, he next turns to the fraternity of Masons for salvation.
But when he tries to put into practice its preachments by improving the
condition of his peasants, he falls into that easy, corrupting illusion of
achievement all reformers know, who think to do a thing without experi-
encing the pain and sorrow of doing it. He delegates the authority to his

steward, which compounds the fraud and, instead of improving their lot, increases their burdens. This effort at brotherhood fails, because it is too private and too worldly. It takes Moscow's burning to restore him to his own. Imprisoned with common fellows, shorn of possessions and power, he suffers in his person the humiliation, the pain, and sorrows of man's common lot. He recovers his humanity through his actual knowledge and sharing of brotherhood. The burning symbolizes Russia's ordeal and his own, and they become one. At this climactic moment the purification by fire frees him of that which has divided him from his own, as the empty, burning city miraculously turns Napoleon's army into a mob and foretells Russia's deliverance. The false leaders, his own false ideas, are literally burned away. The mystical brotherhood between all Russians, at the price of this ordeal, is renewed. Like the good craftsman he is, Tolstoy does not let this happen too generally. He uses Pierre's close companionship with a fellow prisoner in a series of concrete incidents to bring about his regeneration. His other companions in sorrow he later forgot, but "Platon Karataev remained forever in his mind the strongest and most precious memory and the personification of everything Russian, kindly, and round." There is an indestructibility about the almost peasant Karataev. This is the indestructibility of life itself, of the seasonal return, which all men know but which the peasant knows instinctively. He is the Russian Everyman, who prays to horse saints because all life receives his compassion. He speaks like the countryman in proverbs: "Let me lie down like a stone, O God, and rise up like new bread"; of Moscow, "She's the mother of cities. One must be sad to see it [the burning]. Yes, the maggot gnaws the cabbage, but it dies before it's done." Pierre, lying beside him, feels "that the world that had been shattered was rising up now in his soul, in new beauty, and on new foundations that could not be shaken."

What has been shattered are the false illusions, the false education, which have stood in the way of Pierre's true destiny. The means to and meaning of this destiny have all along been about him, only he was blind and divided against himself. Karataev has been the interpreter, as Kutuzov interprets for all Russia. In his presence Pierre rises up like new bread. The maggot Napoleon dies before he can finish his destruction, and dies not from the strategy of foreign generals but of the corruptible before the incorruptible, which is the force of life itself, defined by the Russian's feeling for the land which bears him. Lubbock was right, as far as he went, in saying the book was about the turn of one generation; but this is merely one aspect of the total meaning. The illusion of life was so magnificently done that it misled Lubbock. There is such variety of character and circumstance that the core of meaning is overlaid, but this is just as it should be. Only by such means can the idea become fiction. Behind all this teeming life is the Russian land as the image of the seasonal pattern—youth, middle age, old age, and death; then birth again—the indestructibility of life, whose two extreme phases are death and regeneration. But the physical expanse of land is too great to see, too great even of itself for man to have any feeling about it until he personifies it. For Russia this personification is the image of the Little Mother, as Moscow is the mother of cities.

It is the acceptance of this which regenerates Pierre. Lubbock complains that the story diminishes its effect by becoming the story of the private lives of Natasha and the others, but he fails to see what Natasha, after her marriage to Pierre, represents apart from this privacy. Both she and Pierre have changed, but certainly not to take into account the effect of experience would be false. Certainly Lubbock has made nothing of Pierre's moment of illumination. After his expiation in sorrow, out of which has come his revelation, for it is nothing less than this, every decision he makes is the right decision, for he has now come into his total inheritance. He has no difficulty in deciding on business matters. He is freed by death from the false wife, Hélène. The toast of Petersburg dies of an abortion. By her attempt to evade childbearing, she denies her natural function only to discover nature's penalty and man's incompetence before nature. This is Tolstoy's final comment on Petersburg. Pierre then marries Natasha, and the girl of all time becomes the mother of all time; and Natasha represents in the personal, private, and institutional life which she and Pierre make what Holy Russia represents in the mystical and finally the religious acceptance of the eternal, ever-recurring source of life. And life is indestructible.

And it is this, this particular sense of life, struggling to break through the alien form which the state suffers and, privately, to deliver the soul from its carnal appetites, which becomes the kernel of meaning in the book; or to put it another way, it becomes the image, or rather images, for there are almost as many as the degree and variety of experience permit. Pierre is the most comprehensive one. But there is his counterpart, Prince Andrew, whose most characteristic feature is intellectual pride, that sin above all most difficult to overcome. This pride leads him to worship false gods, to endanger his love for Russia. It almost causes him to ruin Natasha. So great is it that only death can bring him into the right relationship to his love and to his land. Nicholas, the delightful boy of all time, becomes the best master of all time, because his simple heart, almost a natural innocence, has resisted, or has not even been affected by, the false mask which has been the occasion for the action of the book. Like the peasant, he must exhibit and suffer and achieve the virtues man can, since Adam, the first Immigrant, was turned away from the Garden. But his instinct turns him to Princess Marya, who teaches him compassion and pity, and out of love for her he learns self-discipline and restraint, which with his natural gifts and simple pursuit of his interests make him the best master within the peasants' memory.

And so I could go on, but it is not my purpose to burden you with a complete exegesis of *War and Peace.* That would take time indeed. I have hoped to be discursive enough to show an approach to the total reading of fiction as fiction, particularly when it is laid in past time, which, like the other arts, also gives that impression of life as it lifts the reader out of the accidents and the mechanics of living and, momentarily at least, elevates the imagination to the intensity of vision.

In Defense of a Passionate and Incorruptible Heart: Flaubert's Madame Bovary

BEFORE A GROWING NIHILISM in literature I want to talk about a book and its heroine, a book which is now neglected in its own country before the existentialist sense of experience and the misuse of the stream of consciousness by certain contemporary authors. Book and heroine bear the same name: Madame Bovary. These extreme changes in attitude towards fiction are not limited to France. There are those writers in our own tongue who have neglected the fullest inheritance of the crafts of fiction. This neglect is a part of that chill sense of chaos, unseen but felt (chaos casts no shadow), which threatens Christendom. I am using the word deliberately. The servile view, no doubt, would hold it anachronistic; at least outmoded. Certainly it is ancient, but so is the society it denominates. It is universàl but composed of concrete particulars which a term such as *the West*, for example, lacks. As a term for our society *the West* is too geographical; it is to the secular society of our day a submerged half-truth, for the symbolic meaning of the West is death, the grave, the night sea journey; and in spite of the blatant political public assertion

that the West is power, underneath we feel the threat of its eternal mythological meaning. And this makes for a fearful speculation insofar as it is
separated from its completing symbol, the East, which promises renewal of
life and light. This failure to consider together the two halves which make a
whole has to do, remotely but surely, with the present state of letters. I know
I speak a platitude, but never before in our culture have the arts disclosed so
sensitively our essential disorder: in fiction a kind of energetic formlessness,
an intensive enlargement of a part for the whole, an obscene preoccupation
with the personality of the author rather than with his work, and last,
eroticism everywhere replacing love. Perhaps it is all right to publish anything. The only good censorship is that which censors itself (particularly
when the mind is Carthaginian); but to say that *Fanny Hill* is literature and
not what it is, successful pornography which boys have been reading in barn
lofts and beneath school desks for generations, is going a little far. And yet it
is this far we have come.

It seems to me that at this point there are good grounds to look at
Flaubert's masterpiece once more. I will not weary you by saying over again
how Flaubert suffered over *le mot juste*, which he did; nor how he personified
the devoted artist, which he was; nor will I use one of those grand words
such as *realism* or *naturalism*, which to my knowledge never helped anybody
to read. I will go so far as to say that his excessive use of detail almost spoiled
his book, for too much or too little detail makes for an abstraction, and
abstraction is the death of fiction. But he always saved himself from this
calamity, since he never lost the sense of what he was about. This is most
clearly seen in his paragraphs. These, rather than the sentence, seem to be
the units of his structure. They present a succession of shocks of truth,
usually by putting at the end of the paragraph a contrary image or an
involved apposition of what has gone before. Consider, for example, the
dinner preceding the marquis' ball, where the luxury of the board goes
beyond appetite, the overwarm air blending the smells of flowers and fine
linen and truffles, red lobster claws overhanging the dishes, napkins folded
like bishops' mitres (here a controlling image)—to bring into relief this
ritual of sensuality, suddenly, like an apparition, as the paragraph closes,
there is a statue of a woman standing upon the porcelain stove, "draped to
the chin," gazing motionless upon the room full of such life. In the way of
good art, without statement, the reader receives the statue as a threat, a

moral reproof, suggesting both the blind scales of justice and the aloofness of Fate.

But this paragraph only prepares us for a deeper involvement, which brings the action immediately to Emma. At the head of the table sits the old Duc de Laverdiere, the only male at the woman's table. He wears a bib like a child; his mouth drools. A servant behind his chair must name for him the dishes his trembling finger points towards. The rich foods, all the ceremony of the board, the culinary arts that have gone into pleasing the eye and palate are wasted on a jaded taste and the impotence of senility. Brought to this condition by old age and aggravated by a life of debauchery, he is there to warn Emma that those in the happiest worldly circumstances must suffer, along with others, the consequences of folly as well as the common ills of humanity: sickness, old age, and death. But does she take warning? No, for the old duke has slept in the bed of queens, particularly, rumor had it, in the native bed of Queen Marie Antoinette, after M. Coigny and before M. de Lauzun. Instead, Emma turns aside from reality and assures herself in her delusions. This is the technical purpose of the episode. Without it she might have come to accept her common, prosaic life with Charles. But the shine of the splendor of this house convinces her that her romantic longings may be found in actuality. They do exist. She had not only seen but taken part. She will never again be satisfied with her station. Poor Emma!

So much is this so that later, when the atmosphere of the ballroom grows heavy and footmen take chairs to break out the windowpanes, reality leaps into view through the peasants' faces pressed against the openings. The fresh air, the faces, peasant like Emma's own, should this time bring her to her senses, but "in the refulgence of the present hour her past life, so distinct until then, faded away completely and she almost doubted having lived it." The antitheses (at the center of Flaubert's method) are never stated but are presented in juxtaposition, as here. When Emma tells her husband not to think of dancing but to keep his place, we surmise how far she will go her desperate way, having lost the sense of her own place.

Beginning with this paragraph, the juxtaposition of opposites extends itself throughout the action. As the guest of a noble house the focus of vision lies with Emma. The ball comes alive through her wonder and expectation. All the ephemeral stuff of her dreams, her sensible longings, take on substance in this rich house; yet her response alone would too sharply limit the meaning but for the invisible hand of the artist. Emma cannot possibly show more than her wants and needs, who has forgotten her peasant origin and has dismissed her husband out of an insubstantial identity with the marquis' guests, whom she will never meet again as a social equal. The intensity of her nature and the sharpness of her vision are part of the strength of the book, but we always see more than Emma. The author has arranged this. Emma sees only what he wants her to see. An almost too obvious instance of this juxtaposition is in the young viscount's two sets of waltzes. He dances first, you remember, with Emma. In the rapid whirling of the dance the lamps, the furniture, the wainscoting, the floor all turn as if of their own autonomy. It is the first time we see Emma's vertigo, I believe. Now this vertigo of Emma's is very interesting. It is the clue to the meaning of her as heroine *manqué* and to the enveloping action, or the intrinsic meaning of the book.

Emma's dress gets caught against the viscount's trousers. Their legs commingle. He looks down. She raises her eyes to his and is seized with a torpor. She stops. They start again and now with a rapid movement. "Dragging her along," the young lord quickly gets her out of sight at the end of the gallery, where she, panting and almost falling, lays her head for a moment upon his breast. Then very slowly—oh, how cautious must have been this slowness on the young man's part—he, still turning, guides her back to her seat. Emma covers her eyes with her hands. When she opens them, they open upon a formal, pageantlike pose. Three young men are kneeling before a fashionable young lady seated upon a stool, in mock chivalry beseeching her favor. This is the transition between the two dances, and it already foreshows the nature of the difference between them. The young lady chooses the same viscount, and they dance. They pass and repass, her body rigid, her chin bent downward; he keeps his formal pose, figure curved, the elbow rounded, his chin thrown forward. This couple outdances all the others, but never once do they violate the public and formal posture by the slightest suggestion of intimacy. Again Emma refuses to see more than her infatuate bemusement allows. With grudging respect she reflects: How that woman knows how to waltz!

She sees only a personal threat from another woman. She is unaware of her own violation of decorum, her confusion between the public and private thing. And it was this the young viscount must have feared in her, through the ridicule of his friends, for Emma does respond to his true nature, or at least to the habitual appetites he and his elegant fellows enjoy, the half-easy management of loose women and thoroughbred horses. We are asked to notice that "those who were beginning to grow old had an air of youth, while there was something mature in the faces of the young." This something mature is the look of satiety; and since the aging lack a true vocation, merely prolonging the same kind of self-indulgence, there is no mark of struggle or true risk stamped upon their features. The situation in this house, at this ball, is this: we have the manners and lineage of nobility, but a nobility which has lost its proper function, to advise the king and defend the realm.

The feudal lord had long been replaced by a professional army. (On the knowledge of this, Louis XVI tried to tax the nobility, but the lords selfishly fought to retain privileges they no longer earned as defenders of the realm. The king chiefly failed in his efforts because of Necker, a Swiss banker and the father of Mme de Staël, who used this failure to set nobles against king, as he had already set commons against nobles.) So it is that by Emma's time the marquis can claim only sentimentally to belong to an estate of the realm. He and his kind are now a part of the fashionable world of money; indeed they are *haute bourgeoisie* with a title. The one sound at the ball which the music does not muffle is the clink of gold louis at the card tables. The reason for the ball is not a social one; it is to get the marquis elected to the parlement like any Republican. He has given firewood to the peasants, but his political ball gives away the sacred rites of hospitality. He, too, has confused the public and the private thing, as he showed as deep a confusion when he replaced the family château with an Italian country house. No doubt this was the fashionable taste of the moment, but since building is the surest evidence of a culture's self-belief and expression, we know how to judge the marquis. Fashion is closely connected with money; manners with the formal mask of good breeding, the possessor learning charity from responsibility, as well as enjoying protection of person and position from vulgar intrusion. When we reflect upon the reason for the ball, we see the subtle perversion of manners in the way the marquise greets Emma, "as amicably as if she had known her for a long time." The reproof to this change of status comes about, again, by apposition. Looking out of the past, when this family performed its true vocation, the ancestors hang upon the walls of the Italian country house as a sign of what has been lost. Cracked with varnish and age, nevertheless they show no ambiguity about the black letters beneath the gold frames: "Jean-Antoine d'Andervilliers d'Yverbonville, Count de la Vaubyessard, and Baron de la Fresnaye, *killed at* the battle of Coutras on the 20th of Oct. 1587." Again: "Jean-Antoine-Henry Guy d'Andervilliers de la Vaubyessard, Admiral of France and Chevalier of the order of St. Michael, *wounded at* the battle of . . . " and so on. Of course, Emma sees none of this, but she does not miss the buckle above the well-turned calf.

Thoroughbred horses play a distinct role in this chapter. Just before she leaves for home, the marquis shows Emma through his stables, as he says, "to amuse the young woman." There is in this, of course, the contrast between Emma's house and that of her host, since the floor of the harness room is kept better than Emma's parlor. But that has to do with the action proper. The enveloping action has to do with the thoroughbreds themselves. They are the animal counterparts to the portraits on the wall. These thoroughbreds are now kept for sport and pleasure. One hears of purses of gold won by their speed. A young lord is annoyed because a printer has misspelled a horse's name. These animals are better kept than the loose, easily managed women, but nothing so shows the nobles' loss of caste. Once the horse existed to carry the fighting lord to battle or upon the hunt. On the hunt or in battle it was of crucial utility. Now the creatures run because of their owner's vanity, to keep up style or social prestige, idly to show possession. When life, the welfare of the kingdom—not prestige—depended upon the mount, no proper noble would have demeaned himself or the horse by taking a young lady to the stables "to amuse her."

It should begin to be clear that the book is not a story about provincial mores nor a mere flouting of the bourgeois mind. Nor is it a biography, as Allen Tate feels, "of a silly, sad, and hysterical little woman," whom Flaubert according to Percy Lubbock "knows to be utterly worthless." How could this be, when Flaubert himself said, "Madame Bovary, c'est moi." Of course you can't believe much of what an author says about his work. Falubert told the Goncourts that what he really had in mind in writing *Bovary* was the color gray. The author's comments will always be more or less than the work itself. The reader must read the work as if it were done by an anonymous hand. Nothing but the work itself can reveal itself. And so I am going to look more narrowly at Madame Bovary, and never once at her critics, even though one may be her creator.

The bourgeois values, of course, deeply involve the action, but not quite, I think, as we have been led to believe. The disruption of Christian polity in the sixteenth century violated the entire order of Christendom by upsetting the relationship between the lords temporal and the lords spiritual. The outcome gave God one overseer, the king. For the first time the word was made carnal, and how dangerous the word may become, shorn of its spiritual restraint, may be seen in Machiavelli's book *The Prince*. This was the book which showed the princes of Europe that they might rule, free of spiritual counsel, looking only to their wills for guidance. The word remained creative, and it created Henry VIII and his minister Cromwell, who at the time of the rigging of the evidence against Sir Thomas More had a manuscript copy of *The Prince* at hand. Because the drama of this revolution came clearly to focus in Sir Thomas More's imprisonment and death, he may be taken as the great protagonist, the defender of the common good of Europe, and his sense of what was good for England could not be separate from this. When Cromwell, the Machiavellian, lost his head, all he could say was: "I have offended my prince and I die." But not so More. The king feared his probity and the divinity of his language. He cautioned him not to speak too long from the scaffold. More took the challenge, and his words went all around Europe. They closed, "I die my king's good servant, but God's first."

More's death marks the second fall of man, the fall into history. Instead of a theology for the whole, history—man judging man's acts, and explaining them, too—became the reward of behavior. Gradually the world came to be looked upon not as the grounds for the drama of the soul, but as the end in itself. The Christian vision dimmed. Estates became classes; that is, man was defined by his economic status, the heresy being that the economic man assumed the posture of the whole man, the Christian. The state is still Christian. It has entered its Satanic phase of false illusions. A part is taken for the whole. This is the oldest lie of all, appearance not representing reality. Man is made in God's image. To say that man is only matter, only a sensibility, is the subtlest lie of all.

It is this lie which Flaubert pushes to an absurdity in the enveloping action of *Madame Bovary*. He makes a society totally carnal and secular. The bourgeoisie appears not as a class among classes, but as *the* class which has usurped every estate, institution, trade, occupation, vocation, avocation in the world which victimizes Madame Bovary. Having the bourgeois mind as the only mind exposes the monstrous deformity and impossibility of such a world, a world entirely material. The isolated ego, money, physical appetites, the categories of the mortal sins (without promise of redemption)— such do the actors in this narrative show; such is the substance of the composite life parodying the divine scheme, Substance of the very Substance. It follows that the only guide to conduct is selfishness, and so we find it pervading the action, with two minor exceptions: Catherine Laroux and Justin, Homais' cousin whom he treats as a servant. Catherine is given a silver medal worth twenty-five francs for fifty years' devoted service on one farm. Part of the moral is satire: that her devotion should be worth less than an animal's prize money. But the intention is again in the juxtaposition of meaning. She is a Christian in a Satanic world. Her first thought is to give the medal to her priest, because her only thought is of giving. The boy Justin loves Emma as love should love, without asking anything in return. His innocence and incorruptibility feels through the corrupt outward surface to Emma's uncompromising heart. She scarcely notices him, but he doesn't care. He is glad to be in her presence or do her service in the most menial ways. He can refuse her nothing, and ironically he does not refuse her the means of death. Afterwards he alone is her disinterested mourner, grieving at night by her grave in privacy. When Lestiboudois returns for a spade, the intrusion drives the boy away. Again the method: the gravedigger can only think that he has found the thief who has robbed his potato patch, for Lestiboudois is not only the sacristan and gravedigger; he also does odd jobs about the town. And he plants potatoes in the burying ground. They grow very well next to the graves. The priest jests with him, saying you live off the dead. All in this action live off the dead, because they live off each other, and all are dead here, for death in the world is what is left after the spirit departs. In a small way Lestiboudois exemplifies this most clearly. He rents the church chairs for his own gain; he rings the bell for vespers at his pleasure. The Church, instead of being served by him, is a convenience for him; yet he is not entirely happy. He cannot enjoy the fee he gets for digging a grave, for the loss of that much potato ground. The priest is worse because he betrays more; or rather, because of the material usurpation, he does not understand his office. Since meaning is no longer contained by its proper forms, we get the shell without any content, or we get essence distorted by the half form, the sentimental, or even the wrong form. We get this, particularly, in the romantic and sensual images.

Emma in her nature is incorruptible and inviolate. Her drama is this incorruptibility against the false education she undergoes from her society and the abortive flights she takes in her effort to find what will complete her. Her passionate nature, her great capacity for love, has only the vagaries of sentimental and romantic images (her sensuality) as the means for her quest. Her vertigo arises from the abyss where her passions and needs, deprived of proper outlets, must whirl violently about, reaching for the proper forms to allow her nature to function. All she is offered for husband is an oaf and a fool, Charles; the lesser counterpart, Leon; the equally incomplete Rodolphe. Emma does not settle for anything less than reality, and that for her is complete love. So she must follow the Furies and, in her search for what she can never find, grow more and more desperate, subject to the very corruption of the things which thwart her, until she takes her life.

I have tried to indicate what has happened to the lords temporal in the example of the marquis and his companions: their values are money and fashion instead of nobility and service. His class—no longer estate—has played its crucial part in Emma's disaster. But how is it that her parents gave her so poor an upbringing? Emma's mother died early, but M. Rouault, the father, was another matter. He was a farmer of some substance. There is no better farmer than the French peasant, whether large or small. Farming supports the state as bread does life. There was never until recently any misunderstanding among the French about this. "Agriculture," Napoleon dictated to Las Cases, "is the soul, the foundation of the kingdom: industry ministers to the comfort . . . foreign trade is the superabundance" and of secondary importance. This is the exact opposite of the economy of the plutocratic state. Emma's father has lost this sense of his occupation. He complained that no farmer was a millionaire. He suffered the basic usurpation of money. He was losing it every year, but he "more than held his own in the marketplace, where he relished all the tricks of the trade." This is to say that his interests and values were those of the *petit bourgeois*, not of a farmer. "No one was less suited than he to the actual growing of crops and the managing of a farm. He never lifted a finger if he could help it, and never spared any expense in matters of daily living: he insisted on good food, a good fire, and a good bed. He liked his cider hard, his leg of mutton rare, his coffee laced with brandy. He took his meals in the kitchen, alone, facing the fire, at a little table that was brought in to him already set, like on a stage." One begins to understand Emma's hopes at the marquis' board. There was a difference only in degree and not in kind between the spurious marquis' and the spurious peasant's establishments. The difference was not in the need for luxury but money. When Charles proposed, M. Rouault was in the process of selling twenty-two acres of ground to pay his debts. That is an awful lot of land in France to eat up, and a true peasant would have considered it a calamity. It helped him to make up his mind to give Emma to Charles. Being a trader, he knew that Charles was a poor kind of a man, but M. Rouault felt he would make no trouble about the dowry. Also, Emma was not worth much to him on the farm. So it was his care for money, not love, that delivered her to her fate. At the convent the nuns had already failed her: her "nature, positive in the midst of enthusiasms, that had loved the Church for the sake of the flowers, and music for the words of the songs, and literature for its passional stimulus, rebelled against the mysteries of faith as she grew irritated by discipline." Why didn't the sisters instruct her in both discipline and doctrine? One gathers that the sisters, instead of preparing their pupil for her role in the world, sought to make her one of their own; that is, they saw the narrow interests of their order instead of the good of the pupil. She left confused between appearance and reality and with little spiritual discipline.

This kind of betrayal follows Emma to the bitter end. The head of the state is Louis Philippe, king of France. What should be the symbol of authority among kings—a sword, a scepter, the globe itself? With Louis Philippe it is an umbrella, almost as good as an English banker. There is the innkeeper, Madame François. She thinks of her own convenience and is jealous for her inn and longs for her competitor's ruin. The agricultural fair is a public matter common to all, but not to Madame François: the people will not be eating with her. Madame Rollet, who keeps Emma's child, has no love for the child or her work. She does it purely for pay and the small luxuries she can wheedle out of her customers. For pay she becomes part of the deception Emma must practice in her affair with Leon. M. Guillaumin, the lawyer, with the mannerisms and dress of the English bar, who should be the agency of justice, at least subordinate to his client's appeal, is nothing of the sort. He is a sensualist, ill-mannered, given one suspects to shady practices, suing the bar to take advantage, and is so hardened to appeal that he cannot see Emma's desperation when she comes to him for help—indeed he does not stop eating breakfast—but tries to seduce her. His man does seduce her maid. M. Binet, the tax collector, bears a special importance to the action, although his appearance is infrequent. An official of the state, he hunts out of season. This gives him pleasure. His vocation, collecting money he doesn't earn, and his avocation, turning on a lathe napkin rings which he does not sell, both reveal his basic frivolity. He lives off the work of others, and the tool which should aid man in making something of use merely turns to fill the mind's emptiness. The ring he makes is the perfect figure, but here it rounds off the abyss underlying all who take part in the action. In a way he and his occupation stand for the controlling image. Money is a good when it serves as the medium of exchange for goods and services. A machine, when it helps man to make something useful, is a good. When it takes the place of man or serves him in his idleness, it is an evil. To let it turn to no purpose, as it does for M. Binet, is a symbol of its ultimate possibility, man evicted and the machine running in a silent world. As a sound it enters and becomes the substance and definition of Emma's state when she stands before the window of her attic, having learned of Rodolphe's betrayal, looking down into the square below, being pulled to jump by this insistent sound of chaos, Binet's lathe humming and turning in her head, the very sound of her vertigo. Every time she is betrayed by the deformed images of love, her need for the real thing ejects the spurious forms and conventions, leaving her to the mercy of this vertigo.

If Emma fares poorly in her upbringing, her husband Charles fares worse, partly in the paucity of natural gifts, and these quickly abused by his parents. His father is an instance of the derangement which follows upon an absence of any spiritual control. The forms of behavior are all eccentric, and to himself and others they never represent what they seem to be. His only response is to appetite. This led him to the debauch of himself and his wife's property, until at forty-five, eaten up with envy, discontent, cursing heaven, and disgusted with mankind, he shut himself away to live at peace, a condition that would forever be denied him because he wanted something for nothing. This is the first article in the constitution of hell. It is not enough for a man to act: he must be willing to assume responsibility for his acts. And this is not enough either: he must with knowledge assume it, and that knowledge inevitably must recognize that each man is capable of committing all mortal and venial sins. This knowledge, called in mythology the cooperating opposites, must be known and integrated in the total personality of a man. M. Bovary was forever out of balance. His very appearance was a lie; he had the look of a bully with the easy cajoling ways of a traveling salesman. His dress was that of a soldier and its opposite, the man about town. He had been drummed out of the army. He alternated his son's discipline according to whim. At times he gave him a Spartan regimen, at times let him run naked and wild, be natural in Rousseau's sense. Charles's mother was just as bad. Taken in by the sensual appeal of her husband, for which she suffered, she later tried to recover her life through her son's. But to save money, she gave him no proper schooling. When he did go away, he was withdrawn too soon; then, pushed beyond his talents in his professional training, he failed, though later he passed by memory work. She married him to a dry piece of meat, a widow with property. This property turned out to be fraudulent, as the world taken for itself always is. The woman died when exposed, and Charles was free to court Emma. The clue is this: Charles felt some small grief—for his wife? No. He said, "After all, she loved me."

The morning after the bridal night with Emma, it was Charles who seemed the virgin. Emma revealed nothing, so that the shrewdest dame at the wedding could make nothing of it, and this was because Emma was thinking of the words *felicity, passion, rapture*, which had seemed so beautiful to her in books and which indeed should have lasted out the honeymoon. Their absence did not cause her to say: I was mistaken; I will accept what I find. Instead she wondered if there were not certain spots on earth which must bring happiness, as plants are peculiar to sympathetic soils. She sadly thought of herself in a Scotch cottage, drifting about in melancholy, with a lover attired in a black velvet coat and thin shoes. The harsh truth of what the highlands would have done to those shoes or the manure pile to her melancholy she, a farm girl, should have known. When form and content become separate or mixed, the imagination must still do its work. If the proper material is unavailable, it will use what is at hand, even if this is

romantic or sentimentally absurd. Rightly and naturally Emma expected
her husband to initiate her into the felicities of marriage and the mysteries
of life. She showed herself gifted in all domestic matters, even as she was in
those of love—until her patience ran out. Charles taught her nothing,
knew nothing, wished for nothing but the gross satisfaction of his appetites.
An oaf and a fool, he bored his wife with platitudes. His table manners were
disgusting, his bedroom manners worse; and because he was pleased and
flattered by her obvious charms and talents, he assumed she was happy. At
last her patience rejected what was fake and selfish, so that her legal husband in his human and personal failure sent her upon her ill-starred quest.

A quality easily overlooked in Emma's character is her innate modesty.
We get the sense of it when finally she yields to Rodolphe, for in spite of her
concupiscent daydreams, she is slow to come to adultery. Her surrender is
almost a yielding of purity and innocence, the shame of revelation, that
ultimate violation of self which makes the common pattern of life. It was
not merely Leon's inexperience and lack of courage which prevented their
mutual attraction from becoming intimate at first, though she thought it
was. She was eaten with desires, with rage and hate, but it was the common
series of betrayals which were responsible for these emotions—not because
she couldn't have Leon. The sound of his step thrilled her; the sight of him
at a distance filled her with voluptuousness. However, in his presence the
emotion subsided. The reality of Leon was not what she wanted. She was
using at a distance his form and features to receive the images of her
frustration. In reality he was too frail a reed to bear the weight of her
demands. After he goes away, she is afflicted with a disease common to
virgins at a certain time of life: the green sickness. As far as the essence and
being of her nature is concerned, she has not been touched by Charles. She
is still virginal and still seeking a completing love. In despair she turns to
God. She tries to turn to God, and through the proper channel of the
Church ("inclined to no matter what devotions, so that her soul would
become absorbed and all existence lost in it"). But just as the lord temporal
misled her, now the lord spiritual in the person of the parish priest completely fails her. He is a mere functionary, given particularly to the mortal
sins of sloth and gluttony.

In a summary we learn that the Church is rotting at the top, is dominated
by secular authority. Emma happens upon the priest just after he has eaten.

He is breathing heavily; his habit is dirty and greasy and stained by tobacco. She comes upon him as he is about to teach the boys their catechism.

"How are you?" he asks.

"Not well," replied Emma. "I am ill."

"Well, and so am I," answered the priest. "These first warm days weaken one most remarkably, don't they? But, after all, we are born to suffer, as St. Paul says. But what does M. Bovary think of it?"

"He!" she said with a gesture of contempt.

"What!" replied the good fellow, quite astonished, "doesn't he prescribe something for you?"

"Ah!" said Emma, "it is no earthly remedy I need."

This is the direct appeal which almost automatically a priest should respond to, but this false priest doesn't hear, allows a secondary matter such as the behavior of the boys to divert him, and answers her with their biographies instead of responding to what must have been an obvious need for spiritual counsel. Politely he asks after her husband, but she seems not to hear; so he answers for her.

"Always busy, no doubt; for he and I are certainly the busiest people in the parish. But he is a doctor of the body," he added with a thick laugh, "and I of the soul."

She fixed her pleading eyes upon the priest. "Yes," she said, "you solace all sorrows."

This is his answer: "Ah! Don't talk of it, Madame Bovary. This morning I had to go to Bas-Diauville for a cow that was ill; they thought it was under a spell" and so forth. He is interrupted by the boys and says when he resumes, "Farmers are much to be pitied."

"Others, too," she replied.

"Assuredly. Town laborers, for example."

"It is not they . . . " she begins.

"Pardon. I've there known poor mothers of families, virtuous women, I assure you, real saints, who wanted even bread."

"But those," replied Emma, and the corners of her mouth twitched as she spoke, "those, M. le Curé, who have bread and no . . ."

"Fire in the winter. . . ."

Emma gives up, as she has with her husband. "My God, my God," she sighs. "Do you feel unwell?" the priest asks, approaching her anxiously. "It is indigestion, no doubt? You must get home, Madame Bovary; drink a little tea, that will strengthen you, or else a glass of fresh water with a little sugar in it."

As she goes away, she hears:

"Are you a Christian?"
"Yes, I am a Christian."
"What is a Christian?"
"He, who being baptized, baptized, baptized . . ."

The priest has done no better with the boys than with Emma. Baptism is the official entry into a new life of hope, but here by implication it goes no further. The secularization of the Church will be more formidably reinforced at the cathedral in Rouen, where Leon is waiting for Emma. Young men from time immemorial have waited in church porches for assignations with their girls, but never before with such vulgarity. The house of prayer seems to Leon a glowing boudoir.

Forsaken by the priest, Emma allows herself to be seduced by Rodolphe. He has a château, but he is neither a lord nor a rich peasant, merely a bourgeois with a piece of country property. He is lazy and without attachment or feeling of responsibility for the land. In dress he had that "incongruity of common and elegant in which the habitually vulgar think they see the revelation of an eccentric existence." It is at the agricultural fair that he begins his seduction of Emma. The officials and entourage of this fair are made up of an agglomeration of Rodolphes. The vulgarity, the petty vanities, the pompous speeches given with such self-applauding solemnity, the glib patronizing of the farmers by the officials—all this, the insincerity, the disparity between the nobility of the animals and the mean prizes in money which their owners receive, stand for the comic chorus, which reinforces the play of seduction going on between Emma and Rodolphe in the council chamber. The comedy is here, but the reader cannot miss the agreement between the inane mediocrity of the bourgeoisie in its public occasion and the private performance of Rodolphe, whose end is only a sensual interlude. Before he has had Emma, he is already wondering how he can get rid of her. In this instance the juxtaposition of public and private comes to the same thing.

Materialism in its absolute state may be found in the autonomy of the senses. Instead of being the avenues, the means by which mind and heart, imagination and soul inform man of the world and the hope of the hereafter, carnality makes the senses the end in themselves, which inevitably reach exhaustion by overuse, exposing the monotony of lust or any other appetite. This is the history of the first part of Emma's affair with Rodolphe. Its form is as usual the juxtaposition of opposites. The great adultery can only seem good to her at first, because marriage with Charles has been so poor a matter. However, it is true marriage she wants to feel with Rodolphe. She wants to exchange rings and think of their mothers looking down from Heaven in approval. This is a sentimentality, but again because she is allowed to use only the spurious form of emotion and belief. Once this is understood, we find her having all the qualities which love must have or die: she is tender, bold, reckless, giving, imaginative in the arts of love itself, but especially she gives herself without reservation, until she is betrayed. Her need must truly be great to be so long in misunderstanding her lover. Rodolphe is almost saved by her: "This love without debauchery was a new experience for Rodolphe." He is drawn from his lazy habits, but no further than caressing his pride and sensuality, so that their affair is like a continual seduction. In other words his senses are too jaded to be reborn through love. This great lack allows the perpetual seduction to simmer like any lukewarm domestic flame. A letter from her father awakens her to what has happened. She is aware of what she has lost by the way and wonders if it would not have been better to have remained true to her marriage. Instinctively she demands of Charles what all wives demand of their husbands: something to respect, in his case professional excellence. What she forgot was his inadequacy and commitment to folly. His grotesque failure in operating on a club foot set husband and wife finally apart and returns her to Rodolphe and ruin.

The affair is resumed this time with ardor and depravity, in which Emma takes the lead. But she knows the world has failed her utterly. She can think only of going away, as a desperate measure of finding that soil which will allow the true affections to thrive. She almost persuades Rodolphe, but his selfishness is the counterpart to her false vision. He will not exile himself with a child on his hands. His last thoughts are: "And besides the worry, the expense." He consigns her to God and sprinkles the betraying letter with water, simulating tears.

The deception was Emma's self-deception, but the shock is no less severe.

It almost brings her to a premature suicide. It does make her dangerously ill. The vertigo, the various illnesses, must be seen as the passionate, devoted, absolute commitment to love and grace. Thwarted as she is, they measure by deprivation the reality of her need. Again she turns to God, and again the priest fails her. He is frightened by her fervor, her vision of God. His remedy is to write a bookseller for literature suitable for a lady in difficulty, but the very word of God is falsified by a shoddy craftsmanship in writing; and betrayed again by the criminal failure of the priest, she drifts into the pride of devoutness, to an excessive alms-giving, and from this to the final episode of her quest, that passionate wrong pursuit of the real thing.

At each crisis it is Homais, the druggist, who is the agent for the act which drives Emma further towards her ruin. It was he who brought Charles to Yonville; it was he who, reading in the paper about a theory of operating on a club foot, suggested it to Charles. Only Charles's ignorance of surgery would take a druggist's knowledge of it as meaningful. Homais suggests to Charles that the opera in Rouen is the very thing to divert Emma, and this brings about the final episode. He becomes not only responsible for the disastrous affair with Leon, but his vanity actually is able to make available the poison which kills her. So far has Homais to do with the specific action. But his chief role is to represent the enveloping action, that state of society in which the absolute value, the only value, is material. Once the earthly kingdom imitated the divine one. Now there is only the kingdom of this world, and Homais is its first citizen. As devil's disciple he stands for the false appearance of things. His actual knowledge is limited to drugs; yet he prescribes for disease. Not being a dcotor, he can do this only out of opinion—that is, ignorance. By use of the means, herbs, he usurps the end and brings not life but death. His self-assurance, not his knowledge, convinces the peasants that he knows more than the doctors. He stands for every phase of the usurpation—only secular values, information for learning, opinion for knowledge, the confusion of form and content, inhumanity in his human relationships. One quotation will be enough. When asked what farming matters to him, he replies: "Do you think that to be an agriculturist it is necessary to have tilled the earth or fattened fowls oneself? It is necessary rather to know the composition of the substances in question—the geological strata, the atmospheric actions, the quality of the soil, the minerals, the waters, the density of the different bodies, their capillarity, and what not." How is this known? "One must keep pace with science by means of *pamphlets* and *public papers*." This makes him a comic figure, but the comedy turns rather grim when Emma dies of it.

All the secondhand reports of knowledge pass through Homais' mind as through a sieve. He becomes the parody of man trying to exercise what only God can know. To accept the numbering of the arts and sciences for knowledge, as the state does in giving him the Legion of Honor, shows the criminal folly of the kind of education and treatment which brings Madame Bovary to her death. Lest we miss the point, we have the blind beggar of Rouen, the controlling image of this action. He is corrupt throughout with disease: "A mass of rags covered his shoulders, and an old staved-in beaver, turned out like a basin, hid his face; but when he took it off he discovered in the place of eyelids empty and bloody orbits. The flesh hung in red shreds, and there flowed from it liquids that congealed into green scales down to the nose." And so forth; yet Homais promises to cure him if he will come to Yonville. For this corruption Homais offers a pomade. When the blind beggar tells it up and down the highway, the state, which has given to usurped knowledge the Legion of Honor, incarcerates another victim.

The story now quickly ends. The moneylender brings on the final catastrophe. Emma's borrowing (she could have got on without it) represents the blindness of her desperate pursuit, for we all know that money, where debts are involved, has one sure quality: it will take no substitute. It will be paid in the coin of the realm and with interest, usury in a Satanic society being no longer forbidden but the very support of the state. Emma's last appeal to Rodolphe almost renews his passion, until money is mentioned. By now Emma can appeal only in terms of this agency, no longer in terms of herself. But there is one true sense of herself that refuses invasion. It is desperate, blind, but it has not been touched in its integrity; and this is her quest for the sacrament of love. Finding nothing but the spurious, soul and flesh maimed by the opposite of what she has sought, she will not compromise, not even in death. "She stretched forward her neck [towards the crucifix] as one who is thirsty, and glueing her lips to the body of the Man-God, she pressed upon it with all her expiring strength the fullest kiss of love that she had ever given." Then the priest gives her extreme unction.

As the oiled thumb passes, the two parts of the structure are revealed by a kind of final juxtaposition of opposites: the image of her demand for love against the corrupt means by which she has had to seek it. The sensibility, instead of uniting mind, heart, and imagination in the love she sought, has been made to divert, distort, and waste the substance of life. The thumb, "first upon the eyes that had so coveted all worldly pomp; then upon the nostrils, that had been greedy of the warm breeze and amorous odors; then upon the mouth, that had uttered lies, that had curled with pride and cried out in lewdness; then upon the hands that had delighted in sensual touches; and finally upon the soles of the feet, so swift of yore, when she was running to satisfy her desires, and that would now walk no more."

As controlling image, the living disease, the loathsome corruption of the blind beggar of Rouen, is outside in the street as Emma is dying. He is there as symbol of the action, in which the human being is victim of a society totally selfish, carnal, and material. His presence at her death is not accidental. They are equally victims in kind, if not in degree. He is singing a love ballad. It has all the innocence of spring and youth. It withholds the consequences of love. Emma herself is the consequence, and this she discovers as she rises up in bed and cries out, "The blind man," and laughs "a horrible, frenzied and despairing laugh." His presence and his song combine the essence of the action. Emma has to die to learn. Perhaps she learns only the half of truth; perhaps the other half comes quickly with the final illumination beyond death. The priest and the atheist sit up with the dead body to emphasize further the essential meaning. The priest sprinkles holy water; the druggist, chlorine solution. The priest says we will end by understanding each other. They already understand. Bread and wine is spread for their repast. Not the blood and body of our Lord ends the action, but the worldly bread and wine to appease their carnal appetites as it diverts them from the smell of decay, which, being exuded by the dead flesh, becomes the final symbol of death in life, the description of the society that has undone Emma.

Three Ways of Making a Saint: Flaubert's Three Tales

EACH STORY IN FLAUBERT'S *Three Tales* ends in death, and the meaning of each renders the original properties of the Trinity. Although the enveloping action for all is the same, the form for each differs. "Herodias," with its dance of death, Salome's dance, is informed by the First Person of the Trinity, God the Father; "St. Julian the Hospitator," Christ the Son; and "A Simple Heart," the Holy Ghost. The three in one, as they differ in their actions, reveal the distinction of each member of the Trinity not as an abstract definition but as it affects the body of the world; that is, technically not by summary alone but through scenes and all the discrete uses of fiction.

The conditions and place for "Herodias" is the Roman Empire during the years of Christ's ministry. Its material is superficially historic. "The Legend of St. Julian the Hospitator" is legend embodied in myth, but a Christian myth which is a vision. Its properties are medieval, and it is timeless, but like myth its places of action lack any known geography. The subject of "A Simple Heart" is charity as nearly a perfect reflection of divine love as a human being may suffer, and thus the necessity for the adjective *simple*. The adjective is rich in connotation. The story has been called realistic, one of those words fairly useless as a way of reading. It may pertain to the old Western antithesis which split Christendom, but that Realism is not immediate enough to shed light upon this tale. Because of the seeming simplicity of its leading actor, Felicité, "A Simple Heart" is the most human of the three stories, as the common referent can include any of us. Its ground for action is neither historic nor mythical. It is the French bourgeois world of the nineteenth century. In other words, it is the same old world raised to its highest intensity of general acceptance as the desired value mankind wants and seeks. Felicité's role exposes the disappointments attending upon such a pursuit. But there is an irony here which hides at first view a shocking drama that gives her heroic proportions, the more so for the mundane circumstances of the action.

"Herodias," in the chronological order of the three settings, comes first, although it was written last. Power is the subject. The visible kind of power is worldly, its aim the possession and use of the varying objects of creation. The invisible power, of course, is the power of God, who controls both life and death. Man can bring about the death of man, but he didn't make it. He is never more than agent, even when he causes it for his own ends. If power is the subject of the action, then death, with its double, contradictory meaning, is the enveloping action. Its continuing presence, no matter how common as a property of life, derives from the enduring mystery of God. It takes a bold writer and skilled craftmanship to undertake a revelation of such truth and avoid the platitude of statement.

Flaubert manages to disguise the universals of truth; otherwise they would be unacceptable to the reader expecting merely the sensations of an action. He uses the ordinary, the commonplace appearances of things in which the symbolic is immanent. In the first sentence he relates power and death. "The citadel of Machaerus stood to the east of the Dead Sea, on a cone-shaped basalt peak." This seems simple description; but the rock peak, powerful in nature, is crowned by a fortress palace, the housing of power, of both civil and military rule. To emphasize this, there are warrens of rooms dug out of the bowels of the mountain, hiding every kind of military armament. Even deep down in a stable that opens onto the air there are a hundred magnificent white war-horses, a treasure in themselves, hidden against the authority greater than Herod's in his citadel. But as we quickly discover, this basalt cone holds a prisoner representing concretely and symbolically the power opposed to the might of Rome. It is Iaokanann, called John the Baptist.

The action proper—in drama it would be plot—begins with this voice. It reaches Herod Antipas on the balcony of his palace just before day and makes him turn pale. He has gotten up to be alone, to consider the troubles which vex him. He does not want the Jews to know he has imprisoned Iaokanann. They are tired of his idolatrous ways; most are weary of his rule. Below him he sees the brown tents of the Arabs, at war with him for twelve years now because he had set aside their king's daughter to marry Herodias, his brother's wife.

This act of lust, on his part desire for her body, on her part the desire for rule, brought them together in the surge of passion. Iaokanann's voice struck him at the moment he was considering the sorrows which had resulted from their union. Indirectly Herodias' lust was the cause of Iaokanann's incarceration. As she was passing by where he was baptizing, Iaokanann with roaring voice and flashing eyes spat all the curses of the prophets at her. The wheels of her chariot were sunk up to their axles in sand, and she could flee only slowly, cowering under her cloak, her blood running cold from his insults. Nothing she did could cause his death. Her soldiers were ordered to stab him if he resisted arrest. He was mild as a lamb. Snakes were put in his prison. They died. She did not understand. What did he gain by fighting her? His castigations were beyond her only preoccupation: the stratagems of power.

At the sound of the voice Herod summons Mannaei, his executioner. Officially and unofficially, he beheaded, strangled, and drowned, for his masters. Not only is he the agent and symbol of death; he resembles it, "his face as impassive as a mummy's." He is also a Samaritan who hates the Jews. This reassures Herod that he will guard Iaokanann well. Also, Mannaei's feelings towards the Temple at Jerusalem render the selfish animosities of the various religious cults of the region.

The Samaritan temple at Gerizim, intended by Moses to be the center of Israel, has been supplanted by Jerusalem. The executioner looks between a gap in the hills and sees white marble walls, the gold-plated roof shining in the sun: "It was like a luminous mountain, something superhuman, crushing everything else under its opulence and its arrogance." Mannaei stretches forth his arms and flings a curse at it. He had previously polluted its altar by putting dead bones upon it. His accomplices lost their heads.

Beyond the private concerns of Herod and Herodias are death and power and distorted belief, belief rarely more than selfish tribal interests using the letter of the law to carry out their desires. For two hundred years or better the inadequacy of this rule, that of a jealous God through his followers and priests, has haunted the Oriental provinces of Rome. They have looked for the Messiah to free them, not only to free them but to conquer the world and assume its rule. The common hope and expectation is revealed by the temptation on the mount, when Satan shows Christ the kingdoms of the world.

As Mannaei and Herod part, Mannaei reports Iaokanann as saying over and over, "If he must wax, then I must wane." Herod is too disturbed to try to understand what this means. As he gazes at the terrain about him, the mountains like petrified waves, the black chasms, the immensity of the blue sky, the cruel brilliance of the morning light, the desert's contours make the landscape seem like the ruins of amphitheaters and palaces. The hot wind brings the smell of sulphur, "like the stench of the accursed cities buried under the banks of the heavy waters." These signs of immortal anger strike terror in his thoughts, but he cannot connect them to Iaokanann's effort to reveal the failure of accepting the world as the end of all endeavor and belief. The role Iaokanann was called to play has also long been expected among the Jews. All of this Herod feels but cannot see, although the signs are before him.

His elbows on the balustrade, eyes staring, his forehead in his hands—at this moment he feels a touch. It is Herodias. She comes with the old, now too old, motions of temptation and with political news: her means toward her ends. She announces that her brother Agrippa is in Tiberias' dungeons. She announces that prisoners have been known to die there. Neither considers this a betrayal. She tells how she has brought it about, her wide nostrils quivering, her eyes radiant with the joy of victory. She adds: "It was nothing. . . . Have I not given up my daughter?" This makes Herod Antipas wonder. She has never spoken of her daughter before. The radiance of her joy is not pure. It is suspect to the one closest to her.

When she rubs herself gently against his breast, he pushes her away. He has aged. She has made the old appeal at the moment he is aware of what it has cost him. They quarrel. It is the habit of lust to weary of its object but not of the desire for the object. He sees Salome from the balustrade, unaware that she is the daughter. "Who is she?" he asks. Herodias ceases to quarrel. Her plan is working. It does not disturb her that what she intends is incest, specifically forbidden in every instance, by the laws of Leviticus and according to the Justinian code unto the sixth removal in kinship. Nevertheless, cleverly, at a distance, the child is revealed to its uncle in tempting ways. After Vitellius' arrival, when Herod Antipas has come to his wife for comfort, "from under a curtain . . . a bare arm emerged, a charming young arm which might have been carved in ivory by Polyclitus." "Is that slave yours?" he asks. "What does that matter to you?" she replies. Notice that the comparison is made between the carving of a statue and the crafting of a human being. That the mystery of that arm's form might have been of another sort of creation does not enter Herod's thoughts. Except for superstitious fear of the supernatural, no reference exceeds the goods and things of the material world.

What does matter, however, involves a larger drama with more profound reverberations than Herodias can know or expect. Herod has refused her Iaokanann's death, but she does not intend to be thwarted. She rightly fears that the virulence of his attacks upon her threaten her aims among the Hebrew provinces. She wants to be queen. Her anger seems the fury of vanity assailed, but she does not distinguish between vanity and ambition to rule. Perhaps this blind anger is a blind counter to keep hidden her humanity, that which she has in common with human creatures, but which her greed for rule has buried deep within her. Throughout she never shows a glimmer of warmth or sympathy. This corruption lies at the center of her womanly being. The female who bears life should be the source of sympathy for and protection of that which she bears. Herodias has taken the innocence of her daughter and trained it as a tool to be manipulated in her struggle for power.

Herod is a more sympathetic figure. His humanity is not suppressed entirely. He lacks the right expressions for his feelings. The manners and mores of the overwhelming might which he serves and from which he gets what he gets smother his Jewish inheritance. He is attracted to Iaokanann;

he senses some spiritual force but can think of it only as power, not that it might be the forerunner of relief from the sorrows of the world. The prisoner is stronger than the jailer. He who is above is drawn to what is below, something threatening and impervious to control. This paradox is at the center of the action. The carnal knows fears; the spiritual is fearless. Herod confesses to Phanuel, an Essene, that it is he, not Iaokanann, who is mistreated.

The story is divided into three parts. This first part has shown the machinations, the sorrows and uncertain ties which afflict those who have or want the rule. This might be called political lust, the exercise of an office for private ends, not the care for the public thing which has been the moral support persisting through most of the changes undergone by Rome. In human terms this political lust, enfeoffed in Herod Antipas and his consort, has blinded them to the humanity of their subjects. They contemplate goods and people as objects to be used, digits of power made concrete in themselves as rulers. Herodias' lusting after power, she herself once an object of lust to Herod, compounds in her person carnal appetite with that of the will. Even death becomes no more than a tool. But death, of course, has a larger, more indecipherable aspect which the climax of the story reveals. This Herod indistinctly feels. It is his hope for regeneration, but at last it deserts him. Self-interest and the habit of survival prevail.

Herodias and her plans, no matter how crucial to her needs, are merely one part of the action's structure. She is not the heroine. She is not equal to the occasion in so profound and world-shaking a drama. But her part and Herod's are essential. Their private and public affairs represent the desire and aspiration for the world as an end in itself. It is Iaokanann who is the protagonist, but even his role is that of the forerunner, the one who must wane that the other may wax. But insofar as this action is concerned, he is the hero-victim. He is not the Messiah, even if opinion is not quite sure of that at first. He has the passionate anger of the Old Testament prophets, not the charity of divinity.

At this point two things are needed: a specific antagonist to Iaokanann and direct evidence of the might and awe of power itself, not the secondary play we have seen at the court of Herod Antipas. Herod is only a tetrarch, the ruler over a fourth of a province. The proconsul Vitellius is the ruler of the whole, and as he enters Machaerus, he makes Herod feel the full weight of his position. He seems the epitome of Rome, arriving with not only soldiers but with all the impedimenta of rule. Those crowding the citadel for Herod's birthday feast know that the proconsul's office represents a senatorial province. The functionaries attending him enter with that assurance of authority not be be disobeyed, the lictors with their staves and axes ready to punish any infractions by criminals or rebels, the publicans with their tablets to record treasure and taxable items; all are with Vitellius.

In the dust they raise hovers the aura of Rome's hegemony of the world. The legion Vitellius has with him is an expanded lictorship. It shows a morale got from victories, of the knowledge that wherever it sets foot, it walks upon dirt that is its own. The image of this is in its shields. They are protected by covers from the dust of the march. Uncovered in Machaerus, each shows the effigy of Caesar. The Jews are so loud in protest that Vitellius has them recovered. They complain of idolatry. In the Jewish past the golden calf and other inherited images of worship were a threat to their invisible God. The golden calf will be transmogrified into a substantial Messiah, but they, hating Rome, assert the letter of the law. Rome is never equivocal. The world is all. Rome sees no contradiction in deifying its imperators. But that is not the world which has primarily been invited to Herod Antipas' birthday feast.

But there is one uninvited guest who will attend: Iaokanann, buried near the cisterns in his prison hole. Not only does his presence expose Herod Antipas' secret; it precipitates the approaching climax to the action, when action and enveloping action are brought together with the exposure of a truth which is so new that no one understands, but all bear witness out of a common myopia.

Vitellius is not antagonist to Iaokanann. Like Herod he is a functionary. A red litter, carried by eight bearers, ornamented with plumes and mirrors, follows in his train. This houses his son Aulus, upon whose iniquities depend the father's fortune and rule. Aulus is almost Rome itself. He is close to the throne. He is also a symbol, the complete symbol, with which Iaokanann contends. His is the greatest appetite in the world, and he is known and admired for this.

In a very special way Flaubert's method of work suits this subject. Writers of stories of necessity use the senses to bring their actors alive, but Flaubert made it a fictive law: the more senses the greater the imitation of life.

Therefore the care in selecting the right words, for an action to deliver its meaning must advance in a specific way, or else the reader is confused by not having his sympathy controlled and directed. We are told that Mannaei hates the Jews and has polluted the altar of their Temple. That is a statement. As he looks at Jerusalem, we see, because he sees, the Temple framed in the gap between two hills. But further, the sun, an object, makes the marble walls and gold-plated roof shine like a luminous mountain. The sun touches the walls and roof and, in so doing, enlarges the Temple with an image of a power no building can have: the physical power immovable in its natural condition. Two senses, sight and touch (the light does both; Mannaei only sees), reveal the Temple, then, in a particular way. It shines in Mannaei's sight like "something superhuman, crushing everything else under its opulence and arrogance." This is not description. It is an action, because it affects Mannaei. It also suggests the schisms between the sects in their struggle for possession. The full display of this is withheld until the banquet.

There is no sentence that does not enlarge the subject of the action. As the proconsul descends into the mountain and discovers Herod's accumulation of armament, the eye is caught by honeysuckle flowers dangling in the sunlight. It seems shockingly out of place, so insignificant before the multiplication of things to destroy; but right after it, "A thin trickle of water was purling across the floor." This is another kind of power, persistent, everlasting, the power of nature and life, that mysterious, divine force which quietly in the most simple of things continues as the engines of war, the rich ornaments of princes, fall into decay or are destroyed. Here is the method, again seemingly a small matter of description; but the frail, the insignificant, is put against the summary of its opposite to show the paradox of strength and weakness. Sight, touch, smell, and hearing are employed.

The inadequacy of the aims of power to gratify, to supply the full needs of mankind, begins rapidly to inform the impetus towards a resolution of the tensions. The structure is almost burdened by the accumulation of the degrees and kinds of appetites which the pagan acceptance of the world as the end in itself supplies. This is the control and use of goods. Vitellius is suspicious of the crowd of people. Herod Antipas says they are here for his birthday. He feels impelled to prove his words. He points to servants leaning over the battlements and "hauling up huge baskets of meat, fruit, and vegetables, antelopes and storks, great blue fish, grapes, watermelons, and pomegranates heaped up in pyramids." Surely this anticipates the repletion of the belly's appetite, the reward and largesse of rule, not the food of life, but its surfeit. It causes Aulus, who is Rome to this province, to rush off to the kitchen.

Eating quickens and renews, sustains life. It is moved by smell, taste, sight, and touch, in this order, and sometimes by hearing. But gormandizing abuses the sensibility by forcing it to entertain matters beyond its organic need. This is the physical misuse of appetite—lust, its profane abuse. As an object of lust to others, Herodias reduces the sensibility, meant to serve, not be, its physical parts. This wastes it, each self-abuse diminishing the keenness until exhaustion ensues. This is death to our responses to one another and to the natural habitat which surrounds us. Herodias' accoutrements, "cinnamon . . . smoking in a porphyry bowl, and powders, salves, filmy fabrics, and embroideries lighter than feathers, were scattered about" the room. These are not to enhance her appearance, except as her appearance furthers her purpose to rule and so supplants her humanity with her will.

But how impotent they are before the power which has made the world the vessel of life, not its meaning. This impotence is made concrete at the close of Vitellius' inspection. The heavy plate which covers the pit is lifted by Mannaei, stiffening his long arms, strength against age. The publicans think it holds the great Herod's treasure, but what the enormous pit does hold is something vague and terrifying, a human being almost like an animal, his long hair tangled with the skin on his back. Above, looking down, the Galileans, the priests, the soldiers, make a circle. The tetrarch stands close to Vitellius, with Mannaei crouching at his feet. "The sun was glinting on the tips of the tiaras and the hilts of the swords"—these marks of authority against what lies below. Here is the tableau of conflict, those with physical power looking down upon what they can afflict but not affect. The pavement is hot. The doves swoop overhead. This detail is another antithesis and does what the honeysuckle blooms do earlier.

In sepulchral voice a great sigh rises up from the pit. Herodias hears it from the other end of the palace and is drawn toward it. She rests a hand upon the executioner's shoulder. Then in full power Iaokanann hurls his voice through the bars: "Woe unto you, Pharisees and Sadducees, brood of vipers, swollen wineskins, tinkling symbols." His voice is recognized. All listen now with more than curiosity. He threatens them with extinction, "like the snail that melts as it moves," an image which reduces them by comparison to the lowest and most vulnerable of creatures, but the cogency of the image is in the touch that melts the flesh instead of giving life, since touch is the mortal sense without which we perish. Then he specifies a universal destruction. His listeners can only think of Rome. It reminds them of exile and the sorrows of their long history. They cry: "Enough! Enough!"

Then in dulcet tones he promises them a worldly paradise, with a ruler before whom the world will bow down. This is what they all have in their hearts and expect. "Thy reign shall last for ever, Son of David." This makes Herod start. The existence of such a person is a threat and insult to him. Iaokanann ridicules Herod and his pretension to kingship. He tells him there is no other king but the Lord. At this the tetrarch breaks the cord holding his seal hanging at his breast and throws it down into the pit, ordering the prisoner to be silent. The sign of carnal power confronts the embodiment of spiritual power and is ignored. "I will roar like a bear, bray like a wild ass, cry like a woman in labor," he says, and then he tells Herod his incest has already been punished. He is as sterile as a mule. This produces laughter, a thing authority cannot stand.

Clutching the bars, Iaokanann presses against them a face like a mass of brushwood in which two live coals are glowing. There is no hotter fire. It begins to blaze, "Ah! It is you Jezebel!" He makes Herodias burn in shame for her adultery, which surely is no matter to be publicly divulged, and yet all her carnal temptations and devices are exposed. "You took his heart with the creak of your slipper." *Creak* as hearing suggests secrecy, even conspiracy, but it makes even stronger touch, the foot the slipper, the slipper the floor, and the inevitable hand that will remove the slipper. He ends with, "Die like a bitch." Herodias and Herod must suffer the harangue twice over, as it is translated to Vitellius. Herodias looks around for defenders. The Sadducees look away. The Pharisees lower their eyes. She retreats but not in final defeat.

This attack has put Herod Antipas on the defensive before his guests and subjects. He quotes other instances of incest in their history. Nevertheless he must hear his private affairs discussed as a subject of debate. This demeans him and threatens his position.

This is prologue to the banquet. All kinds and degrees of people, occupations and races are present, among them Herod's old soldiers, the sailors of Ezion-Geber, twelve Thracians, one Gaul, two Germans, the principal men of the Greek cities; others are named. This is the world at the world's banquet, the concentration and variety of appetites at the very moment the true Messiah walks the earth denying its efficacy and announcing its doom.

On a dais shrouded by Babylonian rugs, there are three ivory couches. Herod lies on one, painted and dressed, his beard trimmed like a fan, his hair dusted with blue powder and caught up in a jeweled diadem. Vitellius, near the door, keeps on his purple belt. Aulus, in a robe of violet silk spangled with silver, has his sleeves tied behind his back to keep them out of the way of food. From time to time he stretches himself. His large bare feet dominate the hall. Frequently Flaubert ends a paragraph by a sentence which sums up the paragraph's meaning. In one instance it is Aulus' feet, Roman feet, symbol of what can trample and crush all that oppose Roman will. All there, in some way, have felt the march of those feet, and mostly to their detriment. The sentence does more than define the paragraph.

The long banqueting hall, with three aisles like a basilica, divided by sandalwood pillars (appealing not only to sight but also smell), was filled to overflowing. Evidence of riches and strength, what all there either have or desire to have, shows itself in the great height of the ceiling—again, not a description but an action. Candelabra burning the long length of the tables cast a glow over the earthenware cups, copper dishes, piles of grapes, and cubes of snow (the final luxury); but the height, affecting the red glow, makes it gradually fade away, "until the points of light shone like stars between the branches." This comparison of lights to the eternal stars gives power's artifact, the palace hall, the effect of almost a metaphysical power, until we reflect that the light is wasting itself as it burns. The stars are eternal, made by God, not man.

Each guest has in front of him a cake of soft paste to wipe his fingers on: "Arms stretched out like vultures' necks to seize on olives, pistachio nuts, and almonds." As they eat, the guests talk about Iaokanann and people like him—about Simon, who cleansed sins with fire, and a certain Jesus. Eleazar, a priest, cries out: "He is the worst of them all. An infamous mountebank." A man named Jacob comes down from the dais and shouts at the Pharisees that they lie. He reports the miracle of his daughter's cure, which occurred at the moment he pleaded with Jesus in Capernaum for her life. The Pharisees, the tetrarch's friends, the chief men of Galilee, contemporize. There were herbs, but to cure without seeing or touching was impossible unless Jesus used demons. They have reduced the supernatural powers to Satanic forces, which is the damning judgment upon them. Each of the religious sects has forgotten what its rites represent. The rites have become themselves the objects of worship. The Pharisees shuddered when sprinkled with galbanum and incense, reserved for the rites of their temple. Aulus rubbed it into his armpits. Phanuel, the Essene who is trying to free Iaokanann, would not go near the tetrarch for fear of being splashed by oil. These are examples of the strict letter of the law, the substitute of ritual for what it should represent. They also show that these men ignore the power of God and allow the priestly functionaries to usurp it.

The action moves rapidly now. Jacob is asked to justify Jesus' power of healing. "Then you do not realize that He is the Messiah?" he asks. Upon request the interpreter tells Vitellius that the Messiah is a liberator who would give the Jews possession of all goods and dominion over all peoples. He would exterminate the Prince of Evil. This belief makes for the irony of disbelief in the true Messiah, whose miracle was reported by the witness who saw it. The priests argue that the true Messiah will be preceded by Elias. Jacob answers that Elias has come. He has seen him. All have seen him. He is Iaokanann. The Sadducees shrug their shoulders; the Pharisees deny eternal life for the body. At that moment the body they are thinking of, the body with the greatest appetite in the world, turns green. Aulus, sweat breaking out on his forehead, clasps his belly and leans over to vomit. This is a commentary on the action, with complex meaning.

Antipas makes a great show of concern. The Sadducees pretend distress and are rewarded with the high priesthood next day. Aulus has scarcely finished vomiting when he begins eating again, this being not only his but a general Roman habit which required at feasts a vomitorium. The general discussion which follows concerns cabalistic, occult, and other private religious beliefs and suggests the need for the true Messiah. For example, the priests talk of resurrection, Marcellus of his baptism in Mithras—the baptism of blood which almost, instead of Christianity, became the West's religion. Jacim, a Jew, no longer makes it a secret that he worships planets. An almost blind German sings a hymn in praise of a promontory where the gods appear with their faces bathed in light. And so it goes, this scattering of private interpretations of the divine.

At this point comes the crucial knock on the front gate. News has spread that Iaokanann is confined in Machaerus. The road is filled with torches. His name is called. Iaokanann! Iaokanann! It is clear why Herod did not want his captivity to be known. This power of the people, inspired by hope, threatens him and all those in high seats. A Pharisee says, "No one will have any money left if he goes on." And then a thing happens which makes hideous to Vitellius the Jewish temperament. Most of the guests turn upon their host and attack him for his family's crimes. It is the way they do it, their brutish obstinacy, which makes them seem hideous to the Roman. The Pharisees on their couches work themselves into a fury over being served wild-ass stew. They break dishes, while Aulus chafes them about their ass's head. The disorder increases. Members of a sect with egg-shaped heads and the jaws of bulldogs, with scribes and priests' assistants, rush the dias, their knives threatening Herod Antipas. Vitellius, disgusted with this show of intolerance, wants to leave, but Aulus refuses, a reversal of father-son authority, itself another kind of disorder.

Aulus lets down his robe to his thighs to free him better for gormandizing. Soon he is lying behind a great pile of food, too gorged to eat any more but stubbornly refusing to leave it. The guests become more and more excited, speaking of ways to gain their independence, recalling a glorious past and how their Roman conquerors had been punished. "You scoundrels," says Vitellius. Herod brings out the medal with the emperor's image uppermost and shows it to Vitellius.

Suddenly the golden panels on the balcony fold back, and there stands Herodias, surrounded by her particular pomp and circumstance. "Long life to Caesar," she says. This is repeated by Vitellius, Herod, and the priests. Then it happens. From the far end of the hall, there arises a murmur of surprise and admiration. A girl has just come in. It is Salome.

The great dish is now about to be ordered and served up. Salome is veiled as she walks up to the dais with the indolent ease of youth and beauty, with the confidence in a perfection of training for what she is about to do. The last sentence of this paragraph binds together the appointments and ornaments which envelop her, prepared by her mother to gain her ends. The irony is reserved for this last sentence, a skill Flaubert makes best use of in

climactic moments. Salome's little slippers tapping the floor are of hummingbird down. All the other adornments are designed to arouse fleshly
desires, but birds are angelic symbols. The dove we are familiar with, but of
all the birds the one breed most insubstantial is the hummingbird. The
down of its feathers, its size, its rapidity of movement suggest spirit confined, but barely so, by the body. The reader may anticipate, then, that she
offers more than carnal delight.

The child, abused by her mother, preserves at least for this moment a
vision which only an art can suggest. "Her rounded arms seemed to be
beckoning someone who was forever fleeing. She ran after him, lighter than
a butterfly [an image similar to the hummingbird], like an inquisitive Psyche
or a wandering soul, always apparently on the point of fluttering away." This
use of Psyche's quest is delibertate: "Her whole body was so languid that one
could not tell whether she was mourning for a god or expiring in his
embrace." Of course, Psyche did both. She expired in Eros' embrace, in the
dark of luxury that only lust knows. When she awakened, the god had fled.
She mourned but right away sought him. This quest brought her to her
death, the only instance in the pagan world we know of in which a human
dies for and rescues a god. Previously Aphrodite, Eros' mother, represented
only promiscuous procreation. Psyche died, a personal matter, to please her
lover, and changed his lust into love. This act anticipates God's dying on
the Cross for mankind. It is the pagan world's preparation for the great
events which propels the action of this tale. Herod's response to Iaokanann
suggests that he responds at first to the suggestions of the psychic drama,
when the motions of the dance are not those of simple lust, if such there
ever is. The first movement of the dance is meant to release the secret heart
of desire, raising the erotic to divine status.

But then the dance changes to the frenzy of love which demands satisfaction. "The nomads inured to abstinence, the Roman soldiers skilled in
debauchery, the avaricious publicans, and the old priests soured by contro-
versy all sat there with their nostrils distended, quivering with desire."
Herod Antipas' instinct for piety and fear of the Almighty is drowned in this
greed of sensuality. Lust on its way to changing into the unselfish offerings of
love abandons him. Speciously he reflects that if Iaokanann is Elias, he will
be able to avoid death; if not, it is a matter of no importance. Only the
death on the Cross by the God-man can save mankind from this callous
disregard of life. The world's rule, as exercised under the hegemony of

Rome, has been exposed in its mortal incapacity to command or represent the final truths of mankind.

The irony of Herodias' triumph, insofar as the action proper is concerned, lies just here. She feels she is avenged by death, the usual tool of rule. Actually she is a tool of God's purpose. The death of Iaokanann, the forerunner, is necessary for mankind's salvation. Death in this instance is therefore ambiguous. It doesn't seem to be so in the enveloping action. The head is brought in still gory, cut across the jaw by an executioner whose skill has never botched any execution before. It is shown to all, who are mostly indifferent to so common a sight. It is put upon the charger, according to agreement. There it lies, the prime dish of the feast, the controlling image announcing that the feast of appetite is death. It is symbol of the ultimate defeat of Rome, which will not be large enough to devour nature and human nature. The symbol of the symbol is Aulus, who eats and vomits and eats again, until his belly refuses, and the greatest appetite in the world sits at the last surrounded by food which he cannot eat. What had seemed to the world invincible has succumbed to physical nature. He is awakened by Mannaei, setting the head upright before him. "Behind their lashes the dead eyes and the dull eyes seemed to be speaking to each other,—the dead eyes: I am life in death: the dull eyes, death in life."

A story cannot close on an enveloping action. After the lights are out and the guests have departed, Herod Antipas, the tetrarch, sits at the end gazing at the head, in the same posture in which he is presented at first, "his hands pressed against his temples." Phanuel, the Essene, is with him, arms raised in prayer. The two men who have been sent to inquire of Jesus if he is the Christ have returned with the long-awaited reply. They are shown the head and say: "Take heart! He has gone down to the dead to proclaim the coming of Christ."

They all three then take the head and go toward Galilee. It is very heavy, and they take turns carrying it. I think we cannot refuse to accept that the weight is not altogether poundage. The device that Flaubert often uses to end an important paragraph now gathers together in this last sentence the action and the enveloping action, a physical appearance representing an eternal truth.

Unlike "Herodias," the opening sentence of "The Legend of St. Julian the Hospitator" is closer to myth than to history: "Julian's father and mother

lived in a castle in the middle of a forest, on the slope of a hill." The tone
of this evokes all the isolation of the early Middle Ages. Christian peoples
and their rulers also populate this world, but the exact location of the
castle remains unknown, as in myth. There is no final definition of myth,
but most agree, I believe, that it is outside history, consisting in archetypal
stories which concern heroes and saints through actions both supernal and
infernal. Examine the opening sentence again. It might be anywhere, anytime. Its suggestion is faery: Once upon a time, long, long ago, in a far
country . . .

In this lordship peace had prevailed for so long that the portcullis was no
longer lowered. The archer who patrolled the battlements retired to his
watchtower when the sun got too hot and slept like a monk. Grass grew in
the moat. Not only did the perils and stresses of war no longer threaten the
comforts and ease of the castle, but the serfs and vassals were free of most
seasonal threats, such as hunger and cold. Even the disagreements between
neighbors seemed small, for his lordship easily placated those involved,
settling their disputes.

Against the cold, tapestries hung from the walls; the lord's chests were
crammed with linens; his cellars were piled high with tuns of wine; his
coffers creaked under the weight of money bags. The outer defense of the
castle imitated a domesticated Eden, with gardens and orchards, bake-
houses, pasture for the cattle, a pergola for strolls, alleys where the pages
could play ball. In the wintertime his lordship watched the snowflakes or
had tales read to him, such idleness being the opposite of his proper role. He
had married a lady somewhat stern but with the gift for domestic rule. All
dependents kept busy; all things were ordered well. Warlike matters had
given way to domestic and familial peace. We see her ladyship, fair of skin,
the horns of her coif brushing the door lintels, her train trailing three paces
behind her. Sight is used here, but touch, the mortal sense, relates all the
parts. So we see her. But the horns of her coif that brush the lintels will later
brush the top of a wall with disastrous consequences, and not only to the
castle's comfort or domestic ease.

She is a lady who always has her way. She prays for a son, and a son and
heir is born. She does not attend the husband's merrymaking at his
torchlight banquet celebrating this birth. She is awakened in her chamber
to see a shadow sliding down a moonbeam. It is an old man dressed in

homespun. He speaks to her without opening his lips, telling her to rejoice. Her son will be a saint. His lordship at dawn taking leave of his guests sees a beggar rise out of the mists. He is dressed like a gypsy and says: "Your son! Much bloodshed! Always fortunate! An emperor's family!" Then he disappears. The good lord thinks it weariness from loss of sleep. Both man and wife measure these supernatural appearances in temporal terms. She keeps silent, thinking she will be accused of pride; he, thinking he will be laughed at. They do not even tell each other. Reducing the supernatural to a natural order brings them both to their death.

This is human blindness. The lady is told her son will be a saint: she can think no higher than an archbishop, an institutional functionary. The father thinks of military and political preferment. They look for proof of their hopes in the son's actions, each seeing a part, not the whole. Watching his nobility and humility in giving alms, the mother thinks of the churchly preferment. His father hears his cries of delight at the recounting of fabulous wounds, the storming of castles, and the workings of war machines. After the beheading of John the Baptist, after Christ's crucifixion for the salvation of mankind, the delay in a Second Coming brought not the Four Last Things but the necessity of keeping order by two institutions, Church and State, or Crown and Mitre. The world remains and death remains, and before these facts the divine irony has shifted its ground. The promise of salvation remains for all, but a doubt has crept into the mysterious supernal intentions. Or it may be a testing of the soul. As a supreme instance the saints become the chosen of God for this trial. And Julian is one of them.

If Julian were a monster, who with perversity had no instincts but those of a killer, his brutishness would never have made this tale. He would lack the humanity of men without the instincts of an animal, which kills to eat and protect its young. Material for sainthood is never lukewarm. It possesses great passion, often great criminal designs, and is one of the reasons behind the social need for order. Julian is particularly endowed with passion's rapacity, and he is a votary of death. On the other hand his piety and love for his parents are as deep.

These tales have not deprived God of his thunder. Western theology may define evil as the absence of good, but the behavior of men continually measures human action in terms of the cooperating opposites, life and death, male and female, pain and pleasure, love and power, night and day.

It is the task and quest of both hero and saint to balance, to resolve these differences within themselves.

The peace of the castle had lasted so long that it seemed to deny these opposites, which are always ready to shatter the desuetude of peace. The abrupt change never happens in an expected or rational way. It appears as suddenly as Grace, through the most unexpected agency. One day during Mass a little white mouse comes out of a hole, trots towards the altar, turns about several times and disappears. It keeps returning, first to Julian's irritation, then to his hatred of it. Finally one day he drops crumbs, and as it comes out to eat, he gives a light tap with a stick, and it falls over and is still. A drop of blood shows on the flagstone. He wipes it up and throws the mouse away. He keeps his act secret. Hiding is a property of guilt. So he has learned to kill and see blood: his innocence is lost.

To prepare him for his rank of noble his father gives hounds, birds, lessons in venery, all that his place demanded. Hunting in time of peace kept the fighter trim for war. But all the social occasions which involve hunting bore Julian. He begins to hunt alone. This is not brought about suddenly. He begins by shooting peas at birds in the garden. They rain down upon his shoulders, and he laughs at his cunning. He thinks it is his cunning. He is infuriated at a pigeon that refuses to die. He is still a child and has trouble wringing its neck, but he does it in savage delight, and when the bird grows still, he almost faints. To fighters the battle fury comes infrequently. The fury of killing becomes constant with Julian, increasing with each encounter. No weather deters him. He comes in at night, his hair tangled in thorns and covered with mud and blood, and the smell of beasts upon him. To emphasize the meaning of this, Flaubert has him receive his mother's embraces coldly.

The reader is not left in doubt as to Julian's mastery. All the ways to kill he knows: bears with a knife, bulls with an axe, boars with a spear, even a stick against wolves gnawing dead flesh at the foot of a gibbet. This is merely the beginning. One morning he goes forth with his crossbow and a pair of basset hounds. The weather matches his heart. It is cold. Rime clings to his coat. The hard ground rings to the hooves of his Danish jennet. This precedes the episode with a wood grouse. Numbed by the cold, it is asleep upon a limb, with its head under a wing. With a backward sweep of his sword, Julian cuts off its legs, a gratuitous act of cruelty, for he never stops to pick it up or in mercy kill it outright.

Three hours later he is upon a peak of a mountain so high the sky seems black. He is removed from a sensible to a visionary state. He sees two goats on a ledge overhanging an abyss. He stabs one. The other in fright jumps. In trying to stab this one, he trips over the one dead and, with arms outstretched over the abyss, he stares into its depths. The abyss tells him nothing. At once, without transition, he descends to a plain. Having ignored the warning of the abyss, he indulges in an orgy of senseless destruction. He strikes down cranes with a whip. A black-nosed beaver appears upon a gleaming lake. He kills it and is annoyed not to be able to carry off its skin. The bloodlust rushes through his veins. Framed by an arch of trees, out of the forest leaps a roe, a buck, a badger, a peacock. He kills them all, but there is no end. All kinds of birds and beasts appear, and they are named as they circle him, trembling, gazing with gentle, supplicating eyes.

He is in a valley like an amphitheater. It is crowded with bucks, rubbing together to keep warm. He kills them all. The panic of the carnage, bodies and antlers tangled, only makes him wonder at the magnitude of his slaughtering and how he has done it. The author now enlarges his practice of summarizing the paragraph by a closing sentence. Here, he summarizes the action with several paragraphs.

As Julian leans against a tree, wondering about but not understanding the extent of his slaughter, he is arrested by something on the other side of the valley. He sees a stag with a doe and her fawn. The stag is a huge black beast, the doe the color of dead leaves, grazing as the dappled fawn pulls at her dugs. His bow twangs. Instantly the fawn is killed. Now a new dimension is added to the carnage. The mother, looking up at the sky, gives a deep, heartrending, human cry. The cry exasperates Julian. She falls with a shot full in the breast. The great stag bounds forward, over the dead bodies, receiving Julian's last arrow in his forehead. The stag does not seem to feel it. He comes nearer, and Julian falls back in terror. But the huge beast does not disembowel him. He stops and with blazing eyes, "solemn as a patriarch or judge," as a bell tolls in the distance, says three times: "Accursed, accursed, accursed! One day, cruel heart, you will kill your father and mother." His knees then give and he dies.

Up to this moment in his apprenticeship of killing to the swollen bloodlust in heart and imagination, nothing has made Julian aware of his own humanity or danger to his person. This obsession has isolated him from his social equals, and in his senseless destruction of God's creatures his folly is equal to Aulus' gluttony. The greatest appetite in the world can barely diminish a moiety of the world's substance. And so it is at last with Julian's vision of slaughter. The Creator can use anything to give the illusion of reality, substantial animals or those seeming so. It is the mother's human cry of despair and grief which first touches Julian and vexes him to further killing; then comes fear of the black stag, and then the curse, accompanied by the tolling of, we assume, church bells in the distance. Withdrawal from the common life is not monstrous, only temporarily so; the curse changes Julian, restoring his feeling of humanity, without, however, freeing him of the lust for blood.

In his exhaustion and fright, disgust and deep sadness seize him, and he buries his face in his hands. His horse is lost, the hounds are gone, and in fear he sets out across country. Almost at once he finds himself at his castle gate. This confirms the supernal influence selecting him for its purpose. He cannot sleep. The black stag is always before his eyes, for the stag represents the communion of all living things, animal and human, in the attachment to family. He keeps telling himself he can't kill his parents, but then he recollects and asks, Suppose I wanted to? His bloodlust has not been purged. Doctors are brought at great expense and make trivial diagnoses. To arouse him his father gives him a beautiful Saracen sword. In getting it down, Julian drops the sword; it falls and cuts his father's surcoat. Julian faints. Afterwards any naked blade makes him turn pale. He knows its temptation from which he is not yet free. His parents are in distress. Unaware of his struggle, they see him not as a human being but as an heir who is unfitting himself for his place in society. The old monk orders him in the name of God, of honor, and of his ancestors to resume a nobleman's pursuits. Both Church and State therefore betray him. He gives in. With the pages he learns to throw the javelin with such accuracy that he can split the mouth of a bottle. One summer evening he sees what he thinks are stork's wings on top of a wall. He throws his javelin. There is a scream. He has nailed his mother's coif to the wall. Julian flees and never returns.

What Julian flees is what he has refused all along to interpret: his consuming passion to destroy life. This is the criminal aspect of that part of him which loves, at this stage, his father and mother. The two opposites are out of balance. His vision of slaughter (it cannot be actual, no man could kill so many even if he could gather them together) only makes him wonder how he did it. He knows only that he is alive. He does not distinguish between dream and reality. After he hears the stag's prophecy, he actually is on the castle grounds. He thinks he is lost, but do the gates of the castle make him think? In his long sickness he approaches the necessity of self-discovery. He even has the clue. But suppose he wanted to kill them? he asks himself. The question is not answered. It should plunge him into the abyss of himself, so that he could come to terms with the opposite poles of his nature. His parents, the priest, the whole economy of the castle aid and abet his refusal. Out in the world he throws himself into suicidal situations, a selfless commitment to wandering armies and battles. This is everywhere, except there is a suggestion that it may be mythical, since men's hair catches afire from the heat of the sun and their arms drop off from the cold. He protects orphans, widows, churchmen, and old men, acts of piety which aim to expiate an act which has not taken place, clearly the same refusal to confront that inward mystery of the ego harboring a godlike power with only human control.

He becomes famous, with much bloodshed. He has an army of his own, a charmed life, and he marries an emperor's daughter. Given the ambiguity of supernatural pronouncements, these temporal triumphs seem to be what his father's gypsy promised. Julian lives with his beautiful wife in a marble palace where all is quiet and cool, withdrawn from wars into a domestic and princely life of ease. But the one thing he has tried to forget remains. He cannot trust himself to hunt. He is still possessed. By the hour he sits in an alcove and relives the chase and the magnitude of his slaughters. Nothing his wife does, no entertainment she produces, banishes the cloud which dims their marble halls. However, she is persistent out of a doom which she believes is love. At last he tells her about the curse. She answers with reasonable arguments. He listens but still refuses to believe her.

But her words work. One evening in August, as he is kneeling to say his prayers, he hears the bark of a fox, followed by light footsteps under the window. "In the half-light he saw what appeared to be animal forms." We do not know what his prayers were, but they must have been by rote. He takes down his quiver from the wall.

Whose were the footsteps? After he leaves the palace, his father and mother, weary pilgrims, arrive. In search of their son, they are reduced to begging their bread. They convince Julian's wife by the usual marks upon the body, and she feeds them and puts them into her bed, in the room from which Julian heard the fox bark. The scene is set for the consummation of the curse. However, Julian has been given one last chance to recognize and come to terms with his compulsion to kill.

He walks through the forest with springy step, enjoying the softness of the turf and the mildness of the air. This is the feeling of life and well-being. It is brief. From this his possession leads him into a ghostly world. The moon's reflected light casts shadows of trees across the moss, making substance insubstantial. The white patches of light in the clearing turn into pools of water or ponds blending with the grass. All forms become vague, and everywhere there is a great silence, empty of the animals he thought he heard prowling beneath his window. Sight, touch, and the absence of sound make for this disordering of the senses. Then the sense of smell is added: into this atmosphere enervating scents and puffs of warm air, all conducive to dream, prepare Julian for what he is about to receive. It is the world of the dead. He sinks into dead leaves, when from behind, the ghost of a wild boar passes before he can sling his bow, the first time he has not been able to ready himself for the kill. Deeper in the forest he shoots at a wolf. The wolf stops, looks at him, and trots on, always staying the same distance to miss his shots. The message to Julian increases in intensity and number of warnings. He is on a plateau which is a succession of burial vaults broken or violated, across which he stumbles over dead men's bones and worm-eaten crosses. These are the shards and empty hulls of life, out of which hyenas come to bare their fangs and sniff. It does him no good to draw his sword. A mad bull lowers its horns and paws the ground. Julian flings his lance; it shatters as against bronze. He closes his eyes to die; opens them and the bull has vanished. He begins to realize that some higher power is making him strengthless. All he can feel is shame. The power has encased his bloodlust with a human pride so thick as to blind him to the kind of area he moves through. He is the anomaly of a natural man who does not recognize he exists among the inhabitants of the supernatural.

Making his way home, he is given stronger warning. It is as if all the beasts of the Garden had been killed by him and now surround him with their substanceless spirits. The branches of the trees fill with shining lights rained down from the sky. They are the eyes of animals accusing him. They make a ring about him. They sit on their haunches. They follow him. A bear knocks off his hat. A wild boar prods his heels. Their behavior is sly and insulting. Julian shoots his arrows; they land on trees like white butterflies. There could be no more perfect image of a hunter's impotence. Julian still has learned nothing. His lust to kill remains immaculate. He curses; he chokes with rage; he howls for a fight.

As if all his senses were dislocated, he finds himself fleeing, eyes shut like the blind. This remains his condition until the inevitable cock crows and his palace appears through its orange grove. Three red partridges lie before him. He throws his coat over them and, when he removes it, finds his last warning, one decomposing bird. The warnings of death do not warn: they increase his lust to kill, but this time not animals but men. The stage is set by his adversary, the maker of saints.

Finding his parents in the dark, in his bed, the fury of frustration is relieved. Thinking himself betrayed by his wife, he stabs them both.

At this point the legend of St. Julian adds his wife to his pilgrimage. Flaubert's insight makes him go alone. No other being can share his dark night of the soul as he seeks expiation. He shuns wife, all responsibilities, commands her not to look at him nor answer him but to carry out his orders for the funeral. She is to pray for his soul, now that he ceases to exist, that is, now that he still avoids the impulse behind his parricide. Dressed as a monk, not as a mourner, he follows the funeral cortege at a distance. In the door of the church he lies face down, arms outspread as in a cruciform. But to take up the cross will not be enough for him. He will have to ascend it.

He begs his bread all over the world with a face so sad nobody refuses him. Then, out of a need for reprieve from his isolation and for sympathy, he tells his story. The response returns him to his isolation. All flee him, making the sign of the cross; or they stone him. Wherever he is recognized, people shut their doors. The charitable put out a bowl of soup but close the shutters. He then shuns mankind and tries to live as a beast, feeding on wild plants, roots, or shellfish at the seashores. He becomes the thing he has destroyed. But only briefly. His awakening humanity arouses a longing to join his fellows. From a hill he sees the towers and spires of a town. He descends, but the bestial faces of the people freeze his heart. He sees them, having been a beast, as his prey must have seen him. But when the cathedral bells ring for feast days, he longs to become a part of the common life of men. This is the advance of the recovery of his humanity, but for the moment he can only

watch. He sobs and flees to the open country. His need for human communion with his own kind turns him to the foals in the meadows, birds in their
nests, insects on flowers. At his approach they all flee or hide in terror. They
sense an evil thing, a man denying his nature. This refusal of sympathy from
any form of life completes his isolation. Still he does not examine his
sorrow.

He follows the Furies. Alone, he seeks lonely places, as the fallen angel
accepted the abyss. But the wind sounds like a death rattle, dew falling like
the drops of blood. The sunset makes of the sky a bloody canopy. This
arousal of his sensibility causes him, as in his first flight, to try outward
stimuli—a hair shirt with spikes, the climb to shrines on his knees, but the
pitiless thought that he could have done what he did denies him respite
from his grief.

He is beginning that descent to the path for which he has been set aside.
There are no more false visions. He recognizes God's part in his suffering,
but he does not curse Him; he only despairs. His body, upon which the
senses act, becomes repulsive. He does desperate things to free himself of
it—the rescue of the helpless, for example—but in each instance he comes
out unscathed. He decides to kill himself. Looking into a pool, he sees an
old man vaguely familiar, with such sorrow upon his face that he cannot
restrain his tears. The face weeps; it reminds him of his father. All thought
of suicide leaves him. It has taken all of this suffering, every kind that he has
borne, to make him feel pity for another.

From this pity he begins to remember. Wandering for a long time under
the burden of such memories, he comes to a desolate place with a swift river,
a place so difficult to reach that nobody comes that way anymore. There is
an abandoned boat. The thought strikes him to make of it a ferry and spend
his life in the service of others. He no longer thinks of himself and so begins
at last his expiation, that preordained divine pilgrimage, which he did not
ask for, towards sanctification.

Up to this time his penance derives from self-mortification, but now in
this final stage the self engages in a complete submission to the needs of
others, without reward of thanks or pay. His rough hut has a stool, a table,
and three clay mugs. His bed is of leaves. With painful effort he makes of the
mud a causeway. He mends the boat, and people cross by this ferry. He is
abused: he gives his blessing. He is overloaded: he does not complain. Some

give unwanted clothes or a crust of bread. He continues to serve, no matter
the extreme afflictions from nature or man. Months go by and he sees no
one. Often he closes his eyes and tries to recover his youth. Gradually
images appear, a fair-haired boy under a vine-covered pergola, an old man
wrapped in furs, a lady with a great coif—and then the corpses consume
him. He flings himself upon his leaves, weeping, crying out: "Ah, poor
father! Poor mother, poor mother."

The pity he feels this time is not for himself nor a suffering face, but for his
victims and his part in their murder. It is the pity which must always
accompany love and so distinguish that feeling from lust, for lust uses the
object and casts it aside as having no life beyond the seizure of desire or
power.

And now for the final stage of the action. One night while a storm howls,
he hears a voice call, "Julian." It calls three times, the number for betrayal
or annunciation, and the voice has the sound of church bells. Julian rises to
his duty of service, with no hesitancy before the risk of nature in its most
destructive form. As he steps into the boat, the storm allays itself, and he
glides across the water to meet the passenger. He sees a face that is a mask,
"with two eyes redder than burning coals." This is the same image he fled in
his dead father's eyes. He lifts the lantern and sees a figure covered with
leprosy. He sees also a kingly bearing. The passenger steps into the boat, and
it sinks to rise with a bounce. At once Julian begins his strain of endurance.

The water is furious and black. The surf lifts the bow into the air. The
waves hollow out abysses, mountains, and repeat all the places of his physical trials. The senses, particularly of sight, evoke the blackness of hell. The
man-made light of the lantern intensifies this blackness, a human spark
against the everlasting dark, two conditions each of which makes the other
visible. But there is a sharper addition: birds fluttering past the shine of the
lantern increase the meaning of the two images. Each flicker reproduces
primal chaos; and yet the journey ends not in the sump of damnation but in
Heaven. Through the turbulence of the passage Julian sees the eyes of the
leper, motionless as a pillar in the stern.

At one point Julian, exhausted, gives up and lets the boat drift down-
stream. But when the wind takes his breath away (the meaning is ambiguous), the feeling that he must not desert his trust returns him to his labor. He
is now in that transition between life and death. The rattle of the rowlocks

makes a noise above the storm, a thing physically impossible. "And this went on for a long, long time." This sentence, which is a paragraph, lifts the action out of the temporal world. The tone is the eternal tone of faery.

The leper as passenger is the perfect symbol for Julian. According to the Haggadah, the legendary part of the Talmud, leprosy is the mark of Cain, the first family murderer. It punished as it protected the culprit. As expiation Julian had isolated himself from humankind. His only associate is a passenger, corruption eating the flesh, reminding him of his acts, and binding him. At last ashore, they enter Julian's hut.

By suffering, his self-imposed withdrawal from his fellows had returned him to his human condition, but it was his long vigil of service to others that gave to his humanity the perfection of charity and so prepared him for what would now follow. The use of the senses and the interrelationship of objects achieves at this point a moment of high craftmanship. Julian shuts the door (sound and touch) and in so doing shuts out forever the temporal and carnal body of the world. Before him, upon a stool, sits the leper, his only and constant companion. The leper's shroudlike garment falls to his hip. The parts of his body, shoulders, chest, scrawny arms, cannot be seen, for the scaly pustula in eating have reduced the differing parts of the anatomy to the anonymity of the common flesh. Where his nose had been, a hole shows the skeleton. This is death in life approaching the final breathless state. The leper exhales a nauseous fog of corruption into Julian's nostrils. Julian sees; he touches; he hears; he smells; and finally he will taste. Nothing repels his invincible charity.

The leper is hungry. Julian gives him what he has, a piece of bacon, the crust from a loaf of black bread. The author does not say that leprosy destroys life, whether it be human or vegetable. "When he had finished eating, the table, the bowl, and the handle of the knife bore the same marks that could be seen on his body." This is the ultimate literary use of the sense of touch.

The leper is thirsty. Here begins the reversal of opposites. The corrupt indicates incorruption as the water turns into wine. The scent makes Julian's heart and nostrils expand; but before he can drink, the leper empties the jug. The odor of the wine must have been excruciatingly tempting, since the ferryman had had only muddy river water to drink. This is the Last Supper reenacted, but the one guest can only witness, not participate. Yet

Julian shows only deference without the slightest animosity. The action quickly completes the surrender, even the ignorance of all personal wants. The leper says he is cold. Julian lights a fire of twigs. The leper squats to warm himself, but his strength is flagging. The cold increases; the shine leaves the leper's eyes; his sores run; he murmurs, "Your bed." Tenderly Julian helps him there, putting a sail cloth, his only cover, over him. But Julian must immolate any remnant of self. Upon command he lies down beside the dying stranger. This is not enough. He must take off his clothes and warm him with his body. The leper's skin, "colder than a snake and as rough as a file," descriptive of the lust in Julian's soul, touches him. There is still a last act of charity to perform.

Growing colder, the leper asks for Julian's entire body to warm him. On top Julian stretches himself, "mouth to mouth, breast to breast"; and then, clasping Julian in his arms, the leper transmogrifies himself. His eyes shine like stars; his hair spreads like the filaments of the sun. His foul breath suddenly has the aroma of roses, while a cloud of incense rises from the hearth. Superhuman joy floods Julian's soul, and he swoons as the arms of the other grow tighter about him, until the walls collapse and the roof flies off and Heaven unfolds. Julian rises towards the blue, "face to face with our Lord Jesus Christ, who bore him up to Heaven."

Julian had taken upon himself the full knowledge of and expiation of Cain's crime. And so is sanctified. And here is the irony. The divine authority set him aside at birth for sainthood by giving him one crucial property. Julian could not distinguish dream and vision from the conscious conduct of life. His Adamic self rebelled. Instead of caring for animal life, he set himself to destroy the Creator's creatures. To such an extent does the divine power go to show its omnipotence. The irony reverses itself.

Each of the tales gives differing conditions for the making of a saint. "Herodias" uses history; "The Legend of St. Julian the Hospitator," myth; and now "A Simple Heart," the lives of ordinary people. There are no great events, no circumstance of high estate to give occasion for self-sacrifice, only the usual domestic ceremonies and strains of civil life. The society is nominally Christian, but class has replaced the estates. Class, whether upper or lower, always means money. There are, of course, the usual sacraments of the Church's calendar, but a sustaining spiritual belief is submerged within selfish hearts and carnal natures. This seems to be the enveloping action. Madame Aubain as persona is its human representative. The definition for *aubain* is this: one living in a country to which one is not native-born. Madame Aubain is native to France; so it can only mean that Madame is in permanent exile from the once Christian kingdom of the French. The belief in divine salvation, which cost John the Baptist his head and St. Julian the unreserved surrender of himself, Madame Aubain would give lip service to, but other sacrifice she would not understand.

She is not a bad woman. She is selfish. Into her life enters a simple heart, but a heart which is pure in love. No divine sacrifice, no reversal of a criminal nature, but the pure passion of love's wants, complete as caritas and eros. The selfish ego and the loving heart, extreme opposites, are thus brought together and must have presented Flaubert the hardest demands on his skill. The question must have been: How could any human being in the hard-bitten materialism of that day have remained untouched by it?

The answer seems simple enough, but actually the invention has all the complexity of any profound truth. The purity of the protagonist's love is a given. It was a gift from God. No further explanation is possible where the facts are beyond reach. Flaubert then concerned himself with her simplicity, and this meant her isolation from sophisticated influences, such as a formal education. However, he warns the reader that *simple* is an adjective to a noun which is mysterious. He does this by naming her Félicité.

The circumstances of her life isolated her. Her parents died when she was young. She was deprived of the love and care of family life. Too young, alone, she must face the harsh conditions of service to a farmer who took her in. Young as she was, she had to mind the cows. She was beaten for nothing and was treated no better than the animals she tended. She lay on the ground and drank pond water. Accused of a theft she did not commit, she left and was hired by another farmer. She was better treated and put over the poultry, but she learned another form of distress, the jealousy of the other servants. Betrayed by an intended seducer, she left and went to Pont l'Eveque, where Madame hired her to cook and do all the housework. She took her in presumably because her demands were so few.

To this point, although without education, Félicité had been learning from nature and callous human nature. Her world was strictly limited to two farms, where the seasons were good instructors. She was like one suddenly thrust into the wilderness of Time without having undergone the state of innocence. The flora might just have been transplanted and the fauna shifted to its unenclosed pastures, where care of such had never been anything but sweat and sorrow. Her ignorance was almost that of the first day, before the sensibility had thoroughly awakened.

Animals, fowl, the sowing time, and the gathering time, all dependent upon the unpredictable seasons—these she served according to their needs and so understood ends as well as means. Her learning, then, was many small crafts all connected and completing a common body of knowledge. This was the working habit of craftsmanship practiced over the high days of Christendom. Because of her isolation no foreign habits intruded to soil her integrity. The accusation of theft did. By injustice the other part of her nature awakened and so brought her to the beginning of what would sanctify her.

In one way she and Madame suffer common sorrows. All they love is taken from them. Unlike Félicité, Madame, the worldly woman, is helpless in dealing with the world. The man she marries squanders her estate and then dies. After its settlement she has only two farms and a less pretentious dwelling. Her agent steals and betrays her confidence. He shocks her respectability. Her son disappoints her. Her daughter, not only her own but Félicité's delight, dies. She complains to God as if He, her spiritual agent, has betrayed her. Her education, holding money and possession as ends in themselves, gives her information but little learning, and that scattered and disconnected and so of small use to her.

Flaubert never leaves dramatic comparisons vague or too general. To both women he presents the exact curriculum of two farms. Madame's land is inherited, but she feels little responsibility towards it, only taking what it brings her. Privately her love for her daughter is possessive and too personal. Her life is so far deformed. With Félicité the two parts of behavior, formal and intimate, are two parts of the same thing. In their life together the roles of mistress and servant are reversed. When Madame's farmers come to sell her cheese and fowl, it is Félicité who sends them away, after trading, with the profoundest respect for her acumen. I know this is the custom, but Madame is like a relic, to be respected, but apart from the real stresses of life. Félicité tends to everything. Madame rarely leaves her chair by the window, where she sits embroidering or awaits the foot warmer her servant prepares

for the evening card game. Nevertheless it is under Madame's roof that
Félicité finds that her love can flourish. At first it is the children. She kisses
them so much that her mistress protests. She dresses Virginie, puts her to
bed, attends to her clothes. This is the service of love and adds nothing to
all the chores she must do.

But a dramatic episode reveals the quality of their diverse education. The
Aubain family is returning home one autumn night. The moon is in its first
quarter, with a mist over the fields, and they find themselves surrounded by
oxen. "Don't be afraid," Félicité says, and she makes soothing noises with
her mouth and rubs one of the animals on its back with that familiarity of
knowledge which is her guide. But in the next field a bull bellows and
charges the group. Madame runs with her children. "No, no," the servant
admonishes. "Not so fast." And then as the bull's hooves beat the ground
like a hammer, Félicité turns and throws turf and dirt in his eyes. Facing the
animal as she retreats, she calls out: "Be quick. Be quick." With great
courage Madame gets her children in the ditch and over it, while Félicité,
backed against a fence, the slobber from the bull's muzzle on her face, ducks
between two palings just as the bull is about to gore. One last touch, an
image as summary to the meaning: the bull pulls up short in astonishment.

Félicité thinks nothing of it. The incident is, however, a subject for
conversation for many years at Pont l'Eveque. She can manage her world on
its own terms, and she can defend those she loves. And it is this capacity
which instructs her in spiritual matters. She learns her catechism by taking
Virginie to learn hers. At the child's first communion she recognizes her by
her slender neck and devout bearing. When Virginie opens her mouth to
receive the Host, Félicité almost faints. Next day she receives her own
devoutly but without the same rapture.

This submersion of the self into another, unconsciously, is the selflessness
of love. So stimulated, "her simple heart" quickens an imagination rich and
unblemished. And this directly through the senses receives religious images
without which her simple heart could never have been prepared for sainthood. In an apse she sees the Holy Ghost hovering above the Virgin. Lest
this should appear to be too technically obvious, one dramatic image after
another assaults her mind: the Virgin kneeling before the child, Michael
destroying the dragon, "Paradise, the Deluge, the Tower of Babel, cities in
flames, throngs of people being annihilated, idols shattered."

These visions bewilder Félicité. "They filled her with the awe of the

Almighty and terror of His wrath . . . but the story of the passion moved her to tears." The Christ loving little children, being born among the poor and in a barn with animals, goes directly to her heart. Planting seed, gathering time, pressing grapes—this is the life she had lived. The images have one characteristic effect. She begins to love lambs more tenderly because of the Lamb. There is an irony here. The author seems to suggest that the farming world, which involves itself constantly with nature, is the world which best supports Christendom, whereas Madame's world tends to distort it and so lose the meaning of the Son of Man's Passion. As further emphasis the only secular education Félicité is given is from geographical prints Madame's agent brings to the children. Paul, a child, explains them: Bedouins in the desert, an ape fleeing with a maid, a whale being harpooned, et cetera. This world is at least puzzling to Félicité, as later on, when the agent shows the dot on a map where her nephew Victor may be, she asks to be shown the house.

For the action proper, in preparation for turning a dessicated worm-eaten parrot into the Holy Ghost, Flaubert has a slightly different problem. Félicité has no familiarity with the metaphysical world. The Holy Ghost is a flame as well as a bird and at times a breath. But accepting what she has been told and understanding that nature is also mysterious, she resolves what at first she finds puzzling. As a flame He is the light flickering on the edge of the marshes; His breath moves the clouds and His voice makes for the harmony of the bells. In her day bells had not lost all their metaphysical meaning or usage, such as quelling storms and ringing for emergencies.

When Virginie is sent off to school, Félicité feels that Madame lacks feeling, then reflects that such things are beyond her knowledge. To know such limits and to know her place is one aspect of Christian order. But this does not solace her for the child's absence. Each morning she goes into Virginie's room and grows sad that she can no longer comb her hair, tuck her in bed, lace her shoes, hold her hand on walks, nor see her pretty face. The sense of touch is mostly denied, and of the senses touch is the first way to the beloved object. Madame misses the child, too. Letters help; friends console; the other days she reads or walks in the garden. Félicité tries to make lace, but her worn fingers break the threads. She seems to herself no good for anything. She cannot sleep. Not being able to love, she is perishing. She asks that her nephew Victor might visit and distract her.

The boy returns her affection and brings her gifts from his short sea journeys. She brushes his clothes and feeds him and walks on his arm to church until he signs on for a two-year voyage as a cabin boy. Then all of her thoughts are for Victor. On hot days she imagines him suffering from thirst. When the wind shrieks down the chimney, she imagines him in a storm at sea, on top of a broken mast, or being eaten by savages or carried off by an ape. But she keeps these fears to herself.

Even so, Victor does not supplant her love for Virginie. In Virginie's last illness Madame calls for her foot warmer, gloves, and purse and rushes away in M. Poupart's carriage. Félicité first goes to church and lights a candle; then she runs after the carriage, catches up with it, jumps up behind, and holds on by its straps. It is dark and cold, and snowflakes are falling heavily. It comes to her that the yard is not closed. "Supposing thieves found their way in!" And she jumps down. This is the same selflessness she showed with the bull. Also, she knows the way of the world and her responsibility towards her place. Next day she arrives in the diligence and hears the death bell tolling. At the convent she finds Madame holding to the bedpost, sobbing in agony, where the dead child lies. The nuns lead her away. For two days and nights it is Félicité who stays by the dead girl, saying her prayers, throwing holy water on the sheets. As the beloved's face turns yellow, the lips blue, she kisses the sinking eyes. It would not have surprised her if they had opened. Her love does not stop at nature's boundary. She dresses the corpse as she had dressed the child alive, only snipping a lock of her hair for herself. Then she lays the body in the coffin. The two women continue to have the same attitudes. Madame cannot stand the raw grave. Félicité tends it and makes it lovely with flowers. Only then can Madame approach it. As the two women finally must go through the child's relics, Félicité takes for herself a plush hat with a deep pile, though it is moth-eaten. The two women's eyes meet and fill with tears. The mistress opens wide her arms, and the servant throws herself into them. In their kiss and common grief the differences in rank are annulled. Félicité is as grateful as if she has received some actual benefit. Henceforth she serves her mistress with "as much devotion as a dumb animal, and with a religious veneration." She has no thought that it was her love and attendance upon love that changed Madame.

For a while I thought this rescue of the possessive heart by the simple heart comes close to the meaning of the story, in that it exposes the inadequacy of the bourgeois world towards the needs of man. Selfless love is awakened in Madame, whereas the servant is filled with a benevolence towards all who have need. But this carnal, secular, and civil state as final value over against an irrefrangible charity is merely a part of the enveloping action. Not until I began to examine more carefully the controlling image or images (they repeat themselves) did a fuller truth appear.

The two telling images are Theodore, the false lover, and Loulou, the parrot. The name Theodore is the clue. It means the gift of God. But Theodore offers, instead of the compassion and service of a lover, simply lust. When he cannot have his way with her, he abandons her with a lie brought by a friend. This is not what we usually consider a gift. She flings herself upon the ground and succumbs to a paroxysm of grief. But unlike Madame, she neither blames God nor asks why. She confronts what has happened, but after that first betrayal, there are no more outbursts of grief. If we did not witness her restraint, we would not know the strength of her nature. At her nephew's death her mouth is closed, but she beats the clothes at the riverbank with such force the noise is heard throughout Pont l'Eveque. Never does she show the slightest sentimentality in sorrow. As she jumps from the carriage on the way to see Virginie, she resumes life by turning to her usual responsibility of the wash.

Each time God—and so she must have believed—removes the beloved object, her love, impervious to denial, rises from grief increased in capacity, even though her loss has been replaced by an object inferior to the one taken away. Whether it be soldiers she gives cider to, a wretch eaten by disease as he lies in a pigpen, stinking and foul, the two children, or finally a parrot, her benevolence remains the same. Its practice changes in the degree of intensity of feeling, but the giving remains constant. With Loulou, however, love reaches its absolute, even a metaphysical, definition.

The gift of God, then, becomes the opposite of meaning. He continually withdraws what He gives, as soon as Félicité grows attached. So it becomes a contest between the Creator and His creature, but it is not yet clear as to what end. Will Félicité turn cynical and be reduced to despair? Will she curse God and die? So far she has surmounted all the tests, but by means of a bird the action will be resolved into its meaning.

Félicité connects the bird with the strange, exotic, faraway places where her nephew died. And she brings about the gift of the bird to Madame, who finds it a nuisance and disruptive to her social life. In the presence of Madame's world, Loulou ordinarily remains silent; but at sight of Bourais, the agent, he laughs raucously, so that Bourais puts his hat before his face or, like a felon, hides along the wall as he comes to call. The town watches and enjoys the bird's comments. Bourais had laughed at the simplicity of Félicité's questions about foreign places. This now rebounds upon him through the parrot, a symbol of the foreign. Loulou has reduced a commonplace life to low comedy; but also, the bird's causing Bourais to slip hidden along the wall reveals the agent's criminal nature, which later shows itself.

Félicité now has only the parrot upon which to put her exorbitant capacity to love. And so she does. Again the pattern repeats itself. The bird disappears. Félicité returns from her anguished search exhausted, her shoes worn away; and as she sits upon a bench by Madame recounting her useless wanderings, she feels a light touch upon her shoulder. It is Loulou. What in the world had he been up to, a visit among the neighbors?

Although the bird returns, the result is an exhaustion which finally makes Félicité deaf. This is the beginning of her withdrawal from the carnal world. She no longer hears the lowing of cattle or bells. Only Loulou's sharp voice. People move as noiselessly as phantoms. This isolation confines her only to the parrot. Ordinarily such company would become unbearably boring or reduce her humanity and so her capacity to love. It does neither. The two talk together, the bird by mimicry reminding her of the common sounds of Pont l'Eveque, and she replies in meaningless words and sounds. They have enlarged language by a limit which is limitless, the fullness of the heart's voice. As she grows in deafness, Loulou becomes a son-lover almost, walking up and down her fingers, nibbling at her lips. He hangs to her kerchief, and as she leans forward to shake her head, the wings of her cap and his wings flap together, touching.

One cold winter day she finds him dead in his cage before the fire, where she had put him. She weeps so much that her mistress says, "Well, well, have it stuffed."

Parcels often miscarry in the diligence. In the dead, cold winter she walks in her black sabots to deliver the dead parrot to the ship's captain personally. She does not hear the mail cart galloping down the decline where she treads. The driver manages to pull the lead horses to the side, but, furious, he slashes her with his whip. When she regains consciousness, she looks first to her basket and finds Loulou safe. Her face is bleeding. She sits down and staunches it, eats a crust of bread, and takes consolation for her pain in the bird. It is not until she reaches a crest and can see the lights of Honfleur sparkling like stars, and the indistinct sea beyond, that the crucial test is given her, which is at some point always given to those the Godhead has chosen. The Christ asked that the cup be removed, the Buddha that he be spared from teaching. Félicité is tempted to feel sorry for herself: "A weakness overcame her, and her childhood's misery, the disillusionment of her first love, her nephew's departure, Virginie's death, came back all at once like a flood tide, rising to her neck and suffocating her." But the urge to consign Loulou into the hands of the captain of the vessel restores her to her usual self-effacement. After a long while Loulou arrives, perched on a branch fixed to a mahogany pedestal, with his head cocked, and one claw held in the air. He is biting a gilded nut.

How would her love respond to death, a lifeless image of life? She hangs the parrot in the chimney, where at each dawn she can see it; and full of peace, she recalls the days past and each insignificant event, so that the dead bring, through memory, life. More surely cut off now from others, she lives as in a trance. In church she has seen that the Holy Ghost resembles the parrot. This likeness is more marked in a certain picture. With its purple wings and emerald body it seems the very portrait of Loulou. She hangs it in the window so that she can see the bird and the picture with the same glance. The two become associated in her mind, and so the Holy Ghost is more easily understood. God the Father surely would not choose a dove to announce Himself. These birds have little voice. He must have chosen one of Loulou's ancestors. As she prays before the sacred picture, from time to time she turns her head slightly towards the bird.

In this gradual way Flaubert has prepared her for her final vision. In this way the years pass. Paul marries; Madame dies at seventy-two, mourned only by her servant, who feels the mistress's death before hers upsets her sense of the nature of order. The house is emptied by Paul and put up for sale. This distresses her, for it so suited the parrot. Gazing with pain at Loulou, she prays to the Holy Ghost, contracting the idolatrous habit of kneeling before the parrot to say her prayers. At times the sun strikes its glass eye and fills Félicité with ecstasy.

Years pass. The house remains unsold. The roof leaks, and she is afraid to ask for repairs, lest she be asked to move. One whole winter her bolster remains wet. She grows weak and her eyes fail. She catches pneumonia one year, at the time of the festival of Corpus Christi. As she suffers, she worries that she has nothing to put upon the altar, which is set up in Madame's courtyard. She will give Loulou. The ladies of Pont l'Eveque protest the worm-eaten parrot, but no object in itself is worthy to adorn the table of Christ. The object is no better than the spirit of worship or love which informs it. The priest understands that Félicité in offering Loulou offers herself, for to the parrot, dead or alive, she has given her full last love. So then the bird becomes not only the symbol of a simple heart's invincible charity. In Loulou, dessicated, moth-eaten, wings falling awry, Félicité returns the gift given, and with it, her immaculate love.

At the last, as her soul detaches itself from contamination with her body, now as destroyed as the parrot's, its ghostly presence rises to meet, as the Heavens open, a gigantic parrot in all its extravagant color, its wings hovering to receive what ascends. This brings to an end the story of the Trinity, of God the Father loving the child, and the Holy Ghost the love that played between them. This is Pont l'Eveque, the bishop's, the shepherd's, bridge which a simple heart crossed to find under the protection of those vast and purple wings the felicity which in life, as far as the world understood, had been only her name.

She has won the contest. Her adversary has granted her her reward, at least the sanctity He had intended for her. But an irony remains. To be a saint is to suffer desperate and unique deprivations. John the Baptist loses his head; St. Julian dies in the arms of a leper; Félicité is denied the continual joy and communion with what was given. The chosen, then, is that object of a divine secret which remains, with no veil lifted, secret and divine.

The Divinity of Love: Joyce's "The Dead"

JOYCE'S "THE DEAD" HAS OB-
viously been put together by a master craftsman. The form and the
subject make a perfect joinery.
Nothing is left dangling; no part of it
is inert. This is the mark of a master's work. Some of the stories in
Dubliners are more moving than
others, but they all produce that
shock of surprise which comes from
an old truth once again reborn into
the full radiance of its meaning. The
occasion for the action of this story
is that celebration which is Christ's
birthday; yet the reason for the fes-
tivity is forgotten, unnoticed by all
who attend. These are the dead, but
the dead in a Christian sense. Aside
from the stopping of the heart, the
many ways to be dead have as a common ground a spiritual hardening,
to be shown in the action here as a
kind of death in life; and yet as the
action advances, the hardening enlarges its meaning. The guests'
worldly interests, their carnal
natures, so absorb them that the
Word Incarnate, and any sense they
may have had of it, is absent. The
Christian miracle has been interred
in the lifeless forms of Church and
State. The communicants worship
by rote as they would attend

thoughtlessly to any routine. Or they look upon the institutional Church as existing for their private needs. Aunt Kate feels the great injustice done her sister Julia when "whipper-snappers of boys" replace her in the choir, after Julia has been "slaving there in that choir night and day, night and day. Six o'clock on Christmas morning! And all for what?" It does no good for Mary Jane to suggest that it is for the honor of God. Aunt Kate knows all about that.

If the world is all here at the Morkans' party, it is not unlike that world which Christ was born to save—temporal, a universal servility under the hegemony of a great empire. The treadmill of obeisance to this kind of power is symbolically presented by the literal treadmill the grandfather Morkan makes as his horse circles the statue of Wellington, topped by the snow, a symbol of the Irish plight and its hope. The statue is as foreign, as heavy upon the landscape, as must have been the columns of Rome in Israel. There is an analogy between these two small countries, as there is between Rome and England. England's alien rule marks Ireland's great fall, long entombed in history, for once it was the cultural center of Europe and brought the Word to the continent. But upon the night of this party there is a difference, and it is not simply historic. Christ has already come, even if the guests and the hosts have forgotten. The promise of redemption all men now share alike. Their forgetfulness cannot change the sacrament of this promise, for the Word will forever be risen. So it is that snow is the perfect symbol for the Christian dead. It is the waters of life in a state of suspension. Water has changed its appearance. It seems not to be itself, no longer flowing, now stilled, its divine crystals unique, original, and numerous as the leaves and the grains of sand, but it is still water, still the source of life in this world. It awaits the sun, that old symbol for Christ, to melt it and make it flow as water again, resurrected in the flesh of its proper mystical body, ready for judgment.

At first the very words which write the story seem to be deprived of their fullest meaning. They also are in a state of suspension, in appearance restricted to the appetites, to the sensible used as the end in itself, as at this annual party the glory of the occasion lies buried under a profane communion. This is Joyce's irony. It will be the creative power of his language which will resurrect by means of his story the full meaning of the Christian vision. It begins with Gabriel, as once it did. The Muses of the Dublin musical world, the two old aunts and the frigid niece, await the moment, the momentous arrival. Gabriel, the favored nephew, is late. It is he who is longed for, expected, and needed.

However, the hostesses look towards the arrival of another guest with anxiety: Freddy Malins, whom they expect to turn up drunk. Malins suggests *malum*, an apple, the substantial symbol of our common plight, and *malus*, bad. The Misses Morkans' apprehension is immediately a possible scandal which will mar their party. More profoundly they fear him as the representative of them all, shown best by the extremity to which the carnal and sensible can be carried as ends in themselves, short of spiritual grace. Freddy is the boy who has not been allowed to grow up, and his mother is at the party to prove it. Metaphorically thwarted by her old dry dugs, yet not free of his want, he cannot take to the proper food of man; so he takes to stronger drink. At times he stands for a baby devil. With the backs of his fists he rubs his eyes like a sleepy child; he is inchoate when telling a story, like a baby using words before he has learned their sense. He beats time on the table, leading the song "Jolly Good Fellows" with his fork. At the end his fork is upraised like a baby devil's tool. The comparison that comes to mind is this: "Woman, what have I to do with thee?" *i.e.*, you cannot prevent me from doing my proper work. But Freddy, we learn towards the end at a crucial moment, does begin to recover his manhood. It is not in itself a very grand thing he does. He opens a shop to sell Christmas cards, to spread the news of friendly neighborliness, forever promised by Christ as of the first importance. Gabriel has lent him a sovereign to help in this. We may presume this is from the heavenly treasure-house of charity, not alms, for in returning the loan Freddy keeps his proper sovereignty, a man beginning to be responsible for his acts.

But Gabriel arrives before Freddy. He is lightly dusted with snow, and the fragrant air from out-of-doors escapes from the crevices of his overcoat into the hallway. This air emanates from the snow which overlies Dublin. Snow is the visible sign of winter, the dead season. But death is not sweet-smelling. Fragrancy suggests bloom and so promises renewal, as does the archangelic name Gabriel. This archangel is the guardian of the celestial treasury, the messenger of good news, the Angel of the Annunciation, the Angel of Redemption. The name means "God is my strength." He generally bears a lily as symbol of the Blessed Virgin's purity.

Gabriel, the man, in parody of the divine mission, enters the house of the dead—that is, pure matter, appetite, flesh. He is his own announcement of himself; yet his name, which means "God is my strength," is still with him, even though he has lost the sense of its meaning. It is interred in his ego, that part of being which replaces God with man. This reduces humankind to substance. The divine Word, therefore, instead of entering the flesh, is buried in it. Such is the plight of all in this story. But because the Word was made incarnate, resurrection has been promised. The lily, the symbol for purity, is not left pure symbol. The caretaker's daughter is named Lily. At once we get the divine drama reduced to human definition, but in that definition are the qualities of the archetype. Certainly Gabriel brings no lily with him. His entrance parodies not only that of the heavenly messenger; as a lustful man Gabriel Conroy does not practice or understand purity. The lily suggests the place of love, with all the complexity that involves, even to the depravity it may induce or the soilure it may suffer. The Word spoken to the Blessed Virgin, creating in woman the promise of redemption and thereby ennobling her beyond measure, has become to Lily, the caretaker's daughter, a sly means to threaten and betray her own virginity, betray it through the pretense of love. The creative Word has been traduced. All the spittle of lasciviousness has made it slick. The Word is now palaver. "Men is all palaver and what they can get out of you," Lily says bitterly to Gabriel, and he blushes.

It is this blush, the sense of guilt and failure, which begins his redemption. He only feels this guilt and failure now; he is not yet awakened to its meaning—that he has allowed his love for his wife to fall into the easy habit of lust; that as a teacher and journalist he has allowed language by false rhetoric to inflate his good sense of himself, thus failing his office to render and transmit meaning. This failure matches in a secular way what has happened to the divine meaning of his baptismal name, for the O'Mulconreys were hereditary poets and chroniclers of the kings of Connacht. This meaning he will finally have to confront, for no matter how besmirched, how misapplied, a word means what it says. This is its secret power and its danger. It is finally impervious to any other translation than its meaning. Danger to it lies in the place it takes in the sentence. There the word may belie itself, be perverted by its modifiers, become its opposite. It is always subject to an antic threat. That flickering tongue, invisible and harmless until it houses itself in humankind, may make of the beautiful tones of speech a discord. Not an obvious discord to the ear, since that tongue has already separated sight from sound, but the more gravely induced discord to the intelligence. The intelligence is traduced in its very citadel. Language no longer has to have meaning; it only has to sound as if it had. This betrays the Word which begat words, the one means which brings to our poor lot a charitable communion and allows us to move and speak together as human beings, in a temporal state dimly reflecting that of the Heavenly Kingdom.

When language approaches the perfection of this inheritance, all together and separately each and everything stands forth in the fullness of its qualities. This allows for the poetic seizure which takes those who serve it at its highest possibilities. Gabriel's false rhetoric describes failure in both his offices; so he is unsure of himself before Lily. In his confusion, to her confusion, he tips her, as if money could repair the damage to her spirit. He goes upstairs feeling demeaned without knowing why. He waits outside the drawing-room door as the waltz is danced and hears those skirts which touch the private parts of woman brush also the door. Yet this subtle appeal cannot dispel the gloom the serving girl has cast upon him. For reassurance he takes out the notes of his speech; but this brings him no comfort. The "indelicate clacking of the men's heels" reminds him that his grade of culture is better than theirs. He would fail with them as he had failed with the girl. Indeed he would. He had failed himself and so forgotten the common brotherhood of man. Failure is hardly the word: his soul is imperiled by the weight of his vanity. The soul's effort to warn him brings the gloom he feels. He can only feel, he cannot know, the cause, for appetite and false pride is to the soul a foreign tongue whose emphasis of tone may disturb but not inform.

Yet there is hope for Gabriel. The successive advances of the action encourage his sense of loss and guilt. Without this the moment of revelation, that miracle of spiritual rebirth, would fail him. The increasing sense of loss and guilt are not enough in themselves to bring this about. They are negative. It takes a pure heart (Gretta's) to respond both to the word almost forgotten and to the music, hoarse though it be, and resurrect a love which has never been dead but only withheld as in a treasure chest.

The increasing awareness of loss and guilt seems to be Gabriel's plight as he enters the dance, a dance that more resembles the dance of death than the dance of life. Here again the marks of life are present, but in the fullest sense they are inanimate, and the dancers themselves seem in a state of trance. The dance is not a celebration; it is a sensuous movement which stops when the music stops. Even its movement is marred by an alien intrusion: Miss Ivors' propaganda for a dead language, Irish. She dominates the dance for Gabriel, her partner, like some harsh priestess. Propaganda dehumanizes, because it would reduce the full flow of life to an abstraction always less than life. She invites him to go to the Aran islands for a month, not for the pleasure of being there, such as gave delight to Gretta at the thought of going, but because these remote and cut-off islands still speak Gaelic—their given speech, but not hers nor Gabriel's. He says as much. Gabriel quite frankly confesses he goes to the Continent for a change and to keep in touch with languages, not the language of Christendom but the separate national tongues of states no longer Christian except in name.

Gabriel's awakening, once set in motion, proceeds. He is still self-absorbed. He is not even aware that his wife is dancing, but her care for him notices the quarrel with Miss Ivors. He is drawn to the cold windowpane; his fingers touch it, drawn to the coolness outside. He is longing to walk through the snow, breathing the fragrant air. The clue is the word *fragrant*. What he feels is an instinctive need for salvation. He prefers it to the supper table, that feast of appetites only. "I'm sick of my own country, sick of it," he tells Miss Ivors; yet he cannot tell her why. The Gaelic tongue is a dead language. Miss Ivors' commitment to its resurrection is misapplied. It cannot now, except in those remote places where it is still spoken, serve as the means for communion among men. It is English, foreign though it be, which is spoken in Ireland. It is the instrument of communion; as such it needs renewal, lest the faith now sunk within the heart remain forever buried. Miss Ivors has confused, with the best intentions, the instrument with the thing itself. Gabriel rebels against this. Thinking of her, he rewrites his speech in his head, accusing her of being hypereducated—that is, of relying too much upon intelligence. To this he opposes the hospitality of his aunts as an ancient virtue of the Irish. However, in doing so, he exposes the same fault in himself of which he accuses Miss Ivors: "What did he care that his aunts were only two ignorant old women?"

This is betrayal of his kin, betrayal of his office as orator. His words will not have any meaning; they will only seem to have meaning, because they are insincere, largely inflating his vanity.

This brings us to the feast and to what Christ's advent did to the Muses in their multiple meaning. The feast itself would appeal to the most dyspeptic appetite. The appeal to appetite cannot be paraphrased; it must be quoted.

> A fat brown goose lay at one end of the table and at the other end, on a bed of creased paper threwn with sprigs of parsley, lay a great ham, stripped of its outer skin and peppered over with crust crumbs, a neat paper frill round its shin and beside this was a round of spiced beef. Between these rival ends ran parallel lines of side-dishes: two little minsters of jelly, red and yellow; a shallow dish full of blocks of blancmange and red jam, a large green leaf-shaped dish with a stalk-shaped handle, on which lay bunches of purple raisins and peeled almonds, a companion dish on which lay a solid rectangle of Smyrna figs, a dish of custard topped with grated nutmeg, a small bowl full of chocolates and sweets wrapped in gold and silver papers and a glass vase in which stood some tall celery stalks. In the centre of the table there stood, as sentries to a fruit-stand which upheld a pyramid of oranges and American apples, two squat old-fashioned decanters of cut glass, one containing port and the other dark sherry. On the closed square piano a pudding in a huge yellow dish lay in waiting and behind it were three squads of bottles of stout and ale and minerals, drawn up according to the colours of their uniforms, the first two black, with brown and red labels, the third and smallest squad white, with transverse green sashes.

This is the world's feast. Its fruits come from the ancient world and the new, as well as from what can be got at home. It is worthy of our Savior's birthday, but it is not set forth in His honor nor in His name. It is the feast of the dead, because it does not celebrate anything but appetite; its hospitality, anything but the vanity of the hostesses; its humanity, anything but its physical necessities—all ghosts of the sacraments these qualities represent. As the food passes, the conversation turns upon singing. This is a house that lives by music; many of the guests are enrolled in its discipline. The ladies Morkan must have loved it and in a way still do; but the professional cares attending it, the need to make a living by it, have lost to them its mystery— all except for Aunt Julia. The house of Morkan, when pronounced aloud, is powerfully suggestive of the morgue. All of the singers brought forth by reminiscing are dead. They appear at the banquet like ghosts of the past, each one evoked by an individual out of his memory, a private ghost which denies by its presence present song. The Muse, instead of bringing all together at the feast, separates each from the other until each stands alone, isolated by his or her particularity and lack of communion. This is the comment on the birthday, ignored and neglected, of the Savior of mankind. There is the protest by Mr. Bartell D'Arcy. He is a tenor who lives by singing and, as we learn, cherishes it. In this house his voice is hoarse, and at first he refuses to sing, because of a cold. He protests, however, that there must be as good voices now as then; and he mentions London, Paris, Milan, and Caruso by name.

The pudding brings an end to this discussion but not to the subject. It shifts ground to Mount Melleray, a monastery where the monks, withdrawn from the world, entertain it without cost. They do not speak (their communion is with their inward journey, and so they are literally dead to the world), and they sleep in their coffins. Mary Jane tells Mr. Browne, when nobody else can give him a proper answer to a pragmatic question, that the coffin reminds them of their last end. The sweets are now passed and the glasses filled with port and sherry as a prelude to Gabriel's speech and the toasting at the end. Mr. Bartell D'Arcy at first refuses the wine. This is an instinctive, symbolic refusal: the living have no cause to toast the dead. Gabriel arises and begins. His speech, besides belying the language, is entirely about the dead, the lost spacious days, the lost common humanity and humor and tradition of courteous Irish hospitality, dead to and by the present skeptical generation, hypereducated and thought-tormented. He speaks of lost youth, changes, and absent faces. Towards the end he makes a rhetorical statement that living duties and affections claim their time.

Feeling the need nevertheless for something to celebrate besides mortality, he resurrects the myth of Paris and the golden apple. In the "true spirit of *camaraderie*" he refers to his kinswomen as the Three Graces of the Dublin musical world. The myth is certainly a part of our inheritance, but not of our Christian history. The Three Graces are certain mysterious forces of the classical world. They are also the Three Gray Ones (the Morkan ladies' physical description is gray), the three Muses, the three Fates. Their powers were extensive, far beyond music and dancing. They presided over oratory, letters, prophecy, healing, the fearful making and withdrawing of life; they invented certain letters of the alphabet. But their language is not ours. We may fear death, but no one fears the shears of Clotho.

Acting for Gabriel as the Three Graces, the Morkan ladies represent the goddesses Athena, Hera, and Aphrodite—Wisdom, Uxoriousness, and Love. Gabriel appoints himself to the role of Paris. This usurps the power of Zeus, but it is all a metaphor. Zeus' thunderbolt threatens no one, least of all Gabriel. But he shows he has forgotten his own true divinity, affirmed by the passion of Christ. And so Gabriel not only parodies the pagan myth—he parodies himself, seeing himself only in his natural attributes. But like Paris, he has taken the love of another, as the gift this time of death, not love. Aunt Kate's wisdom is all practicality. There is a suggestion of Athena's warlike capacity as she orders the feast, the decanters serving as "sentries" and the "squads" of stout and ale and minerals drawn up in their "uniforms." Like a soldier, she accepts rules without understanding their purpose, as illustrated in her reply to Mr. Browne concerning the monks who sleep in their coffins. Mary Jane must surely be the miscarried Aphrodite, with her wasted gifts of youth, not having a man but doing his work as chief bread-winner for the family. She plays perfectly her Academy piece, not missing a note, missing only the purpose of music, for, alas, she plays it only for herself. It has no melody for her uncle nor for the young men whom she should attract. They slip away for refreshments and return to applaud the loudest as she finishes and folds away her score. Her playing is what her uncle calls thought-tormented music. Its melody and tone are lost in the execution, which makes of it a meaningless discipline.

To change the order of the goddesses, who this night offer no golden apple to Paris-Gabriel, I take Aunt Julia last. With her slow, cowlike eyes she must be Hera, a Hera without a Zeus. And yet it is her singing which arouses the genuine response, sure flight that it is, not missing even the grace notes. The applause brings a faint flush to her cheeks. This blush carries the same promise of salvation as do Gabriel's blush of shame and Aunt Kate's nut-brown hair. Momentarily she arouses in her guests the sense of a hallowed force, even though "her slow eyes and parted lips gave her the appearance of a woman who did not know where she was or where she was going." Life has not fully engaged her; though she has never wed, her song, "Arrayed for the Bridal," transposes into music the great gifts of womanhood, the queenly knowledge, that have gone unused. This burial of life the guests feel strongly, because in her they recognize their common plight. The irony belongs to another level of reading. She, an old woman, will not wait in vain; the groom will arrive, and soon. He will seem to be Pluto, not Zeus; and yet he will be neither. In a Christian sense death can never be a bridegroom. He is the eternal eunuch. The groom whom Julia may expect will be of the highest estate.

Finally the myth as Gabriel uses it loses all its meaning. He does not award the apple. There is no apple, and therefore he cannot take the risk Paris took. The golden apple is merely a metaphor of a false invention and a convention of a senseless speech. It is that other apple, offering the choice of salvation, he should have thought of on this birthday of the second Adam. But the promise adhering to this birthday is not yet awakened in him, and the forms of the Muses are ghosts of themselves, since Christ the Word has altered the Fates and silenced the Muses of oratory and letters. Christ, who came singing and dancing, has lost us the chants and dances of the choral odes. His birth has made anachronistic all prophecy; his miracles have made useless the sympathetic healing of magic. Unaware of his true role, Gabriel blunders into a peroration as fatuous as his speech: "To their health, wealth, long life, happiness and prosperity." Upon this profane toast the guests rise and lift their glasses. The words are verbiage. The possibilities of wealth and long life have already passed the aunts by. With the approach of old age health does not seem promising. We have watched Mary Jane repel in the young men the agencies of happiness and prosperity. If Gabriel's words are gaucheries, the gratuitous cruelty of the song lifted in the ladies' honor makes a travesty of the feast. "For They Are Jolly Good Fellows" is a bachelor's song. To call the Morkans by what they lack to complete them as women is a brutal reminder of their plight. The refrain, "Unless he tells a lie," makes this clear. All have forgotten upon this birthday that there is no final joy but in Christ.

The party ends shortly after midnight: "The piercing morning air came into the hall where they were standing." It is this air which Aunt Kate fears will bring Mrs. Malins her death of cold. Tradition has it that Christ was born exactly at midnight. The spear which pierced the side of God as man let out water and blood, the substance and symbol of matter as temporal life to be resurrected into life eternal, our manhood into his divinity. Air as life now strikes Mrs. Malins, the bad or corrupt apple. The death feared for her is the world's evil, metaphorically pierced to spill into the world that which is the world's own by the spirit which is salvation. Time and space become one in the eternity of Christ the Word, the Just Sun, which is again about to rise and dispel the darkness and make shine the promise of salvation to all creatures. This means hope for Mrs. Malins, Freddy her son, and Mr. Browne, an enigmatic figure in the action, wizen-faced, with a grizzled moustache, and of swarthy skin, who leaves the party dressed in a green overcoat with mock astrakhan cuffs. All the things that make up the world as the end in itself—appetites, disbelief in the supernatural, comfort, sensuality, the rational acceptance of matter as the only value—Mr. Browne represents. "Browne is everywhere," Aunt Kate says, lowering her voice. And she further says that he has been laid on here like the gas all during Christmas—gas, the artificial and man-made light and warmth, aeriform but, unlike air, deadly by itself; in other words, Browne is symbol of that which has allowed them all, Morkans and guests alike, to forget the true light and substance. The green coat may stand for his predicament: green as corruption and verdure. All the laughter about getting a cab seems beyond the occasion, even a little hysterical, until you reflect that the guests are now leaving the house of death and darkness to enter the morning, still dark, of the new day. Amidst the confusion of directions given to the cabman, Mr. Browne tells him to drive up bang against Trinity College gates. This is another example of Joyce's tactics. A place of learning may have uses for words, made perhaps useless for the loss of the Word. However, the word *Trinity* is there awaiting regeneration, as the astrakhan wool cuffs, both false and foreign, remind us that perhaps, after all, Mr. Browne is the Shepherd's lamb, even if among those who go astray.

In the very depths of the winter solstice, in the darkness of the night of centuries, the Light of Lights and King of Kings was born. So it is that in the spiritual darkness of the Morkan household life, in its form of true music, is awakened.

Gabriel had not gone to the door with the others. As protagonist he has been held back below, in the dark part of the hall, gazing up the staircase, that metaphorical temporal upward flight all sinners must confront. This is the moment for the beginning of the great change in Gabriel. His mind has been somewhat prepared for this, but he is still in his fallen condition. He sees a woman standing in shadow on the first landing. He can see the terracotta and salmon-pink panels of her skirt, warm and lively colors which the shadows have reduced to black and white, good and bad. It is his wife, and he sees only that part of her, the lower part, which arouses his lust. The sovereign part of her being is obscured by shadow, but "there was grace and mystery in her attitude as if she were a symbol of something." She is the symbol of life and love, into whom the Grace of the Holy Ghost is about to descend. This is the mystery of the awakening which leads to salvation.

It is her stillness which first attracts him. Tradition holds "that at the moment of Christ's birth all Nature was still as if time itself had paused in its course, and that this shock of stillness was so sudden and strange it made universal the revelation of the Incarnation of God." The entire Host of Heaven came down to earth and shone around the cave with a brilliance that turned night into day. Hardly had the intense throb of silence passed when all the nine choirs of Heaven cried out, singing: "Gloria in excelsis— Glory be to God on high, and on earth peace to men of good will!"

It is almost a parody to reduce this earth-shaking moment to the stillness of a woman listening to a simple piece of music, sung with a hoarse voice and haltingly, as if the singer were uncertain both of words and music. But she is the one in all the party of that night who is full of life, and all that Gabriel can do does not destroy it. In her very entrance to the party we are told how he tries to insulate her from life. He makes her wear gutta-percha things which protect from water, the substantial symbol of life. She laughs and says he would like to make her wear a diving suit—that is, to insulate her completely. This makes a grim comment in that he would like to keep her entirely for his own pleasure and usage. But he has failed in this for the simple reason that she is life itself. A country girl, her human nature has been nourished by the mysteries of nature, only secondarily by the laws and habits of man. Her joy will be the joy of this knowledge, and her grief will be its grief. She is called "country cute" by Gabriel's mother, that bourgeois mother who sees no further than worldly success for her sons; yet it is Gretta, out of her natural sense of charity, who nurses this woman through her last illness.

Caught in that ambiguous balance of light and dark, the controlling opposites of our fallen condition, which is the stress we know as life, Gretta is listening to the song which will release the miracle buried in her heart. It lies there distant from her usual habits of living. However, it is that music which is the joy of life and its promise of perpetual being. The archangel Michael's trumpet will sound the resurrection of all those in that state of

suspension called death. In imitation of this, in an action which foresees the
reverberation which will precede the Four Last Things, it is not a trumpet
but a song of the old Irish tonality, of the ways which Gabriel praised
rhetorically at the dinner, which will awaken and raise up in Gretta the
perfect hope promising us our salvation but certainly bringing our moment
of final judgment. In the inverse way in which the situation is propounded
in this action, Michael Furey, the prototype in name of that archangelic
splendor so dimmed here at the Morkans, the boy who died for love of
Gretta, is in the simplest way, from an old country song, to be resurrected
through Gretta's memory. Memory through recollection into song is the
pagan definition of the Muse. The agency is Bartell D'Arcy, who, hoarse as a
crow, haltingly through song strikes the note in Gretta. It is the note of love
which never lets itself die. It is the pagan god of love, Cupid, buried deep by
Christ's mission; and yet Christ's very mission will transform the god of love
into permanent meaning. It cannot be by accident that Bartell D'Arcy
derives from *bois d'arc*, that tree the French thought best for arrows. Its familiar name in this country is bodark, the mock orange, whose blossom
can only mock that marriage which is no longer sacramental but carnal.
So it is that for Gabriel his wife, standing where she stands and listening as
she listens, reminds him of Distant Music—distant from him, but music,
as the agency of the divine, will transform them all. From this moment the
trumpet of revelation draws rapidly near.

She has to ask Mr. Bartell D'Arcy the name of the song (the music she
recognizes). It is, he says, "The Lass of Aughrim," a song about a woman
who grieves for her dead babe, who lies in both the falling rain and the dew.
Rain as life falls coldly upon the baby now, but as symbol, its falling promises
life eternal, since the song itself is to release this promise again to Gabriel
and the universe. The Blessed Virgin lost her son momentarily by death to
receive him deathless. Because of this, the unwed mother in the song in
imitation will assuage her grief; and, as song, will resurrect in the actors here
the promise which has been thought dead but is, only so far as it can go in
the world, deathless. In spite of the imperfection of our mortal conditions,
we may hope for the miraculous descent of Grace because we cannot escape
the hope the Crucifixion gives us.

Gretta stands apart, unaware of the lugubrious talk of the others just
before parting. It is much about the dreadful cold of Mr. D'Arcy, who is

"hoarse as a crow," who must be "careful of his throat in the night air" because, "Yes, everybody has colds," says Aunt Kate, "everybody." And there is poor little Mary Jane. Before the latent meaning in the song, already setting to work to release the final revelation, Mary Jane, a woman in name only, a virgin who has known no ghostly descent nor indeed any kind, can only say the conventional mannerly thing: "It's a very nice air," and "I'm sorry you were not in voice tonight." This is what a thought-tormented music has brought her to. Lily, the caretaker's daughter, in another time, could be found at the foot of the Cross; but any hope Mary Jane has is Martha's hope. Her sterility stands forth in apposition to the fullness of life that Gretta has. Gabriel turns to his wife and sees the "colour on her cheeks and that her eyes were shining." This is the blood of life and the radiance of love now being released from the depths, where it has lain in waiting for this moment. The sudden tide of joy leaping from Gabriel's heart will bring his salvation, but not yet. His condition is still ambiguous, as the good-nights of parting show. The good-nights contain the opposites light and dark, good and bad. This makes the transition from the darkness of the spiritual apathy which is the world to that moment of universal awakening.

There is no trumpet yet. The first sentence of the next paragraph continues the fusion of opposites: "The morning was still dark." But this is the morning of the last day. The snow underfoot is losing its shape. It is not yet water, but no longer snow: it is slushy. It is on the way to becoming water. The lamps burn redly in the murky air; there is a dull yellow light brooding over houses and river, over nature and human nature. The palace of the Four Courts menaces the heavy sky: the Four Last Things—Death, Resurrection, Heaven, Hell.

As they walk along in the slush, Gretta on D'Arcy's arm, Gabriel stays behind where, by watching her, he can feel the blood she has aroused go bounding through his veins and his thoughts go rioting through his brain, "proud, joyful, tender, valorous." What has seemed killed by the dull years together shows death not as pagan obliteration but death in the Christian sense of suspension in the unconscious. There is a summary of the acute awareness of nature and man which love's joy can give, and its seeming folly is an obliteration of the world. Gabriel now becomes poetic in his thoughts. The moments of their secret life together shine in his memory, like the tender fire of stars. His awareness grows: household cares, children, his writing have not quenched his soul nor hers. He remembers a sentence from an early love letter: "Is no word tender enough to be your name?" Brought forth from the past these words make him long to be alone with her. They find a cab and descend at the hotel, parting with Bartell D'Arcy. He is no longer needed, having done his part. Saying good-bye, Gretta leans upon Gabriel's arm as lightly as when they danced together. He had felt proud of her wifely grace and carriage, but now the kindling of so many memories, "the first touch of her body, musical and strange and perfumed, sent through him a keen pang of lust."

He has not yet reached his ordeal, but he is on the way. The controlling opposites (of lust and love, in the present instance) which all humankind knows as life now enter the forever renewed struggle which must end in either loss or gain. This is the drama of the soul, to make the sensible body of the world its housing, not the opposite of this, where the house stands alone, all shut in. The early joys have rekindled in Gabriel the fires of lust; the earliest joy-sorrow of Gretta's, the love of Michael Furey, is renewed in her soul. Lust wants power over, wants to use and then discard. Love always arouses pity; and its joy never loses its shadow, except when the sun is at the meridian. The greatest example, of course, is Christ's death, which is to be mourned; but since that death destroys death, the mourning turns into a celebration of eternal gladness. It is this obvious paradox that is close to the heart of the action and final meaning of this story.

The old porter asleep in his hooded chair arises to take them to their room. As Gretta climbs upward, her head is bent, her frail shoulders curve as with a burden, her skirt is tightly girt about her. Her burden is twofold: Gabriel and the grief over her lost love, now that it has been resurrected through song. Her posture is that of the first, the primordial position of copulation. Gabriel behind her "could have flung his arms about her hips and held her still, for his arms were trembling with desire." He restrains himself by *digging his nails into the palm of his hand.* The porter halts to adjust the guttering candle. I take it this light suggests two things: the obvious phallic symbol which has at this point usurped Gabriel's mind, the phallus as the tool of lust and power; also, it is literally man-made light. Before the immensity of the dark we see how frail a thing it is. The meanings complement each other and arrive at a larger meaning of the world's defeat, for man and wife all unknowing are climbing out of the sensible into the supernatural world. Once in the bedroom Gabriel has the candle removed; the electricity is out of order. The two of them are alone, with nothing artificial to aid their vision.

Nothing in the room, but from outside through one window the street-light lays a ghastly shaft as far as the door. The crucial word is *ghastly*. Lurid and wan, it is the path into this room of the ghostly hosts who will presently enter to do their work. Gabriel turns away to calm himself, and then he turns and sees his wife before the large swinging mirror. He calls her name; she walks "along the shaft of light towards him." She is now within the influence of the ghostly world, apart from her husband. He will never rejoin her until he, too, enters this world, to his salvation and to the only knowledge of love. His situation is still ambiguous. He longs to cry to her from his soul and at the same time crush her body against his. Now that she is under the control of that other world, which she has called forth by her resurrection of her youthful lover, Gabriel will each time be thwarted in his lustful longing. Each time the cry from his soul will become stronger.

She kisses him for his generosity to Freddy Malins. It is the kiss of charity. Still unknowing and not able to recognize the true feelings of his wife, he wonders why he had been so diffident, now that she has fallen to him so easily. This self-absorption causes him to miss the mark. Thinking she is longing for him as he is for her, he asks the question which should bring her to him. It brings the Lass of Aughrim and presently Michael Furey. Instead of falling into his arms, she flings herself upon the bed and hides her face. He follows, puzzled, and catches sight of himself in the mirror. This is no longer self-absorption, but the beginning of self-illumination. He does not yet understand, but he begins to see himself objectively. With a kinder note than he intended, he asks her why she cries. She begins to tell him about the boy, and "a dull anger began to gather again at the back of his mind . . . the dull fires of lust began to glow angrily in his veins." He then accuses her of lustful thoughts of adultery, but the truth and simplicity of her replies stop him. At first Gabriel feels humiliated by the failure of his irony; then he begins to see: when he was full of memories of their life together, she was comparing him with another. He sees himself as the ludicrous figure he is, "a pennyboy for his aunts, a nervous, well-meaning sentimentalist, orating to vulgarians and idealising his own clownish lusts." He turns his back to the light lest she see his shame. This is proper humility. Each question shows him more clearly himself and leads him deeper into the metaphysical world now hovering just outside the window. She answers his query about Michael Furey's death—"I think he died for me." From shame this brings him to a feeling of terror.

The terror is vague, arising from his feeling of his rival's triumph. That one absent in death could threaten the living might well bring terror: "Some impalpable and vindictive being was coming against him, gathering forces against him in its vague world." He hears her finish the story, how Michael Furey comes to her from his sickbed, out into the rain. Standing by a tree near the end of a wall, he casts a pebble to her window. She comes down to him and tells him to go home, he will get his death in the rain. He replies he does not want to live, and his eyes tell her why. Choking with sobs, Gretta flings herself upon the bed, sobbing into the quilt her muffled grief. Now the great reversal comes over Gabriel: from shame to terror to self-judgment and humility. He takes her hand in friendship, holds it irresolutely and, "shy of intruding on her grief," lets it fall and walks quietly towards the window, through which has entered invisibly but surely the Messenger whose name he bears. When he returns to his wife, she is asleep—the suspension of life in imitation of death (as the snow outside is nature's imitation of death), the Christian paradox. Her hair is tangled, and her mouth is, like Aunt Julia's, half open, and her breath is deep. Earlier this would have fired his blood; but now, as he gazes curiously at her, curiously because he only now begins to see her as herself, it "hardly pains him to think how poor a part he, her husband, had played in her life." He watches her sleeping, as if they had never lived together as man and wife. There could hardly be a greater self-effacement. Wondering about her girlish beauty and how the seasons have changed it, barely wondering, but in "a strange friendly pity," he knows that her face now is not that which caused Michael Furey to risk death. Pity is the crucial word, for it is that which transforms lust into love.

The carnal world is dead to Gabriel. The disarray of Gretta's clothes once would have quickened his desire; now it merely makes him wonder at the riot of his emotions an hour before. He clearly sees it as coming from the multiple stimulation of appetite which his aunt's supper aroused. The mark of his changing condition is that appetite is no more than a ghost of itself. His pity is about to extend itself boundlessly, but it begins, as it must, in an understanding of a person in the singular, first his wife and then his Aunt Julia, whose haggard look as she sang "Arrayed for the Bridal" foretells her entry into the ghostly world very soon.

That world is already nigh. The air of the room grows chill and sends Gabriel beneath the sheets, beside his wife for comfort but more than comfort, for she is the one who has brought forth out of her memory the ghost which is love. No mortal may bring it forth in its body. That is saved until the end. One by one, Gabriel thinks, they were all becoming shades. "Better pass boldly into that other world, in the full glory of some passion, than fade and wither dismally with age." He can think with sympathy, with no feeling of personal loss, of Gretta's lover's eyes when he told her he did not care to live. Tears come into his own and with them the final abasement of pride and selfish need, for he recognizes that he himself never had felt so towards any woman, "but he knew that such a feeling must be love."

This is the final confession of the world's defeat, the final acceptance of that brotherhood in Christ which prepares for life eternal. Out of the semidarkness, blurred by his tears, the form of a young man standing beneath a dripping tree, the tree of life, also the tree of knowledge in that fateful garden—this impalpable but clear form enters into Gabriel's imagination. The imagination is that in each of us which can receive the divine Word because the imagination alone is that part of the mind which mysteriously makes images, transmits to the eye and hence to speech the body of life. Having evoked out of his humility, his understanding and charity, his rival Michael Furey, he has overcome his feeling of his own identity as something separate and special. Having evoked one ghost, he can evoke the entire shadowy world. Other forms grow about him: "His soul had approached that region where dwell the vast hosts of the dead. He was conscious of, but could not apprehend, their wayward and flickering existence." His own identity fades into this world, and the solid world of matter dissolves like him and dwindles.

"A few light taps upon the pane made him turn to the window. It had begun to snow." This is the most brilliant invention Joyce has conceived. It is not only moving in itself; in the concretion of the symbol it fuses the separate parts of the action into one coherent meaning. As Gabriel Conroy is entering the ghostly world, Michael Furey, the shade, is returning to the substantial world to renew the promise of life eternal. * In life he threw a pebble against a windowpane to bring his love to him and hastened his death. From that impalpable world where he now is he throws flakes of snow against the windowpane, calling again to Gretta but also to Gabriel to renew the promise of hope—that death as cold snow does not mean extinction but the eternal waters withheld.

The archangelic meaning of Michael is "like unto God." Furey suggests the Greek forces of retribution and vengeance. Like unto God, the boy Michael died for love. He suffered and died for one human being, as God the Son suffered and died for all. He had acted out as nearly as he could in his mortal condition the immortal mystery and paradox: to die is to live. Michael the Archangel obliterated the Furies. Unlike the Furies, he does not pursue and rend. Upon the final day he will judge all the living and the dead, but as Protector of the Church Militant he pursues not those who fail in love but that old dragon Satan. Michael the boy is secure, as he is like unto God. His mortal name of Furey is no more. There is only now the brotherhood in Christ, one individual who has become the paradigm for all. As Michael he does not judge Gabriel Conroy. His act of love has quickened the sense of charity in Gabriel and causes him to judge himself. It is the epitome in mortality of the saving grace of the Word. Both Michael the boy and Gabriel the man, even though neither understood that their names meant more than something to answer to, are words, and words have their absolute eternal meaning. Gabriel Conroy had been made dumb by his carnal nature, but every time his name was called, it repeated this truth. By analogy Gabriel is Joseph the husband, and Michael, Gretta's true love in Christ. Even though she is a woman and a carnal woman at that, the divinity of love has been buried within her as in her virginal self. This is as close as human beings can come to the passion of the Cross. Continually mankind will forget, as the guests at the Morkans' party had forgotten. But music, the invisible but heard tones of life that is love, will always penetrate

---

*Some years ago Larry Vonalt, a brilliant student of mine at the University of Florida, suggested that the snowflakes against the windowpane were evidence of the return of Michael Furey as ghost. I disagreed; I saw no further than the death of all here in the action, not comprehending then its complexity. But his words sank and lay buried in my mind, to be resurrected at this reading of the story.

the ear, and these tones in all their multiplicity are the inflections of God's voice speaking the unknown but not unfelt tongues.

So once again the true vision has been granted by life to seeming death. As Gabriel sleepily watches the flakes fall, he senses, certainly feels, the promise in their movement. What he senses is their universality and invincible recurrence. This releases the poetic language about to be resurrected in his half-waking mind, restoring to the name and man Conroy his proper inheritance of the ancient office of poet and chronicler. Not journalese nor false oratory, but only poetry can contain the truth of final things. "Yes, the newspapers were right: snow was general all over Ireland. It was falling on every part of the dark central plain, on the treeless hills, falling softly upon the Bog of Allen and, farther westward, softly falling into the dark mutinous Shannon waves. It was falling, too, upon every part of the lonely churchyard on the hill where Michael Furey lay buried." As a sign of what has happened to the symbols of salvation, "it lay thickly drifted on the crooked crosses and headstones, on the spears of the little gate, on the barren thorns. His soul swooned slowly as he heard the snow falling faintly through the universe and faintly falling, like the descent of their last end, upon all the living and the dead."

The Hero as an Old Furniture Dealer: Ford Madox Ford's Parade's End

PARADE'S END IS FORD MADOX Ford's second masterpiece. *The Good Soldier*, using a smaller scene, is a more intensive rendition of a common subject. The actors in *Parade's End* make a microcosm of the enlarged drama, whose enveloping action is the end of European civilization. It is a tetralogy. The first book, *Some Do Not . . .* , divides English society between those who will sustain the inherited manners and mores and those who will not. The Tories (not just the political party), that is, the king's men, that is, those who uphold and defend the traditional English ways, once ruled the kingdoms according to feudal codes and the empire at least by means of the ceremony and regalia and the discipline of a long-standing public service.

This belief and habit have been increasingly threatened by the arrivistes, especially during the nineteenth century, men who think first of their private interests and afterwards of the public good, or even regard the res publica and their interests as one and the same thing. They occupy government bureaus and financial institutions. They infiltrate society. This has been a slow but continuous process ever since the fifteenth and sixteenth centuries, when the prospering merchants felt they wanted more than the countinghouse and the odors of their trade. It was natural to want to share the rule of England. The feudal world, though changing, was able to absorb them. After all, they were merely shifting their knowledge of craftsmanship to another occupation, Christendom being an agglomeration of crafts, from king to yeomen.

In time the newcomers were indistinguishable from the gentry. But the industrial revolution and international banking introduced a new kind, an abstract, irresponsible kind of power. A population settled on the land, where the seasons set the pace of work, could and did without impairment take in outlanders without changing too fast its cultural habits. But the new money was a different matter. Its control was outside the county communities and often England itself.

Christopher Tietjens, the hero, is an example of the indigenous manner of change. The Tietjens came from the Netherlands with William. The head of the family got Groby, a rich country estate, from an English Roman Catholic family, in a way which put a curse upon the place. In time the Tietjens were absorbed in the usual way. They are now all English and all county family, with coal mines as well as land. And they are Yorkshiremen. To emphasize this, Macmaster, Christopher's roommate and friend from his college days, stands for the initial phase of infiltration, but with a difference. He is in a sense a foreigner, that is, a Scotsman. His birth is low; Christopher's is not. But the specific difference is his attachment to those who administer the state, and these administrators lack the sense of feudal honor or care for the public thing. He and Christopher are in the same bureau of statistics, but their attitudes are not the same. In their persons, beliefs, and associations the two men contain the antitheses which operate throughout the entire action. For the sake of truth and proper rule, Christopher complains of the hypocrisy and dishonesty of his superiors, as they manipulate statistics. Macmaster feels that his friend is needlessly throwing away his opportunities, as he did at school in mathematics. Although the best head at it, he came in second. He did not want to be known only for this skill. Macmaster would not dare contradict a superior or refuse to obey. His hope is to be accepted as a man close to the inner workings of rule, with the end of being safe. His interest is selfish; Christopher's is not.

No More Parades, the second book, is largely placed in France during the catastrophic world war. No more parades means no more ceremony, no more formal behavior either in public or private, no more religious rites, workable conventions, all those forms which confine the natural man's instinctive and intuitive behavior towards Christian order. This war goes beyond professional armies. Entire populations, unlike the close-order tactics of the eighteenth century, are subjected to slaughter. The millions of casualties will assure the selfish men who played it safe at home their places of political and economic power. The dead do not protest. Those who still ruled before the war fought it and died; the administrators at home manipulated their interests. It is they who resisted the single command for the Allies. Had they succeeded in this, Christopher feels, the Germans would have won. In explaining to General Campion why he will not be able to return to his job after the war, he says that those who remained safe at home will penalize those who fought for their country. Not only will they resent the better manhood; they will want the women and the jobs.

It is France rather than England that is the epitome of European culture. The French are practical. They understand money and know its limitations. A Frenchman will put a penny in the poor box at night to have a penny to spend in the morning.* Few would confuse industry with progress. On the verge of the war the population was largely peasant, at least with a peasant understanding. Mark's French mistress is petty bourgeois, but she could as easily fit into a peasant's life, which for a while she does in the Tietjens' household after the war. A peasant will put hard money in his sock and hide it when times get perilous.

Christopher tells Valentine Wannop in their intimate tête-à-tête why he despises the oncoming war. Since his private life is ruined, he had thought of joining the foreign legion as a private. "One could have fought with a clean heart for a civilization: if you like for the eighteenth century [France] against the twentieth. But our coming in changed the aspect at once. It was one part of the twentieth century using the eighteenth as a catspaw to bash the other half of the twentieth." He goes or rather returns to the war and there exhibits how a man could stand up, the title to the third book. The fourth and last, *The Last Post*, indicates with a devastating irony the price he and his beloved, Valentine, must pay to do so. What they pay is the measure of what England has lost.

* Djuna Barnes, *Nightwood* (New York, 1937).

The action itself is the concrete incidents which reveal this enveloping action, that is, the universal truths which underlie this fiction. It has to do in a seemingly simple way with the loves of men and women. And how historic change, through war, exemplifies publicly the same tensions. To oversimplify: the hero, Christopher Tietjens, resists and is ruined by those powers which bring to an end an ancient Tory's idea of England. For Christopher so sees himself. More discursive than *The Good Soldier*, the scenes are interspersed with panoramic summaries, often in the reflections which comment upon or elaborate the drive of the action.

The conflicts are all set forth in the first book. Sylvia Tietjens, his wife, is the antagonist. At once almost we discover that she has married Christopher to give a name to another man's child. And afterwards, bored by her husband, she goes to France with a lover. She soon discovers that this is not what she wants and writes to her husband that she is willing to return to him. Her mother, Mrs. Satterthwaite, has followed to prevent an open scandal. She waits with Father Consett, the family priest, at a remote spa in the Black Forest of Germany, which Father Consett suggests is haunted by evil spirits. Indeed, the last Crusade towards a Christian conversion was directed here. The hotel is a grand duke's former hunting lodge. The priest comments on the wall decorations, gore and globs of blood of the huntsmen's kills. Nothing sporting, only the bloody kill. This bloodlust controlling industrial might contains the threat to civilization, as it stands for the destructive forces in private life. It is here Sylvia, leaving her lover, joins her mother and the priest.

There is a singular history belonging to mother and daughter. They both married good men, and they both hate them. The mother did; the daughter does. This also is an English Roman Catholic family, which means that their place, since Henry's assumption of both mitre and crown, has been restricted. The history of the English Roman Catholic differs from that of the rest of the English. He cannot have the same understanding of his past. For a long time he was deprived of his political rights; he does not forget the persecution by the Cecils, the calculated injustice in the courts, by which Groby was lost to the Tietjens; most of all the prohibition of the mass, the sacrament crucial to Christian worship. By the time of the action of this book, the social position of the English Roman Catholic is secure. Why then do mother and daughter hate their husbands and Sylvia complain of boredom? I suggest this: since the English Roman Catholic cannot exercise all his rights, his sovereignty is to that extent impaired. If what a woman wants of her man, according to the Wife of Bath, is his sovereignty, she in this instance cannot have it whole.

Father Consett knows man's imperfection and with charity toward this imperfection ignores the schism by advice which could mend it, at least for those in his care. He tells Sylvia to be a good wife, look after her husband, and bear him children. This is what she would like to do, have a man to respect and share domestic felicity. But in her confusion, she cannot at first see her husband in this light. A man secure among his peers would be for her one belonging to the very group Christopher detests, the arrivistes. Although Christopher is an Anglican Catholic, his plight is not unlike that of the Roman Catholic gentry whom the Cecils persecuted. Without the physical torture, he throughout will be put to all the ways of being ostracized and so exiled at home. And so she will not receive him in the full pledge of matrimony. And when she would like to, it is too late. So she is bored . . . bored . . . bored. She does not know why, but her priest does.

Christopher agrees to take her back on his own terms. She accepts because she intends to torture him the rest of his life. She tells the priest that, if necessary, she will corrupt their child—it turns out to be his. At this Father Consett threatens to burn her with holy water, and she comes to her senses. The extent of her misdirection has brought her with certain of her intimates to tamper with black masses. Father Consett does not take this seriously. It's not much more than fortune-telling or table-thumping. He says: "It's volition that's the essence of prayer, black or white." When she leaves the room, he tells her mother that her hell on earth will begin when her husband (since they will not be living together *maritalement*), a young, full-blooded man, will go running head down after another woman. And she—"the more she's made an occupation of torturing him the less right she thinks she has to lose him." This proves to be true, with complications not stated by the priest.

Ford does not intend this fiction to prove anything historically. He is rendering the given moment of history as people make it and, in peacetime, the cultural conditions through which and by which all human beings are effectively moved. The affections, the biological needs, make the greatest effects. By no means, however, do they shape the full-rounded meaning of what happens to the hero and the heroine in their persons and as they reflect the matters common to what was Christian Europe.

There are constants we all recognize: betrayal, envy, the dishonesties of appearance. General Campion, the hero's godfather and of like caste, sees largely as a professional soldier. To him men go wrong in three ways—sex, money, and drink. Certainly sex and money have to do with the complications of this book, but not quite in the oversimplification an institution like the army would make. Seeing behavior in platitudes delays General Campion's understanding of Christopher. It is never quite clear that he fully solves the behavior of this Tietjens.

Earlier in life Christopher has wanted to be a saint, an Anglican saint like his mother. Of course saints are not made this way. The name Christopher means he who bears Christ, from a legend of a gigantic saint who carried the Christ child across a river. The word was originally applied by Christians to themselves, meaning they bore Christ in their hearts. And it seems that this is what this Tietjens wanted to do and what he meant by being a saint. By the nineteenth century England had so fallen away from religious worship that a follower of Christian beliefs subjected himself to a kind of martyrdom, as an earlier saint of the same name suffered. Christopher himself thought of his aspiration as being sentimental; he might have thought anachronistic. He tried to practice the cardinal virtues of justice, prudence, fortitude, and temperance. To those who were carnally disposed this was unforgivable. In one of the most moving scenes in the book, after he has assured Sylvia that she is honorable and did the right thing to find in him a father for her child, a thing any woman should do, she says to him there is only one man "from whom a woman could take 'Neither I condemn thee' and not hate him more than she hates the fiend." At this point she has come to love him and knows it is too late. That a man could act out of principle her experience of her physical charms will not let her believe: this is the affront direct. She knows who the other woman is.

Christopher makes a kind of pilgrim's progress. The two ways are not theological, not up or down. They are middle class and genealogy: money or family as the basic structure of the state. The middle-class belief is in money as power and as the ultimate good, even though belief in it must be variable. Genealogy is the history, the persistence, and the description of family, that force for stability and prudence in a continuing order. The predominance of one or the other, on the public scene, has to do with history. Personally, it is what a banker can do to evict a man from his place in society. A small check Christopher has given to his club is returned for no funds. He resigns from the club. The funds have been manipulated by the banker's nephew to ruin Christopher, as he lusts after Christopher's wife. The banker, when confronted by his nephew's perfidy, relies at first on a technicality—the account was overdrawn. He is not a bad man; he likes Christopher and the way he has acted, and he promises to rectify the abuse. Christopher tells him it is too late. The news will be all over the city. He is ruined. This is a clear instance of how the power of money specifically can destroy. It can have no morals. The immorality of the act, the nephew's act, can always be disguised by the technical, amoral laws of banking.

When Christopher refuses to allow the banker to explain to his club and reinstate him—it is too late—the banker is shaken. Where will it end and what will be the repercussions? For a man to resign from his club under a cloud, that masculine assurance of social standing and intimacy, means his exclusion from those houses that have always received him. Because he has not been untrue to his beliefs and principles, Christopher is willing to abide by this ruin. It is this that alarms his wife and the banker and misinterprets him to those who should know better. The returned check is merely an instance of how Christopher's character is sullied. All the offensive charges in politics and human behavior are attributed to him: socialism, selling his wife for pay (apparently not too uncommon), seducing the daughter of his father's friend.

The failure of belief in a divine order of the world established, of necessity, materialism as the ultimate support of the English nation. Earlier Calvin had defined this change most cogently. As God's minister, he became the sole interpreter of God's will, and God withdrew into some inner chamber. Who were the elect? Obviously those who prospered in a material way. Business as a total definition of man supplanted the Christian man as image of what he should be. Charity gave way before the selfish will. Practically, the ministry played Calvin's role to the Crown. This is what Christopher meant when he told Campion that his loyalty as an antique Tory was so old that nobody would understand it.

The succession to and opposition to this old view of England are intrinsic to industrialism, scientism, and international finance, et cetera. This tension clearly shows itself in the distinctions between Macmaster's point of view and that of the Tietjens. This egocentric view of matter tends to separate man from nature. Of all the attendant ills of industrialism, et cetera, this fact is the most vicious. It makes preeminent that which dies as man lives, that is, the ego, and neglects that property which is eternal and survives matter as dust. At least this is the Christian promise. Mrs. de Bray Pape, the woman who has inherited the Maintenon's soul, is the archetypal example. She lays flat with her skirts the Tietjens hay, ignorant that she is walking through hay or that it will make it hard to cut.

This is done easily, without making a point of it, as the county landlords and farmers are shown with intimate knowledge of, as they care for, growing things and animals. Mark's one passion is following the races, and we do not get the sense that he does so just for betting. He studies the forms assiduously, that is, the genealogies of the thoroughbreds. This interest comes from his county background. But it is Christopher who shows most clearly the attachment to and understanding of animals. He has lived with them and by them. He whipped one of his father's grooms for turning the horses loose in pasture with curb bits on, making it painful for them to eat. He gave advice to a cabman about feeding his horse; he saw what made Mrs. Wannop's animal seem vicious and corrected it. Later, when General Campion ran into the same horse in a fog, as he and Valentine were returning to her mother's, he knew what to do to save its life, if not its usefulness. In the army he was asked to handle a captured horse. He violently protested against the officer in command of a depot of horses. This involved the action of sending him to the front, which seemed to be death, as he could not be put under the officer's charge.

Sent by the cabinet minister to persuade the policeman not to pursue Miss Wannop, Christopher not only carried out his mission but mended the broken leg of the policeman's wife's canary. He also learned to distinguish a dog otter's spoor from a gravid bitch's.

More directly the dog cart and the horse and the fog, animal nature and nature, gave harmony to the night journey that Christopher and Valentine, human nature, took to deliver the suffragette to safety. The clop of the hooves, the smell of animal and harness and the noise, quiet, natural to the two human beings being driven, instinctively (their wills at first protesting) drew them together. Their bodies kissed without kissing with an instant transferral of this knowledge of mutual feeling. Riding through the invisible fields and orchards led the man to renewal of his deep love for the countryside of England, the nostalgic setting for English maid and man. The fields, the moors, the animals grazing, the orchards became to Christopher parts of his being. It is this a man fights for, when it is threatened.

Macmaster had no interest in, knowledge of this close intimacy between man and beast and growing things. He was a townsman, with little experience beyond the cobblestones of certain streets. He is not a bad man. His actions (or the motives for his actions) are based on nothing more profound than ambition and private needs. The inadequacy of this the action judges. He thinks no further than his anger at Sylvia for her adultery. He urges his friend to divorce her, calling her the cruelest beast. This advice ignores the institutional and sacramental aspects of marriage. It is all feeling. Christopher rebukes him, reminding him that he is talking about his friend's wife. "You can relate a lady's actions if you know them and are asked to. You mustn't comment. In this case you don't know the lady's actions even, so you may as well hold your tongue."

He tries to instruct Macmaster about monogamy. The stability of society depends upon it. Adultery embarrasses intimate social gatherings, formal ones too, by intruding a too private matter, making public private intimacies. He defends monogamy even after his own private struggle with anger, humiliation, and the temptation to do what Macmaster suggests. But his sense of justice prevails. And when he tells his wife that she is honorable, he also rebukes her, not for the white lies she has let her son tell but for teaching him bad manners. The boy is heir to Groby, and he should not put a frog in his nurse's bath. She is an old and familiar retainer whom he should respect and treat with respect. County manners against the private will, which Sylvia understands but Macmaster cannot.

With no family behind him, a solitary in town, Macmaster must have something outside himself (he is not religious) to sustain him. He takes to literature, not out of any love for it but for what good it will do him in his competition for place in the statistical bureau. His choice was Pre-Raphaelite. This suited the circumspect, that is, the cautious middle class to which he belongs. He is doing a monograph on Rossetti, and it is this which brings him to adulterous dealings with the woman whom he will later marry, as he seeks her husband, an intimate of Ruskin's, for help in his research. Ruskin was the popular writer of the late nineteenth century. He also told his wife as they drove to their honeymoon that they would live as the angels. His disciple, whom Macmaster sought, imitated the master too literally, and so led Macmaster to his involvement with his wife.

Christopher has argued that both adultery and war threaten the peace. Macmaster, parroting his superiors, announces there will be no war. "We . . . the circumspect classes will pilot the nation through the tight places." Christopher answers him with war is inevitable, since his kind are such hypocrites. There is no country in the world which trusts England. "We're always, as it were, committing adultery—like you fellows—with the name of Heaven on our lips." And he quotes from Macmaster's monograph: "Part till we once more may meet/In a Heaven above."

The comparison throughout between the loves of Tietjens and those of his friend Macmaster is almost a little allegory. Duchemin, the familiar of Ruskin, is a rich and paranoid priest, who frequently turns to violence. He not only imitates, to the distress of his wife, his master's celibacy, but at a trying breakfast, given so that Macmaster might learn what he needs to know, Duchemin enters shouting *"post coitum triste"* and later quotes from the *Satyricon*. He is seated behind tall silver candelabra, heavy silver dishes, and tall beautiful flowers, to protect the guests. This rich assemblage of artifacts of "culture" is largely for the enveloping action, since it removes from the ritual of food, a ceremony given to social amity, a mad priest who is a literary, not a religious, authority. To the same purpose the flora serve madness: art and nature abused. Under such conditions does Macmaster find his love, in adultery and later in marriage. A decadent literature and rich artifacts are no substitute, however, for divine and institutional guidance. This ornament becomes the pattern of their life together, first the masked meetings, after marriage her salon, this time surrounding her "celebrities" with her appointments, especially at the tea table. These celebrities of hers have accidental reputations. To make this evident, when Mrs. Wannop, the only real novelist since the eighteenth century, arrives, she is isolated and insulted by her hostess, in spite of the fact that her daughter, Valentine, is serving the tea. The moment comes, fortunately, when those who know gather about her, to the chagrin of the hostess, whose falsity is exposed.

The contrast to the love between Christopher and Valentine is almost too obvious. Like Mrs. Duchemin-Macmaster she is also her lover's feminine counterpart: she is the true English maid. Her acts are generous and loving and charitable. She comes as close to selflessness as is believable. Her father, an eminent professor and dear friend of Christopher's father, dies and leaves his family almost penniless. Valentine works for small pay as a domestic slavey so that her mother can keep at writing. She sleeps under the stairs because she will not sleep with the drunken cook. She sees depravity but remains untouched by it. She hates injustice and risks herself aiding a suffragette friend. Her courage contrasts visibly with the Englishmen, hangers-on of the arrivistes, some of them the great selfish themselves, who go about with sticks looking for suffragettes to attack.

She and her friend had merely disrupted a golf game, a purely masculine affair, as a symbol of protest. No other way could the women make it so clear that they were in earnest. This weekend pleasure and social climbing of Londoners coming down to the country already describes a decline. The county social hierarchy is openly threatened, but not by suffragettes. General Campion, along with his companions, is shocked at the loose and loud talk of the club's guests. As president he rebukes them for their manners, which had revealed in vulgar fashion their private affairs in a too public way.

The suffragette affair brought Christopher and Valentine together. She turns to him to defend her and she turns to a man. He trips the policeman who is pursuing her, and she escapes by hurdling the dyke. Afterwards, having persuaded the policeman to turn in a No Can Do—he was anxious to oblige—Christopher learns that she is a member of the community in high standing. For several years she has managed the constabulary's wives' and children's annual tea and sport. She is a good sport herself, holding various records in running and jumping. Her true kindness and interest act in the interest of others. This is the basic Christian and feudal virtue, especially when the act is sacrificial, as when she gives up, they both give up, their first try at concupiscence to bring home her drunken brother and put him to bed. The sacrifice is measured by Christopher's going out to France the next morning, perhaps to be killed. Lust would have ignored the brother.

It is obviously Valentine's nature to serve. The other property of her nature is innocence. It cannot be tarnished by the multiple sins and vices that perforce become the milieu of her movements. Although she is a witness, her idea of sex remains pure idea: men are brutes, insatiable, lustful. Her profound giving of herself to Christopher, without concupiscence, remains untouched. Nor does she understand her own sex too clearly, and this is because of her innocence. She has abetted Mrs. Macmaster in assignations, an abortion, cared for her in her afflictions imposed by the paranoid priest, served almost as a domestic, and was so treated, in the salon of marriage and ambition. The return was not what she had thought it, loving friendship, but the casual acceptance of her service as the due of patronage.

This continued until Edith Ethel (Mrs. Macmaster's given name) insulted Valentine's mother in her daughter's presence. Even then the daughter was slow to understand the cruel and brutal ego which her supposed friend was. There was a passage of frankness at which Edith Ethel reviled her with false accusations, one of which was that she had had a bastard by Christopher. In a suble way the vilification described her own character and experience. Even under such an attack Valentine did not think of her own self-esteem. In charity she sought for the cause of this violent denigration of herself, decided it was from jealousy. Christopher had been Edith Ethel's lover, so little did she understand human behavior at this time. This allowed her at first to feel sympathetic towards it. She was thinking of what it was to love Christopher. When the crucial moment comes, however, and her own nuptials are threatened, she acts unhesitatingly to prevent interference. She resists her mother, thinking of her, and Sylvia thinking of herself. Christopher had wavered. This was the beginning of her acceptance of the realities of life, as opposed to her abstract ideas of war and men.

It is Armistice Day. The war is over and Christopher is back in London. She and he are trying at last to be alone together. Sylvia has stripped the flat of furniture, except for some books and a cabinet. In a sense this defines the two lovers' predicament; this emptiness of a dwelling place is society's abandonment of them. The ill will and bad luck which have afflicted Christopher at war follow him here. He has no money. They meet in parting as he rushes out to sell the cabinet to raise forty pounds. He tells her to wait. Her mother calls to dissuade her from their intention. Her mother talks with him to the same end. The Armistice intrudes and delays. The men who served him in the last months of war enter to celebrate. There is a frenzy of despair in the falsely festive mood from those released from the trenches, blemished, with marred bodies and minds. And with the ghosts of the dead misting their eyes. At last she and he are alone together, abandoned to themselves. She wonders if he will murder her, and her courage is equal to the total risk. Of course there will be a murder: her virginity. This absolute innocence now will be lost in their predicament.

The greater part of the action of *Parade's End* takes place at war, with the exception of the last book. The action is largely scenic, long scenes interlarded with panoramic summaries, just when such comment or reflection is needed to give greater substance to the dialogue. The scenes, discursive as they are, are among the best in the book. They give a rounded sense of the body of the world as it is afflicted by a power selfish and alien to Merrie England, or what is left of it. The confusion in the strategy of the Allied armies derives from a cynical political game, which threatens the French with a withdrawal of troops for another theater of war, towards English prestige in the Middle East after the disaster at Gallipoli: in other words, towards a selfish end. The French respond with railroad strikes to let the English know what to expect if they try to withdraw. The same ministers oppose a single command and so prolong the war and its casualties. This is the public evidence of the rule which Christopher protests.

The private intrudes its domestic wants into the military through Sylvia. She conceives of the front as one large bawdy house in which her husband, along with all soldiers, spends his time fornicating. She thinks he has brought Miss Wannop there: he has not written to Miss Wannop in two years. Sylvia becomes a disruptive core to military discipline. She descends upon General Campion's headquarters as if to a county weekend. She has come driven by a sexual obsession for her husband, with the constant aim to destroy or force him to return to her. It is not entirely sex. She has come to understand that sex is a part of the total man, which she finds her husband to be.

Being a whole person, Christopher has fixed beliefs and a large comprehension of human affairs. Neither he nor Mark expected to inherit Groby. What transport came to mean to Mark, knowledge of English life and England's role in the world was to Christopher. These were matters that those who ruled England should know. His private irony, or rather the irony of his role, showed how well he could serve, limited to small and scattered areas of performance. General Campion tells him he is no soldier. He does not look the part, but his commands are run in a military fashion, even to untangling general and specific confusions which attend this war. Trench warfare is like a siege that need have no end, because its rear is open to the transport of supplies and reinforcements. It is slaughter rather than war as professionally known. Crowding together underground, deep in mud, and the shattering sounds of artillery produce psychic shock on much of this civilian army. With patience and sympathy Christopher solaces and cares for these afflicted and still untangles contradictory orders, the perpetual waiting to move that allows the men to think of death—all of this to his exhaustion, which he cannot give in to.

There are two successions of scenes which reveal the disorder and its cause that are the heart of the action. The first results in the train of Sylvia's appearance. She brings with her the malignant gossip about her husband, and this damages military discipline. General Campion should have sent her home as soon as she arrived, but there were personal ties. She was thought to be his mistress; and so authority was corrupted at its source. The scandal she provoked involved her former lover, a general of police, and Christopher, representing two of General Campion's dicta, women and whiskey.

General Campion acts decisively and quickly. He sends Sylvia home and comes to Christopher, who is under arrest, to learn the truth. He is still offended by his godson's sloppy appearance, but he respects him and begins to see, or suspect, that he has been maligned. He comes dressed as if for parade. As a professional soldier he knows the value of regalia, medals, parades, shining boots, and the wearing of a crop, his magical wand, to support men under fire. The colors to dress on in a charge sustained the effectiveness of close-order drill. When guns shot only a hundred yards, the line had to remain solid, closed up, to pass through that much lead. Trench warfare was another matter; nevertheless the general, slim and neat in all his formal dress, could be a symbol to citizen soldiers as he was to the profession. He signified not just a man fighting but a man in his office, where lay the command of life and death. His very neatness and frailty before the mud and filth in which his men struggled, their grossness, suggested a kind of purity of authority, impervious, stainless, and paternal. The French colonel often addresses his privates as mon enfant. He represents throughout, but particularly in this long scene, the feudal inheritance, the secular office which once was knighthood. In essence this is so. The changing conditions, which he will fight, have changed him. But, insofar as he can, so long as they do not interfere with discipline, he practices the cardinal virtues. He is just: he comes to Christopher to know the truth. He shows fortitude; he will resign and run for Parliament, sacrifice his career for a greater purpose, if certain things take place. He is prudent, allowing neither scandal nor dereliction of duty to affect the efficiency of the army; nor will he disturb the balance prematurely. His temperance is less convincing.

If Christopher is an Anglican saint who practices the Christian disciplines to the point of martyrdom, or prolonged abuse, if martyr is too strong a word, then the meeting between the two joins the secular and the religious offices to withstand strained circumstances brought about by hostile forces. They see alike on public issues, the crucial one of the single command, even down to the same language; but Christopher will not discuss his private and familial affairs. His explanation of the personal attacks on his character he clarifies to the general's seeming satisfaction. The general had shown, as had his father and brother Mark, a too ready belief in his depravity.

At the end they part in understanding and agreement on General Campion's course of action, if certain things take place. The general makes it clear that the only decision open to him was to send his godson to the trenches, but with a promotion, to show that he was not to blame for the scandal. About to part, Christopher reminds the commander that officially he had come to inspect the kitchens. Sergeant-cook Case had been in the professional army with Campion. He remembers him as a good soldier broken to the ranks over desertion because of a woman. He came to live with her as his sister.

The inspection is referred to in religious terms. The kitchens are bright and clean, the cooks goggle-eyed at attention. The "cook-house was like a cathedral's nave, aisles being divided off by the pipes of stoves. . . . The building pauses, as when a godhead descends." With short steps he walks up to "a high priest who had a walrus mustache and, with seven medals on his Sunday tunic, gazed into eternity." The general taps a good conduct ribbon with the heel of his crop and asks, "How's your sister, Case?" Every ear is

attuned to the question. We know at once here is a commander of an army
that men will obey, even in his errors. To Tietjens "this was like the sudden
bursting out of the regimental quick-step, as after a funeral with military
honours the band and drums march away, back to barracks." It is the funeral
of Tory England and Europe that he has in mind.

Christopher does not go to his death in his new command. The colonel
has cracked up, and so Tietjens commands as second in command. The
colonel and his major, McKechnie, have turned a public office into a private
performance. They looked upon themselves and the regiment as pals. But
they did not command pals, that is, friends, but a distinct part of an army.
Their positions were official, not personal. Here again is the confusion
between public and private. The soldiers recognize it when Christopher is
actually in command. The pals had made no contact with the regiments to
their regiment's flanks. Among other military needs Christopher attended
to this. To act alone when you are a part of a whole is military disaster,
which would have overtaken the regiment when the Germans made their
push in the spring. This is a small incident and comments on the lack of a
single command.

Self-interest against the common good, the confusion between public
and private, operates throughout as the controlling impetus towards the
undoing of civilized Europe. McKechnie, the nephew of Macmaster, feels
that his uncle has betrayed him by not keeping him out of the army. He
affronts Christopher with all the gossip Sylvia and London have spread
against his character. He does this because his ambition is thwarted by
having Christopher outrank him. Seeing everything from a personal interest, he can only believe that he is outranked because Sylvia is sleeping
with Campion. To him there is no public good.

He took in college the chancellor's prize in Latin, the very kind of thing
Christopher refused in mathematics. To McKechnie, the prize is for use in
the competition for place, his uncle's own kin. For Christopher Latin is a
habit of reading. It is expected of one of his station in life. There is the
memory, also, that Latin once was the universal tongue for the officialdom
of Christian Europe. McKechnie forces Christopher, out of his by now
paranoid necessity, to compete, to bet on who could write a Latin poem
faster. It is easy for Christopher, but not until after the war does
McKechnie come up with his. To insist upon it during the Armistice cele-

bration shows him on the verge of cracking up. To reprove him, Christopher tells him to show it to Valentine, who is a fine Latin scholar. The point here is this: all the military who come to celebrate seek him out because he has been a good officer to all of them. Even the pals, ruined as they are, arrive. This is the final delay for the lovers' nuptials, which take place as the first three books end.

The Last Post was published after the first three books. Certain opinion holds that the three books were complete in themselves. It is true that parts of The Last Post, certain of Mark's long recollection, is repetitious and somewhat contradictory to the others, but without it the ending would have emphasized the union of the two lovers beyond the meaning of the whole. The lover gets his woman, but the obstructions remain. The bugle call, the last post, taps in this country, in this connection is the death salute. It is played badly by a younger brother of the bugler. The noise irritates Mark. The death salute should only be played ceremonially, on parade. The boggling of it, in a domestic situation, describes the nature of the death of England. An official sounding off has been reduced to the discords of an untrained child playing at home.

The end of England is the end of feudal Christendom, the war and Armistice being merely the final blow to what remained of its structure. Cast out from being a part of life in London, Christopher brings his mistress, now pregnant with his bastard, to the country. He has bought a cottage, a showplace of what an English cottage should be. There is some land to it, allowing for a garden, an orchard, and pasture, from which the household gets part of its living. Of the county, they instinctively return to the land. It is still there and some of its old structure remains, concretely shown in the persons of a fox-hunting landlord and his hind, who has been whipped and cast out for betraying his wife at a delicate time. He then serves Christopher in the old way. And so Christopher's household finds shelter and a living, but not quite. He is in the old furniture business, as partner with an American Jew. Macmaster, since it was fashionable at one time, took as a fad the pretended pleasure and understanding of old things. Unfortunately they were usually fakes, which Christopher pointed out. As for Christopher, the actual things were the furnishing of his life, by which he had always been surrounded. So it was that he could recognize and buy with authority.

This is the irony to which the action arrives: he must live, not by living among old and sound works of craftsmanship, but by selling them. His cottage was bought to live in, certainly, but not entirely. Being the fine example of a period, it displays his wares in a convincing setting. But the catch is, the furniture never remains the same. Valentine sorrows that her home is not her home. Will the marriage bed be taken from under them? Or more outrageous, will the cradle in which she rocks her child, her bastard child, be sold as she rocks him to sleep? And to make the situation unbearable, Sylvia has moved into the neighborhood to pursue her vendetta.

This resolves at its peak about the rental of Groby to a rich American woman, muchly set on sunshine and health. The woman has rented Groby, and she and Sylvia between them will cut down Groby Great Tree. But they have to get Mark's permission. The nephew, Christopher's son and heir to Groby, much against his will, at his mother's insistence, arrives with the woman. The renter is a preposterous caricature. She believes she is the spiritual descendant of the Maintenon, assured by the leader of a cult that the French king's mistress's soul has entered her body. The woman even as a caricature is hard to believe, except that she represents the kind of world that has triumphed: she is ignorant and believes that riches are all-powerful and give to the owner the sanction to instruct, judge any who enter her presence. The ignorance is so profound and dangerous it defines the last position of Puritanism. As the opposite to such a person there is Lady Tietjens (Mark, at his brother's suggestion, has married his mistress) with her firm grasp on the essentials of life.

The burden of the movement is Sylvia's descent upon her husband's ménage. Her curiosity about what goes on allows her to commit the vulgarity of talking to the wife of her husband's carpenter. "It had struck him [Mark] as curious taste to like to reveal to dependents—to reveal and to dwell upon, the fact that you were distasteful to your husband." She would like evidence that Tietjens, as the cottage is called, is a moral chancre in the countryside, to the end of having the local magnate, Lord Fittleworth, drive them away. She makes the error to impute to Mark's illness the sins of his youth. Lord Fittleworth is an old friend of Mark's, of the same cast and performance for the good of England, one of the old gentry, and a hard fox-hunting man.

Mark lies under a bush arbor with roof but no sides, day and night, near the cottage. He never speaks and is treated as if he has had a stroke. Whereas the post of observation of the first books might be called the Hovering Bard with its restricted omniscience, the view here is the Roving Narrator, the action opening in a stream of consciousness in Mark's mind, from which it roves to Lady Tietjens, and without a jar to Valentine and others. Mark never speaks after two happenings. The Armistice which ended the war without invading Germany he considered a betrayal of France by its Allies, a waste of his work in transport which stood for all the blood and treasure England had spent to no good end. He foresaw it had all to be done again. The other matter was his discovery that Christopher meant not to take any money or Groby from Mark or his father.

Refusing to speak put him in a perfect position for observation and reflection. His situation is almost godlike, observant but unreachable. He communicates by batting his eyes. It allows him, as he watches the action about him, to judge it but also to judge himself. Christopher with loving care had nursed him through pneumonia. They became very close. His younger brother showed his love but also that he would not forgive the betrayal. Mark's roommate, Ruggles, half Scottish and half Oriental, brought the gossip to Mark and he to his father. As the two were discussing the matter, Christopher entered the club. His father pretended not to see him. This was the betrayal, not to give his son a chance to know the rumor and hear him out. The shock of his brother's stubborn decision forced Mark for the first time to think beyond his selfish interests and pursuits. He did not blame Christopher. He came to accept that his own indifference had caused all the trouble that gathered about Christopher. And this allowed him to view with understanding and a Christian forbearance all the people who descended upon Tietjens.

Both younger sons, neither was prepared for the responsibility of Groby; yet both would inherit it. Mark refused to become attached to it. This was his way of not being denied what he could have loved. He withdrew into a life of his own from which grew an indifference to his kin and an ultimate betrayal of his brother. To repair somewhat the damage, he had moved into his brother's place to sustain him with his name and fortune.

Christopher as younger son, inheriting from his southern mother a great capacity for love and being loved, not expecting to be master of Groby, looked upon the place with sentimentality. The proper sentiment of a landlord was to care for men and beasts, pay taxes, keep up his station, and hand it on unimpaired to the next generation. Christopher's sentimentality gave him the knowledge of old things from which he could make a living. It caused him, however, to attach his thoughts to a part, such as to Groby Great Tree or to the violation of renting Groby furnished to a stranger. The welfare of the whole estate should have been his prime consideration. He gave it to his son, falsely believing or forgetting that a man who cannot rule his family any better than he had, would be incapable of ruling an estate, which was a small community. He took to heart that his name was infamous. He forgot the ancestor who died in a whorehouse, another who, being drunk, killed himself falling from his horse. His father presumably committed suicide, unequal to disaster. (Mark in his reverie decided this was not so.) Christopher's sentimentality, a part of his sainthood, disallowed to himself the usual human frailties and vices, and this is the grimmest pride.

Sentimentality, being more or less than the occasion requires, misled Christopher in his basic responsibility to himself and his wife and child and his mistress. Making Valentine his mistress and giving her a bastard was not sentimentality, but to think that they could live as if legally married was a form of it. He seemed not to realize, he who pretended to all knowledge, almost supernatural guidance, the simple social misfortune he would bring upon his mistress and their child in gratifying the common needs of sexual congress. The bar sinister is nothing new in society. Armorial shields have its markings. That Christopher is willing to accept isolation from his kind is one thing, but what of the child? And what of the neglect of his legitimate son? Under his care would young Michael-Mark have said that Marxian communism is the thing, a contradiction both to his religion and his responsibility as a landlord? Surely as he grew, the heir to Groby needed his father's counsel.

It seems, in a way, that Christopher was bitten by the snake whose poison had entered the common bloodstream. Under the most adverse circumstances he performed his public service with efficiency and kindness. War's violence did not undo him. But domestically he allowed his private feelings to neglect his office as heir to Groby. He forgot Groby was a large estate which the landlord did not own in fee simple but ruled as trustee in his generation, to be cared for and passed on to the next trustee. He refused it as if it were money, for a personal reason, and he had good cause. Yet it showed him acting like those whom he considered the destroyers of Europe. Ashburnham committed suicide; Christopher withdrew from society. Ashburnham's act drove his beloved to madness; Tietjens' act revealed how far his idea of an Anglican saint failed to resist the archetypal betrayal, upon which depended the salvation of mankind.

But this is Mark's book. Christopher does not appear until the end. Mark's self-examination under the aspect of eternity removes the core of selfishness and returns him to his humanity. And this takes him to his childhood at Groby. At the age of twelve he shot under his grandfather's eye, a fluke shot, several birds at once. These were encased at Groby, and the children of the family referred to them as Mark's bag. This he considered to be his claim to immortality. He meant by this, I think, that the family is the one thing which lasts and by which you can be defined in your fullness of being. Sylvia confesses to him the abandonment of her persecution of his brother. She has had Groby Great Tree, symbol of the family, cut down; but she will not cause harm to Valentine's child, any woman's child, and with tears she lets it be known that what she wanted was to feel again the softness of a baby in her arms. This is the family definition, its fructification and continuance. She will divorce Christopher, and this means to Mark that his brother and Valentine can be married and bring up their child as legitimate issue of a marriage. He pities Sylvia and speaks, he who had not spoken— "You poor bitch, you poor bitch, the Riding has done it."

The riding is an administrative part of a Yorkshire county; it is a legal and social communion of families of all degrees, the earl, Fittleworth, his hind Gunning, the carpenter, all, in spite of change, tenacious in their habits. Lady Tietjens, Mark's wife, makes cider in a French way, and the carpenter's wife feels she is a threat to the countryside and ought to be arrested. The inherited way seems at the end of the story to be hard to abolish. In Mark's reverie: "Well, if Sylvia had come to that his, Mark's occupation, was gone. He would no longer have to go on willing against her; she would drop into the sea in the wake of their family vessel and be lost to view."

The night before, "a great night, with room enough for Heaven to be hidden there," all the animals in the county stampeded and broke through hedges, it was said, because of an earthquake only they could feel. Mark knows better. It was God walking on the firmament. From this mysterious response of animals to the land that sustains beast, flora, and human beings, the supernatural makes a fusion of lasting things. Man is not capable of resolving the complications he brings about. Even Sylvia before her decision feels through Father Consett that God is on the side of the family and the good, else how could his creatures persist, if the family is not there to bear the young. The end seems to promise a reprieve from suffering. Fittleworth arrives before Mark with Marie Léonie at his elbow and says, "I've driven all these goats out of your hen roost. . . ." Cammie sends her dear love. As soon as he was well to bring her ladyship down. He reassures him about Sylvia's intentions. They could all be a happy family. Anything Cammie could do. . . . And because of Mark's unforgettable service to the country. . . . Marie Léonie sees his sweat. Fittleworth says joy never kills, but so long, old friend. It is not joy that kills him but his release from the family responsibility, which he has taken up, but with the Tietjens stubbornness, a little late.

Then Christopher is at the foot of his bed, face white, eyes stuck out, blue pebbles, with a piece of aromatic wood in his hand. He tells the tree is down, half the wall, Mark's bedroom is wrecked, his birds thrown on a rubble heap. Then Valentine, breathing hard as if from running, appears and tells him where he has left the prints, but mainly with a desperate reproof, how are they going to feed the child if he does things like that. "How are we ever to live?" Christopher heavily, because he is exhausted in body and mind, slowly turns his bicycle around.

> "Now I must speak," Mark said to himself.
> He said:
> "Did ye ever hear tell o' t' Yorkshireman. . . . On Mount Ara . . .
> Ara. . . ."

His tongue is thick and his mouth twisted. This is a family saying which she knows. A Yorkshireman speaks to Noah and says it will clear up, in spite of the water. And then he tells her to put her ear near his mouth. He whispers an old song his nurse sang: " 'Twas the mid o' the night and the barnies grat/And the mither beneath the mauld heard that." "Never," he says, "thou let thy barnie weep for thy sharp tongue to thy goodman. . . . A good man!" He asks her to hold his hand, and quickly dies. Valentine tells the doctor it is too bad it could not have been his wife. "But she did not need them [his last words] as much as I."

The four books close on this. Pomp and circumstance, the confusion and sorrows of the world, family pride—all is reduced to the simple language common to all, a nurse's admonition, of bearing and forbearing for family amity and the love for the child, the inheritor of life.

Index